THE METAPHYSICS
OF MEDIA

THE METAPHYSICS
OF MEDIA

Toward an End to Postmodern Cynicism
and the Construction of a Virtuous Reality

Peter K. Fallon

UNIVERSITY OF SCRANTON PRESS
Scranton and London

Library of Congress Cataloging-in-Publication Data
Fallon, Peter K.
The metaphysics of media : toward an end to postmodern cynicism and the
construction of a virtuous reality / Peter K. Fallon.
    p. cm.
Includes bibliographical references and index.
ISBN 978-1-58966-202-5 (pbk.)
    1. Reality. 2. Metaphysics. 3. Mass media. 4. Postmodernism. I. Title.
BD331.F19 2009
110--dc22

                                        2009038140

Distribution:
UNIVERSITY OF SCRANTON PRESS
Chicago Distribution Center
11030 S. Langley
Chicago, IL 60628

PRINTED IN THE UNITED STATES OF AMERICA

So says science, and I believe in science: but up to now has science ever troubled to look at the world other than from without?

Pierre Teilhard de Chardin
The Phenomenon of Man

To the memory of my father,
James Patrick Fallon (1911–2001),
a man of strong residual orality.

And to my dear friend and wife,
Mary Pat Fallon,
for throwing light upon a reality
once invisible to me.

Metaphysics: a division of philosophy that is concerned with the fundamental nature of reality and being . . . a study of what is outside objective experience.

Webster's Ninth Collegiate Dictionary

Metaphysics . . . a broad area of philosophy marked out by two types of inquiry. The first aims to be the most general investigation possible into the nature of reality. . . . The second type of inquiry seeks to uncover what is ultimately real. . . . Understood in terms of these two questions, metaphysics is very closely related to ontology.

Routledge Encyclopedia of Philosophy

Contents

Preface

In 1964, Marshall McLuhan published his groundbreaking book *Understanding Media: The Extensions of Man.* It would still be about ten years before I read it as a sophomore in college, majoring in a field that, arguably, McLuhan and this book helped to invent: communication studies. Like many others, my life was changed by that book, because the structure and focus of my thoughts were changed.

And yet, as I read more of his work over the years, I couldn't lose the uncomfortable feeling that something was missing, something was wrong, something didn't make sense, something was incomplete. Even though McLuhan believed that studying and understanding media was a vitally important activity because of the ways that media change our relationship to one another and to the world, he nevertheless once said, "A moral point of view too often substitutes for understanding in technological matters."[1] While I understand the point he was making and take his criticism seriously, I choose to believe in the potential of human free will in the same way I believe in the potential of human intellect: it is better to recognize them and use them than not; but it is better still to use them correctly. And so the "moral point of view," while not a substitute for understanding, ought certainly to be seen as its adjunct.

As Neil Postman has observed about the eighteenth century, there was at that time no shortage of evidence of human ignorance and imperfection; there was, however, for the first time, a glimmer of hope that we as a species might be perfectible.[2] And Jacques Ellul has shown us that, while human beings may suffer incoherence in a flood of information, we have the power to reestablish coherence by reclaiming control over our experiences.[3] These are but a few of a number of thinkers who moved beyond observing, theorizing, and reporting to trace a connection between human means and media of communication and social and individual values. They even had the temerity to make judgments and to offer suggestions about how to approach the problems of communication presented by new technologies. I have always appreciated their insights, their wisdom, and their counsel. It is, I hope, within this tradition that I write this book.

A Plea for Understanding

In the interests of the truth that this investigation claims to revere, I must acknowledge the limitations I have chosen to place upon myself in undertaking such an examination and the significant limits that naturally fall upon me based on my own incalculable ignorance. This is my plea for understanding and indulgence. I am neither by education nor training a philosopher, nor am I credentialed to call myself by that name.[4] I am by education, training, inclination, and disposition a media ecologist, a communication generalist, most naturally and comfortably an interor multi-disciplinarian whose interests and concerns include the ethics, morality, and spirituality of mass communication.

I began the various tasks of thinking about this book, researching it, and writing it several years ago with a great deal of trepidation—intellectual, professional, and personal. My thoughts, and the arguments that give them voice, swim against the currents of postmodern culture and will appear to many to be arrogant, intellectually imperious, reactionary, and naïve. (I can say this with considerable authority, because in presenting portions of this book publicly over the last several years I have already been called all these and more.) Furthermore, I concede, there does appear to be a measure of intellectual arrogance involved in any attempt to construct what appears to some (correctly or not) to be a normative philosophy, and even more so when the one attempting it is not, strictly speaking, a philosopher. To some extent, I am forced to plead guilty to these charges.

Yet I don't undertake this task lightly or arbitrarily, and it is my most sincere intention to be guided not by my own subjective opinions, but by the objective truth. I have tried conscientiously to cover a great deal of historical and philosophical ground in the last several years, and in taking up this challenge I have reduced my own (still formidable) ignorance greatly. Even at this late date, however, there remain far more philosophical works that I—a student and teacher of mass communication, former electronic journalist, and a now-middle-aged "Irish kid" born and raised on Long Island and transplanted to Chicago—have left unread than I have been able to read. Therefore, the reader far more versed than I in the philosophical, ethical, and moral debates discussed in this book will no doubt be aware of its various and manifold faults, for which I apologize humbly and sincerely. But I had to try to describe what I see occurring: this media-induced blurring of reality, this shifting boundary between objective and subjective experience, this growing ignorance—on a mass scale—of the world around us, for no one else seemed to be doing so, and I believe that this argument needs to be heard.

I caution the reader to approach this work, as I have, in the spirit described by Jacques Ellul:

> Do not look here for some scholarly study on iconic expression or syntagmatics or metalanguage. I am not pretending to push forward scientific frontiers. Rather, I try to do here the same thing I do in all my books: face, alone, this world I live in, try to understand it, and confront it with another reality I live in, but which is utterly unverifiable. Taking my place at the level of the simplest of daily experiences, I make my way without critical weapons. Not as a scientist, but as an ordinary person, without scientific pretensions, talking about what we all experience, I feel, listen, and look.[5]

Several years ago, I labeled the preliminary draft of this paper "a work in progress." Subsequent drafts have borne the same subtitle. Realism (such as it is) demands the intellectual honesty to admit that it may remain a perpetual work in progress, even after its publication. Although I have heard, seen, and read no one else making the arguments I make here, I am hopeful that others more qualified than I might eventually expand on the philosophical, moral, and ethical themes which I lay out today.

I also acknowledge that any discussion of the role of media in creating and supporting specific views of reality can lead one down a dark, poorly paved, and largely uncharted road which will of necessity branch off in numerous directions, leading the investigator down equally ill-defined routes, many of them dead ends. For the purpose of clarity of argument, and at least minimally to ensure that I do not end up permanently mired in an intellectual cul-de-sac, I will confine myself to an examination of the immanent[6] and the transcendent[7] within *three* distinct cultural modalities, representative of four of the five major eras in communication history:[8] the oral (pre-literate), the literate (alphabetic and print), and the electric/electronic (post-literate/postmodern).

Acknowledgments

I would like to acknowledge the help, over the last several years, of scholars and friends who have read drafts of this work in progress and provided me with invaluable and sometimes painful advice and criticisms: Dr. Michael Russo, Associate Professor of Philosophy, and Dr. Stephan Mayo, Chair of the Philosophy Department of Molloy College in Rockville Centre, New York; Dr. Kenneth Amann, Coordinator of the Graduate Social Work Department of Molloy College; Dr. Clodagh Weldon of the Theology Department of Dominican University in River Forest, Illinois; Dr. Tim Weldon (Chair) of the Philosophy Department of the University of St. Francis in Joliet, Illinois; and my friend and wife, Mary Pat Fallon of the Graduate School of Library and Information Sciences at Dominican University. All have read drafts of this book and offered sensitive and intelligent criticism that I have tried my best to respond to. Whatever faults remain a part of this book are mine and mine alone.

I would also like to thank Jeff Gainey of the University of Scranton Press for taking a chance on a somewhat unusual manuscript, and for his sensitive and deft hand at helping me see it in print.

Finally, I must also give posthumous thanks to the late distinguished Georgetown University Professor of Theology Monika Hellwig, who was gracious and generous enough to read an early draft of one of this book's chapters (the epilogue, Chapter Nine, In the Dark: The Survival of Ignorance in an Age of Information) after we presented together at the "Women of Spirit" Symposium sponsored by the Siena Women's Center at Molloy College in 2002. She gave me both critical advice and encouragement, and urged me to finish this work and get it published. I am grateful to her for her support, and sorry that it took me this long to do as she urged.

Why a Metaphysics of Media?
Why Should Anyone Care?

I was born a first-generation American of Irish immigrant parents. The America I grew up in was not the America of my friends and classmates; it was something far greater, far more important, far less to be taken for granted. The streets, while not paved, as in Irish mythology, with gold, were nonetheless paved, and for my parents that alone was nothing short of miraculous.

My mother and father each came separately from a land that was poverty-stricken and wracked by warfare. Some in my father's own extended family—uncles, aunts, cousins—found it necessary, as a result of their loyalties to Britain, to exile themselves from Ireland during and after the 1916 uprising and war of independence—"run out of Ireland in their nightshirts," as one family legend tells it. My father, after living the first eleven years of his life in Tubbercurry, County Sligo, finishing only a few years of grammar school, came to the United States in 1922 and worked for the next seventy years.

My mother's family—staunch nationalists all—suffered no political displacement, but my mother was forced by hard economic circumstances to move away from home to find regular work, first in Longford Town, then in Dublin, and finally, in 1939, in New York. She moved not merely to support herself, but also her family back home in Gubbadoorish, County Leitrim.

When they met, my mother was "downstairs help" in the home of a wealthy family in the "Five Towns" of Long Island; my father worked delivering groceries for a small market nearby.

They met at the back door—the service entrance—and the rest, as they say, is history.

My parents felt blessed—indeed, one might argue that they certainly were blessed—to be living in the United States of America in the middle of what Henry Luce, the founder of *Time* magazine, called, "The American Century." America had achieved unparalleled and unquestioned global preeminence—military, economic, technological, diplomatic— by the end of World War II, at just the point my parents were married and starting a family. Jimmy and Mary Fallon, immigrants from Tubbercurry, County Sligo, and Gubbadoorish, County Leitrim, remain to this day—years after their deaths—the most enthusiastic, patriotic Americans I have ever known. This was their life. This was their objective reality.

In my childhood household, there was no question that the United States of America was the greatest nation upon which God had ever shed His grace. Everything that America did, everything that America said, everything that America invented, everything that America produced was, by its very nature, a gift from God and therefore inherently good. American agriculture, American arts, American business, American education, American government, American health care, American innovation, the American standard of living, American technology—all were the best humans had ever devised and the envy of all the world.

In many ways, this was all true. It was true for no one more than my parents who had grown up with family recollections and stories of famine and with the reality of poverty; who had seen neighbors, friends, and family members leave Ireland forever or stay and die of diseases that could easily be treated there today, or in the United States of America one hundred years ago; who had lived through a civil war and the bitter peace that followed only to be frustrated and demoralized by both a stagnant economy and a repressive culture. I actually heard the name *Ireland* very rarely as a child; "God bless America" was a nearly daily prayer.

That God had blessed America was, to my parents, a proposition beyond argument. It was objectively true. The blessings were everywhere self-evident and seemed self-motivated and self-perpetuating. America was the fabled "land of opportunity," and the opportunities were constantly expanding; our technological prowess ensured constant improvement in our lives. Progress was one of the objective hallmarks of American life, a life drastically different from the lives my parents left behind. This is the rough conceptual framework and worldview of my childhood—a childhood so "American" that I wondered where my friends' parents came from, because they didn't seem "American" at all, as my parents were.

Ironically, as you might already suspect, my family was the strangest, oddest, funniest, most peculiar collection of creatures you could ever imagine. Everything we ate was boiled until gray. Our clothes were bought in thrift stores and handed down, from brother to brother, brother to sister, sister to brother. We knelt in our living room in the early evenings of my life reciting the rosary. We had frequent *ceilis*—evenings of music, singing, very bad dancing, skits, and story-telling—Dad with his accordion, brothers with guitars, trombones, tin whistles, and pots and pans, Mom presiding over the chaos with a cigarette in her hand, a broad smile on her face, and the sound of her constant laughter filling the rooms of our house, words of mischievous encouragement delivered with a still-thick, deep brogue. The spectacle amused some of our friends, alarmed others. In some of the less respectful quarters of Long Island, my parents were known as "Mr. and Mrs. Deedle-dee-deedle-dee-dee."

And yet, there can be no denying that, as odd as it was, I

enjoyed a thoroughly American childhood. My brothers and I may have played jigs and reels at home, but in our friends' garages and basements we were playing rock and roll—my older brothers, the music of the Surfaris, the Ventures, Bo Diddley, Elvis; and myself, some years later, the music of Chicago, Tower of Power, and Santana. We may have sometimes been on our knees saying prayers we didn't really understand, but in my school bag was a *Batman* comic book or a copy of *MAD* magazine. And we all may have gotten to feel comfortable telling stories, performing skits, reciting silly rhymes, and singing songs written a century before we were born, but when we weren't so engaged in nineteenth-century "party pieces," we were sitting together in the living room watching that fruit of American ingenuity, that quintessentially American medium: television. And we thought it was great.

Some of my earliest memories involve television. As difficult as it is to measure empirically, I'd have to say that some of those early televisual experiences were every bit as responsible for making me the person I am today as my siblings and my parents were. Even though I was born into the age of television, I was a first-generation television child, and I think that this first generation intuitively sensed that we were experiencing something objectively new and revolutionary, another one of God's unquestionable gifts bestowed upon us. Exactly what we were witnessing and just how revolutionary it would eventually turn out to be, however, we had no real idea.

Many of my early recollections of television are mundane and, perhaps, even banal. *The Mickey Mouse Club, Sky King, Howdy Doody, The Arthur Godfrey Show, The Soupy Sales Show, Candid Camera, and The Twilight Zone* (yes, I was way too young to be watching that, and inevitably had nightmares about Martians who wanted to import us to their planet as food:

humans as take-out and earth as a galactic Dean and DeLuca's). Endless repeats of the cheesy 1932 classic *King Kong*. Speedy Alka-Seltzer, Arthur Godfrey, Tony the Tiger, Sandy Becker, and the Ipana Toothpaste mascot Bucky Beaver were just some of the characters—real and imaginary—with whom I grew up.

Some of my memories, however, stand out beyond the mundane. I remember watching television with my father one evening long ago. We were watching scenes of soldiers, with bayonets fixed upon their rifles, holding back an angry, shouting crowd of what I remember thinking was an otherwise normal looking group of "grown-ups," while a group of students—my father called them "Negroes"—walked into a school. I didn't understand what I was watching, but my dad explained it to me. These Negro students wanted to go to school, but the white students—or was it their parents?—didn't want them to. So the President of the United States, my father explained to me, sent soldiers to make sure the Negro students could go to school. To my young mind that seemed like a good and decent thing to do. I was glad that the president of the United States sent those soldiers. The president was Dwight D. Eisenhower. The school was Little Rock Central High School. The year was 1957. I was three years old. And I remember it as though it were yesterday.

I remember one night a few years later sitting with my entire family watching a "special" that was airing the night after Thanksgiving. I saw pictures of men, women and children—some white, some "Negroes," and some who seemed to be neither white nor black (indeed, race was a concept that was difficult for me to grasp, for on a used 1950 black-and-white Philco, everyone appeared merely as slightly different shades of gray)—traveling in the backs of pickup trucks, living all together in something that looked to me like big one-room shacks, and working in hot fields, sweltering under the blazing summer sun, picking oranges, apples, berries, and all sorts of vegetables. They looked poor, and I remember someone of my family saying that the children didn't have a school to go to. That didn't sound "fair"—a significant moral concept to a child. Not really understanding everything the stern-looking narrator said, not really fully comprehending the story that was being presented to us that evening, I can still remember seeing a look on my parents' faces that today in my memories I can only describe as "discomfort." The stern-looking narrator was Edward R. Murrow. The program was the CBS News special, "Harvest of Shame." The year was 1960. I was six years old.

Earlier that same year I remember sitting down with my parents and my entire family to see what my folks said was a really important television broadcast. I remember seeing two men standing behind podiums on a stage of some sort, answering questions they were being asked by a TV newsman. They were talking about things that no six-year-old could possibly ever understand,[1] but I don't remember that it mattered much to me. I watched with great interest because my parents were intensely interested.

Of the specifics, however, I remember little more than this: I liked one of the two men, and I didn't really like the other one. One looked "nice" and one looked sort of "scary." One looked "friendly" and one looked "mean." One seemed "calm" and the other seemed kind of "nervous." One was, you could say, "handsome" with a "pleasant face," and the other, well, wasn't. Oh, yes—and one was Irish-Catholic and the other wasn't. Their names, my parents told me, were John Fitzgerald Kennedy and Richard Nixon, and one of them would be the next president of the United States of America. Without really knowing anything about them other than these impressions of "niceness" and "not-niceness," I remember hoping that the one named Kennedy would win the election. And in retrospect, I can see today something I was unable to see nearly a half century ago: I reacted to this debate—as a six-year-old child—in pretty much the same way the "grown-up" American electorate did:[2] on the level of impressions and emotions.

I remember, too, seeing images of the civil rights movement as a nine-year-old in 1963. I remember seeing pictures of American citizens—still called "Negroes" but soon to begin referring to themselves as "black"—marching through Birmingham, Alabama, in peaceful protest against "Jim Crow" segregation, being attacked by police dogs, beaten with billy clubs, and knocked off their feet by powerful water cannons. I remember seeing—and hearing—the Rev. Dr. Martin Luther King, Jr. address hundreds of thousands of people at the Lincoln Memorial in Washington, D.C., thundering above the din of the crowd that he had a dream about people being judged not by the color of their skin. but by the content of their character. Like so many millions of Americans, I was moved by both the words and the images. I started to realize that the idealized America of my parents' imaginations was not an objective reality, and that the real America of objective existence was far from perfect. But I also began to realize that in television—that great gift of American technology bestowed upon a deserving people by a loving God—we had a powerful tool for finding, investigating, and fixing our problems.

Then came November 22, 1963. Like all Americans of my age, and like most people across the world, I will remember that day for the rest of my life. I remember the Dominican sisters who taught in my grammar school leading us in a somber recitation of the rosary for our young, Irish-Catholic President who had been shot in Dallas, Texas. We prayed until, at about 2:00 PM Eastern Standard Time, we were sent home without explanation as the sisters broke down in tears. I remember reaching home and finding both my mother and father sitting in our living room leaning on each other, crying inconsolably, a sight I had never seen before in my life. I remember them telling me that President John Fitzgerald Kennedy had been murdered, and I remember crying with them. And I remember a stark feeling of numbness, of being disconnected, suddenly, from reality.

Two days later, I remember being one of the tens of millions of Americans who witnessed for the first time the murder of another human being, live (if you will) on television, as Jack Ruby shot Lee Harvey Oswald in the Dallas County jail. I remember thinking, at the ripe old age of nine, that the entire world had gone mad, and I remember being very frightened by that fact.

I remember, as I entered my teenage years, the images of mayhem entering my home every evening as television covered its first war. I remember seeing images of GIs lighting grass huts on fire. I remember seeing wounded GIs on stretchers, and as the war dragged on I remember seeing images of demoralized soldiers getting stoned at the front, some of them shooting heroin into their veins; seeing images of the aftermath of massacres such as that perpetrated at My Lai; being sickened by truly horrifying images of General Nguyễn Ngọc Loan executing a Viet Cong prisoner on the streets of Saigon during the Tet offensive of 1968.

I remember watching as television brought us images of Martin Luther King expanding his quest for civil rights into a crusade against mindless warfare, and of Bobby Kennedy, the murdered president's brother, former attorney general, and senator from New York, becoming an outspoken anti-war candidate for the presidency of the United States of America. And I remember watching, numbed, the news reports that told me that they had been assassinated within weeks of one another.

And I remember seeing the change in public opinion regarding the war, a drop in public support, a growing mandate for ending the war, as measured by the increasingly strident and self-confident anti-war protests being held on an almost daily basis by a maturing anti-war movement. And I remembered the America I grew up in, my parents' America, and tried to be optimistic, tried to put the best face on what seemed to be an increasingly dire reality. I remember telling myself that America was experiencing growing pains but that, while the world and our place in it looked bleak at this moment, we would learn from our mistakes, recover from our self-inflicted wounds, and go on to do amazing and important things for ourselves and for the world.

On July 20, 1969, we did just that. I watched, along with the rest of the world, as the United States of America accomplished what is still arguably the greatest feat of technological engineering in the history of humankind—the landing of two humans, Neil Armstrong and Edwin "Buzz" Aldrin, on the surface of the moon. No other human engineering accomplishment—not the pyramids, nor the hanging gardens of Babylon, nor the Brooklyn Bridge, nor the construction of one-hundred-story skyscrapers—comes close to this epic achievement, and when Walter Cronkite took off his glasses as the lunar excursion module touched down on the moon's dusty surface, ran his hands through his hair, breathed a sigh of relief, and chuckled contentedly, all of America, and much of the world, rejoiced with him.[3]

I remember seeing all of these things, and so much more. And I remember thinking to myself at a very early age[4] that I wanted to be a part of this revolution in mass communication, to take part in the process of change, to make a difference in the world. Much to my delight, excitement, and eventual despair, I eventually got the opportunity to do just that.

After college and a five-year apprenticeship making educational and training videotapes for the New York State Office of

Mental Health, I began work at NBC News in July 1982 as a "vacation relief" electronic journalism editor. By the spring of 1983 I was hired permanently and spent the next sixteen years working for the *TODAY* program. I was thrilled to be a part of television journalism, to follow—at a respectful distance, to be sure—in the footsteps of so many of my heroes, Fred Friendly, Edward R. Murrow, Walter Cronkite, Roger Mudd, Edwin Newman, Frank McGee, Chet Huntley, David Brinkley, Nancy Dickerson, Reuven Frank, and so many thousands of others who worked behind the camera; to share in the legacy of "Harvest of Shame," "See It Now, NBC's *TODAY* program, *The CBS Evening News with Walter Cronkite,* the coverage of the space program, and the investigation of presidential wrongdoing known as "Watergate."

But almost immediately upon my entry into television journalism, things began to change. Television, like most other American industries, began a long process of deregulation in the 1980s that continues today. The cable networks introduced greater competition for viewers' attentions and profit became a powerful criterion for programming. Information—news as well as entertainment—became more and more a salable commodity rather than the civic responsibility of a free press. The news began to "soften." There were more human-interest stories, more stories that might make the viewer laugh, or shock the viewer, or anger the viewer, and fewer stories that I, at any rate, would consider newsworthy. News interviews became shorter and shorter until they achieved (if that is the appropriate word) the status of "sound byte," ten- to twenty-second blips of disjointed information, more emotion than fact. As time wore on, there were fewer and fewer serious original news documentaries on the "big three" major broadcast-news networks until, finally, there were none at all.

The last decade of my tenure at NBC was dominated by coverage of the murder trial of O.J. Simpson, the inconclusive investigation of the murder of Jon Benet Ramsey, the various tribulations of P. Diddy, and the $64,000,000 political witch hunt known as the Whitewater investigation, that alleged to have been an investigation of the financial improprieties of then-President William Jefferson Clinton while he was governor of Arkansas (no such improprieties were found), but ultimately culminated in his impeachment for lying under oath—on national television—about his relationship with a White House intern, Monica Lewinsky. And I started to see myself not as a part of a powerful agent of social change, but as a cog in an enormous machine of mass entertainment, a powerless functionary in a powerful mechanism of social stasis.

But since those days, my attitudes about television have become even further refined. I have been forced to reconsider my earliest and most closely held beliefs about the role of television in society. I have begun to question whether, even when it is functioning at its highest level, at its most professional, with its greatest degree of journalistic integrity, with its most serious and dedicated reporters (there are a few left), television can ever be seen—as I once saw it—as a medium of enlightenment and as an agent of change, or if it has in fact fulfilled its *true calling* as merely another electronic medium of inane distraction from the harsh realities of life.

I began to question if this medium, and other human technological innovations we have vainly and chauvinistically labeled "American," were the gifts from God that I had once imagined them to be, or if they did not instead constitute some sort of moral challenge. For television, along with other electronic media, has presented such a challenge to us all. Television has so sped up the flow of information to and from humans, while at the same time increasing the volume of information we receive (thereby distorting its meaning for us), that all hope of coherence in mass communication seems lost.

Discrete "bits" of information, delivered without benefit of context or organizing principle, assault us minute by minute, day after day. Cultural chaos and social discord appear to spread all around us. The possibility of an objective view of the world recedes into the distance, and all we can see are diverse and disjointed points of view. Television, along with other electronic media of the "information age," can leave us feeling dazed, confused, impotent to understand—let alone address—the world's problems. We are exhausted, overwhelmed by an endless series of apparently disconnected events swirling around us, powerless to control them—let alone change them.

Worse still, television, as the dominant medium in our electronic culture, has changed the way we *think* about the world, about our place in the world, about our nation, about our values, about ourselves and our relationship to one another. Because of the powerfully presentational structure of images,[5] we have literally allowed the rational thought processes, which took millennia to develop, to become atrophied—while reinforcing and giving renewed power to those instinctive, intuitive, and emotional processes that we share with our evolutionary ancestors.

At the same time, a new discourse (if that is even an appropriate word to descibe it) has emerged in our culture—and not just the American culture, but an increasingly global culture—that is difficult to think of as discourse at all. It is a very strange set of exchanges that seems to value controversy for its own sake and conflict for the sake of dramatic appeal. It is a sort of discourse that presents two people with diametrically opposing viewpoints who argue or yell at or even insult each other, and gives the viewer no real opportunity to approach anything like an understanding of the issues which are being "debated."

It is a free-market sort of discourse valued most for its appeal to the senses rather than to reason, a sort of discourse whose primary concern is the attraction and maintenance of an audience, not the identification and dissemination of information that might add quality to our lives or help us to see and think about complex ethical issues. It is, most importantly, a sort of discourse that puts the patently untrue on an equal footing with the empirically verifiable. It is a sort of discourse that has displaced its predecessor, rational discourse, by force. And it is a sort of discourse that has mistaken the absence of *any* point of view for objectivity.

And so I look upon the current era of television, the broader era of electronic communication, and the much vaunted "information revolution," with a skeptic's eye. Has the age of information improved our lot, made the earth a safer place or humans any more compassionate? Has global, instantaneous information made us more appreciative of the miracle of our own human intelligence and more likely to use our intellectual and physical capabilities to change the world for the better? Has exposure to different cultures and different points of view and different aspirations and different needs made us more tolerant people?

Or have we indulged ourselves (those few of us on Earth who can afford such indulgences) with new toys, new games, new amusements, new entertainments, and used the very technologies with which we indulge our whims—television included, and all that appears on television—to shield us from the consequences of our egoistic self-indulgence? Do we see reality more clearly and understand it more fully as a result of global mass communication, or have we escaped into a different reality, an alternative reality, a virtual (but not necessarily virtuous) reality?

Has the age of electricity left us, paradoxically, in the dark? And has any other medium that came before the age of electric communication done any better, or will any that follow it? And, in the end, does it really matter? Questions of ethics, questions manufactured and asked on the basis of values, questions of "right" and "wrong," "truth" and "falsehood," "justice" and "injustice"—are such questions at all appropriate anymore in anything other than a functional, utilitarian, or pragmatic way? Is the very idea of truth as an epistemic end, a pursuit of truth, anything more than a quaint and obsolete notion (like human rights in a time of terrorism, like the Geneva Conventions at Guantanamo)?

Different Media, Different Realities

In order to answer these questions, it will of course be necessary to make some sort of judgment about the media that human beings have used throughout history in order to gauge the extent to which humans were helped or hindered by them. We will also have to make other, more subjective judgments about what constitutes help or hindrance.

This is likely to be a contentious discussion, not least of all because of our human cognitive, intellectual, and emotional diversity. We don't all see things the same way; that is objectively true. But it doesn't follow logically, therefore, that all points of view are equally true—in spite of what the postmodernists are telling us.

Human beings, alone among all the creatures on earth, have the capacity of language: the use of meaningful, abstract, and shared symbols to process, store, manipulate, recall, and transmit experiences. As a consequence of the abstract nature of these symbols, we are also the only creatures to have an awareness—perhaps no more than an inkling, a vague sense, a desperate hope—of a reality beyond our physical, sensory experience. That we believe things and "in things" that we cannot ever experience through firsthand sensory perception is a defining characteristic of human intelligence. Both our daily understanding of "reality" as constructed by our various news media, interpersonal contacts, and firsthand experiences, and our propensity either to envision ourselves as spiritual beings with immortal souls or to reject such a vision, are part and parcel of symbolic thought. Just as important a consequence, however, is the fact that we are the only creatures with the ability—and the technologies—to confuse our realities. Walter Ong tells us:

> The technological inventions of writing, print, and electronic verbalization, in their historical effects, are connected with and have helped bring about a certain kind of alienation within the human lifeworld. This is not at all to say that these inventions have been simply destructive, but rather that they have restructured consciousness, affecting men's and women's presence to the world and to themselves and creating new interior distances within the psyche.[6]

At least since the time of Descartes, we have been aware of the critical role of the human mind in the invention, construction, and comprehension of reality, in both its sensory perception and in the intellectual processes of making meaning. If one were to propose, therefore, that media of communication had a strong influence on human perception and the intellectual processes of meaning-making, and furthermore that different media influenced the processes of perception and reasoning in different ways, one would certainly be inclined to conclude that we will think about things—at the very least—*differently* as a result of using one medium of communication rather than another. It is therefore necessary to examine the role that these media play in both the construction and the confusion of reality, in the restructuring of consciousness, and in helping us sort out the "real" from the "unreal."

It is in the nature of any reality that is inherently "beyond the physical" to be difficult if not impossible to comprehend fully. That has not stopped human beings from claiming to have a full understanding of such ideas, and claiming further to have a monopoly on such understanding. Throughout history humans have contemplated, theorized, created myths about, dogmatized, denied, argued, fought, and gone to war over metaphysical "realities" (*"Gott mit uns"* was a German rallying cry of World War I, and we remain at this very moment engaged in what appears to some observers to be a holy war—a "crusade" in the words of George W. Bush[7]—supposedly between the abstract and absolute concepts of good and evil). At the same time, we have often behaved similarly with respect to "facts" which have little or no foundation in physical reality—things that we want so badly to be true that we believe they are true in spite of either evidence to the contrary or no evidence at all.

This is nothing new and not at all unexpected. All things distinctly human about our species—love and hate, dreams and aspirations, art, literature, music, superstition, government, commerce, science, idealism and cynicism, and religious faith—spring from this innate capacity to understand and engage the world through abstract symbols. The greatest human accomplishments and the most barbaric atrocities are attributable to symbolic thought and language.

Even the fact that we have culture—distinct sets of ideas, attitudes, values, and behaviors that we transmit down the ages through formal social institutions—is a powerful index of the potency of symbolic thought. Richard Leakey and Roger Lewin remind us that, as creatures of culture, "we can impose our will on the environment and on ourselves, depending on the social rules we choose to make and follow."[8] It is important to acknowledge that this is as true of the information environment as it is the natural environment. The power of culture to reflect and perpetuate one view of reality over another, one set of assumptions, values, attitudes, and behaviors over another set, is truly formidable. "Each one of us," Leakey and Lewin continue, "is born with the potential to live any of countless different lives, but we live just one, the one shaped by the rules of the culture in which we grow up."[9] And so, historically, because it matters, but also biologically, because we were born to be creatures of culture, we human beings have tried to conserve, preserve, and perpetuate those things (including ideas) which we value, which have some functional utility, or which we find beautiful or aesthetically pleasing.

Within and through our culture we have also, however, handed down from generation to generation our hatreds, our prejudices, our rational and irrational fears, our jealousies, our greed, our self-righteousness and—dare I say it?—our stupidity. These intellectual effluvia—flotsam and jetsam of the mind—pollute our perceptions and understanding of reality and the ways we hand down those perceptions and understanding to future generations. Some of these noxious elements (racial prejudice, for instance) are based on ignorance and can therefore be remedied. Critical scientific thought, since its advent, has allowed us to examine our assumptions and test their validity. What is true, from an objective, empirical point of view, is good to know. What is not true, from this perspective, should be discarded.

Other negative influences, however, are not based on ignorance *per se* and confront us with problems more difficult to address. It can be argued that greed, for example, signifies a faulty system of values. In such a case, a person may have all the empirical knowledge he/she needs to function effectively in society, but assigns a greater value to self-interest than to the interests of others. As a compassionate society, we might be expected to say that such a person is "wrong" and "selfish." But who is to say, many argue, that a particular value system is more valid than another? In fact, from an empirical point of view it could be demonstrated that greed, as a value, has advantages over many more other-centered virtues—as a survival tool, for instance.

In either of these cases, it is important to note, knowledge is an important factor in decision making. Consequently, the quality of the knowledge ought to be of concern to us. Steven Jay Gould in *The Mismeasure of Man*[10] illustrated how even empirical knowledge, collected using consciously or unconsciously biased methods of measurement, can be used to reinforce racial prejudices. Yet little more than a decade later Richard Herrnstein and Charles Murray in *The Bell Curve*[11] resurrected both bad science and subtle racism and produced a best seller, albeit a controversial one.

And the question of unknown, hidden, or suppressed knowledge—information that for one reason or another never reaches us—is one which should not be ignored when considering the social construction of reality, and conversely, society's construal of "un-reality." Our mass-mediated information age, an age of promiscuous, profligate information, an age where we find ourselves literally inundated with millions of discreet bits of disconnected data daily, an age where we *appear* to be more connected to one another than at any time in the history of humankind, is not, unfortunately, an age in which we have witnessed the demise of ignorance. On the contrary, the very incongruity and incoherence of information overload may make ignorance a growing phenomenon. This phenomenon grows at our peril, for what we don't know about ourselves and about the rest of the world *can* hurt us.

Ignorance, Vincible and Invincible

In his *Nicomachean Ethics,* Aristotle discusses the phenomenon of ignorance with an eye toward ameliorating the blame of one who chooses to do wrong in the absence of certain facts not in his/her possession. Aristotle sees all human actions as either voluntary or involuntary—the former resulting in praise or blame for the moral agent, the latter in pardon or pity.[12] His is certainly a humane assumption. Involuntary actions may be the result of coercion, duress, or some other form of force, in which case we—as judges of those actions—are naturally inclined to forgive or otherwise attenuate our reproach; or involuntary actions may be the result of ignorance.

Aristotle moves to further fortify his moral position by differentiating two conditions: acting *in* ignorance and acting *due to* ignorance. Acting *in* ignorance is akin to derangement or stupidity: "A man's action is not considered to be due to ignorance when he is drunk or angry, but due to intoxication or anger, although he does not know what he is doing and is in fact acting in ignorance."[13] And if he is not entirely culpable for the acts undertaken in such a condition, he is certainly culpable for the condition itself. But acting *due to* ignorance is a different story entirely:

> Now every wicked man is in a state of ignorance as to what he ought to do and what he should refrain from doing, and it is due to this kind of error that men become unjust and, in general, immoral. But an act can hardly be called involuntary if the agent is ignorant of what is beneficial. Ignorance in moral choice does not make an act involuntary—it makes it wicked; nor does ignorance of the universal, for that invites reproach; rather it is ignorance of the particulars which constitutes the circumstances and the issues

> involved in the action. It is on these that pity and pardon
> depend, for a person who acts in ignorance of a particular
> circumstance acts involuntarily.[14]

This sets a stage for a set of moral circumstances which distance us from culpability for our behaviors which don't *appear* to us to be connected to any other events going on in the world which don't have a clear and obvious connection to them. And in a world of global markets, global labor, and the global distribution of both commodities and information, the particulars of human relationships are obscured by their very ubiquitous immanence, and can appear to be random and unrelated to our choices; in such a case, we might just be skating on some thin moral ice.

There is a set of old jokes built on a template that begins, "I have some good news and some bad news . . ." Well, I have some good news and some bad news for anyone reading this book. First, the good news about ignorance, defined in the *Catholic Encyclopedia* as a "lack of knowledge about a thing in a being capable of knowing,"[15] is that it "is said to be invincible when it cannot be dispelled by the reasonable diligence a prudent person would be expected to exercise in a given situation"[16]—that is, when we've done everything we can, morally speaking, to learn the truth. Invincible ignorance is always a valid excuse and excludes us from culpability since the agent is "unaware of the nature of a situation or the obligations it involves."[17] Now the bad news: we may be in trouble (theologically, in "a state of sin") if we allow the existence of evil *even when we are ignorant of it,* if that ignorance is vincible, "that which could be dispelled by the application of reasonable diligence,"[18] such as a sensible and prudent person would use under the circumstances. Ignorance may be bliss, but it is certainly not a virtue, as it does not in the slightest add to a comprehensive view of reality. Nor, on the other hand, does recognition and acceptance of transcendent "truths" (belief in God, for only one example) *necessarily* imply ignorance or superstition or anything else inconsistent with enlightened, rational thought—although it certainly might.

In this book, I invite you to accompany me in examining the metaphysics—the conception of things within and beyond sensory experience—promulgated and supported by different media of communication. It is an assumption of this book that

- because of their physical and symbolic forms;
- because of the way they structure information and challenge us either to respond on an intellectual or emotional level;
- because of their speed, direction, and quantity of information flow;
- because of the conditions that they present us with in order to use them and to attend to the information they make available to us; and,
- because of the various ways in which they create and support conceptions of time and space,

different media engender different conceptions of reality and therefore corresponding conceptions of what is not real.

More specifically, we will want to investigate this problem within two distinct subdivisions of philosophy: *ontology,* the study of the fundamental nature of being; and *epistemology* the study of knowledge, of how we know, and of what is worth knowing. Together we will try to answer the following two questions:

Because of their sensory and intellectual biases, do different media support different conceptions of what is ultimately real? (Ontological question).

Because of the tendency for monopolies of knowledge to form around specific media, do different media reflect in their content the different political, economic, or social agenda of the social class that controls them? (Epistemological question)

Looking closely at the form, structure, and biases of media, we can use these questions to help us understand more fully why we know what we know (and why we don't know what we don't know), why what we believe (or don't believe) is worth knowing, how and through what means we come to this knowledge (or not), and, ultimately, what sort of a picture of reality we carry with us in our heads. These questions may be unusual for students and researchers of mediated communication. They are, indeed, questions of the metaphysics of media. I propose it is time that we started getting used to asking them, and consider deeply the questions that they, in their turn, suggest to us.

Chapter One

On the Utility of the Media Ecological Perspective as a Tool in the Study of the Metaphysics of a Culture

The concerns of metaphysics have traditionally been the domain of philosophers and theologians. Many academics would like them to remain so. Studying the belief or unbelief in things seen or unseen, the existence or nonexistence of absolutes or ideal concepts, the ultimate foundation of human values, and, of course, the nature of reality has been seen for roughly the last generation—as the postmodern concept of education has shifted towards a market model—as somewhat esoteric and impractical. "How can I use this," most students ask, *"in the real world*? How will this help me have a successful career?"

The metaphysical question, however, not only refuses to go away, but is increasing in its urgency. It is one that we are confronting more frequently in disciplines that were once foreign to such discussions. A world of six billion people living lives increasingly connected by technologies seems to demand a greater demand for ethical decision making than ever before. And being able to see those connections—for good and for ill—becomes a paramount ethical concern, something we've only begun to do. For instance, acknowledgement of the role of technologies of communication—*without regard to the content which they deliver to us*—in creating and supporting socially-constructed views of reality is barely a generation old. The role of communication technologies (like the role of all technology) in society was once clear or at least appeared so; media of human communication were more or less innocent, objective, and "transparent" instruments for the dissemination of information. They could be used to spread truth, or they could be used to spread lies, propaganda, or other "harmful content," and that was the extent of our concern. We very much wanted to use our media to spread "truth" and not "falsehood." We had no conception that perhaps the medium itself, through its very form, might bear a powerful influence upon us beyond its content; that, as Marshall McLuhan said, "The medium is the message,"[1] or, as he explained, "This is merely to say that the personal and social consequences of any medium—that is, of any extension of ourselves—result from the new scale that is introduced into our affairs by each extension of ourselves, or by any new technology."[2]

Like all members of a culture that learns more to depend on their technologies than to question them, we naturally believed our media of mass communication were a manifestation of human progress. Today, we are not all so sure. One of the significant contributions of postmodern thought to the global *Weltanschauung* has been the (seemingly) moral imperative to see clearly the structures of thought, of language, and of power that support culture and its institutions, and to understand their role in the social construction of reality. Those roles, postmodernists have decided, have not always been positive. I am inclined to agree with what I see as their objective appraisal.

My major premise in these pages is that different media impose upon the societies that make use of them different specific and identifiable—though frequently invisible—metaphysical "frameworks" through which we understand ourselves, our lives, our societies, and our world.

In the last half of the twentieth century, social and cultural critics from a number of academic disciplines began to recognize the role of technology in shaping culture, not just in a historical sense, but also in an intellectual one. Anthropologists (Hall, Malinowski), sociologists (Ellul), historians (Eisenstein), psychologists (Watzlavick, Beavins-Bavelas, Jackson), linguists (Goody, Watt, Johnson), classicists (Havelock), economists (Innis), and many others have created an expanding body of literature which has become a core curriculum for a new field of study: media ecology.

Media ecology is, according to Neil Postman, the study of media as information environments:

> It is concerned to understand how technologies and techniques of communication control the form, quantity, speed, distribution, and direction of information; and how, in turn, such information configurations or biases affect people's perceptions, values, and attitudes. Thus media ecology transcends several subjects of wider acceptance, including, for example, psychology and sociology, since it assumes that the psychology of people and their methods of social organization are, in large measure, a product of a culture's characteristic information patterns. . . . When we talk of the psychology of a culture or its sociology, we are talking about the effects of information forms.[3]

Media ecologists have looked particularly closely at the powerful influence communication technologies bring to bear on social institutions like education; on the formation and perpetuation of values; and on the shaping of a society's peculiar epistemology—those concepts, attitudes, behaviors, beliefs, etc., which a given society sees as being worth learning, knowing, and preserving. They have also noted that different media impose peculiar cognitive and affective limitations on the very types of information they can handle, and these limitations in turn influence the shape, the structure, and the manner of the culture.

Media Ecology is broad in both its scope and its methods. There is no one specific way to "do" Media Ecology. Some theorists (such as Innis) believe that emergent technologies change the balance of power in a society, upsetting established "monopolies of knowledge" based on already dominant media, and creating new ones.

Harold Innis, working from his unique vantage point as a historian of economics, showed us several consequences of the introduction of the printing press into late-medieval Europe that were as much (if not more) related to the physical form of the medium alone as they were to any question of its content. Innis saw print as a "space-biased" medium, one that led to the effective expansion and consolidation of political power across vast regions. Consequently, "the effect of the discovery of printing was evident in the savage religious wars of the sixteenth and seventeenth centuries. Application of power to communication industries hastened the consolidation of vernaculars, the rise of nationalism, revolution, and new outbreaks of savagery in the twentieth century."[4]

It is also, Innis tells us, in the nature of a space-biased medium like print to frame itself in opposition to time-biased media, which facilitate the growth and spread of institutions whose concerns are of the spiritual, the unchanging, and the eternal: "In England . . . [abolition] of the monasteries and disappearance of clerical celibacy were followed by sweeping educational reforms. The printing press became 'a battering ram to bring abbeys and castles crashing to the ground.'"[5] "By the end of the sixteenth century the flexibility of the alphabet and printing had contributed to the growth of diverse vernacular literatures and had provided a basis for divisive nationalism in Europe."[6]

Other theorists (for example, McLuhan and Ong) see the influences of media upon the cultures that use them as psychic and structural. To these researchers, the propositional structure of print (to use an arbitrary example) actually changes human thought patterns, changing at the same time the structure of society itself, the relationship among individuals within the society, and among individuals and social institutions. The eventual discovery of electricity and the development of electronic media will yield different psychic effects with different consequences.

Marshall McLuhan, speaking of the rise of nationalism following the development of print, tells us:

> There was no nationalism before the Renaissance, and we have now seen enough of the character of print technology to know why this should be so. For if print made the vernaculars into mass media, they also constituted a means of central government control of society beyond anything that even the Romans had known with papyrus and alphabet and paved roads. But the very nature of print creates two conflicting interests as between producers and consumers, and between rulers and ruled. For print as a means of centrally organized mass-production ensures that the problem of "freedom" will henceforth be paramount in all social and political discussion. [7]

Of print's powers to engender a new European concept of individualism, McLuhan says, "Print is the extreme phase of alphabet culture that detribalizes or decollectivizes man in the first instance. Print raises the visual features of alphabet to highest intensity of definition. Thus print carries the individuating power of the phonetic alphabet much further than manuscript culture could ever do. Print is the technology of individualism." [8]

Electricity creates a new type of human, however, and changes his/her relationship to the world:

> The new environment of simultaneous and diversified information creates acoustic man. He is surrounded by

sound—from behind, from the side, from above. His environment is made up of information in all kinds of simultaneous forms, and he puts on this electrical environment as we put on our clothes, or as a fish puts on water. [9]

The alphabet (and its extension into typography) made possible the spread of the power that is knowledge and shattered the bonds of tribal man, thus exploding him into an agglomeration of individuals. Electric writing and speed pour upon him instantaneously and continuously the concerns of all other men. He becomes tribal once more. The human family becomes one tribe again.[10]

Walter Ong takes a similar—if somewhat more systematic and focused—approach to that of McLuhan, focusing on the psychic and intellectual influences media impose as a result of their specific forms. For example, writing, Ong tells us, restructures consciousness by (as Plato argues) inducing our rejection of "the old oral, mobile, warm, personally interactive lifeworld of oral culture;"[11] by shifting our intellectual dependence on memory to preserve the past to written records;[12] by creating an objective distance between the knower and the thing known;[13] by changing the human sensory balance from ear dominance to eye dominance;[14] and by bringing on an expanded interior life impossible without the act of reading. "Technology is important in the history of the word not merely exteriorly, as a kind of circulator of pre-existing materials, but interiorly, for it transforms what can be said and what is said. Since writing came into existence, the evolution of the word and the evolution of consciousness have been intimately tied in with technologies and technological development. Indeed, all major advances in consciousness depend on technological transformations and implementations of the word."[15]

But other theorists (for example, Eisenstein, Postman) take a more measured social or ecological approach to judging the influences of media on human culture and society. What societal or cultural institutions, they might ask, will be affected, positively or negatively, by the introduction of a new medium? What institutions will find a natural ally in, say, print (science and education perhaps) and what in television (commerce and industry)?

Eisenstein takes issue with both McLuhan's deterministic exposition of the power of the printing press and his stereotyped view of the new "print-made man": "McLuhan's eighteenth-century man who is 'locked into a closed visual system' seems to be symptomatic of the very ailment he purports to diagnose: a print-and-paper creation, a fit companion only for McLuhan's other ingenious creation: the mechanical bride."[16]

And yet she does not, it must be said, disagree with McLuhan, for at the same time she chronicles—citing abundant historical documentation—the growth and progress of Enlightenment thought, aided by the parallel growth and progress of a European printing industry:

> From the days of Castellio to those of Voltaire, the printing industry was the principal natural ally of libertarian, heterodox, and ecumenical philosophers. Eager to expand markets and diversify production, the enterprising publisher was the natural enemy of narrow minds.[17]

> When setting the stage for the Enlightenment, metaphorical "citadels" and "fountains" are too insubstantial to serve as props. Real presses and printing firms made it possible for Grotius, Descartes, Richard Simon and John Locke to make a permanent impression on the European mind.[18]

Eisenstein's point—it appears to me—is that McLuhan has made some very interesting and valid points that both the average person and the mainstream academic are missing, probably because of difficulties with McLuhan's highly intuitive and creative, but equally confounding, aphoristic method. Her approach appears to be to take McLuhan's highly intuitive, "right-brained" observations and clothe them in a mantle of historical facts.

Similarly, Postman's measured approach echoes McLuhan's intuitive one but tempers it with reason based on historical insight: "In the eighteenth and nineteenth centuries, print put forward a definition of intelligence that gave priority to the objective, rational use of mind and at the same time encouraged forms of public discourse with serious, logically ordered content. It is no accident that the Age of Reason was coexistent with the growth of print culture, first in Europe and then in America."[19]

Still other media scholars (such as Perkinson) believe that a medium's content—the messages that flow through it and pervade a mass culture—can have a powerful positive or negative effect on that culture. Speaking of television's power to bring about the moral improvement of human beings (and their civilizations), Henry Perkinson points out:

> Television provokes feelings more than thought. Our criticisms, therefore, take the form of "this is good" or "this is bad," rather than "this is true" or "this is false." Television therefore educes moral criticism, and that criticism focuses primarily on the relationships encoded on the screen—relationships among people and relationships between people and nature. [20]

> In the political realm, such criticism comes in two varieties. One form of moral political criticism exposes the evils, the injustices, the bad consequences of the policies, practices, and procedures, carried out by the government. The second kind of moral political criticism chastises the government for not doing what is proper, good, or just.[21]

Each of these few Media Ecological perspectives that I have used as examples differs in its approach and in the problem it seeks to address, but each of them acknowledges the relationship of media and culture to be an ecological one. That is a good thing, because that relationship is, in fact, ecological. The relationship of a culture's belief systems with its technologies of communication is also ecological.

The particular theoretical framework upon which this investigation will be based is of this Media Ecological sort: that is to say that it utilizes a set of six characteristics of media which have been identified and validated through observation and empirical research by media ecologists. The six characteristics[22] can be summarized as follows:

1. Communication media differ in their form. Form includes *symbolic* form and *physical* form. Symbolic form refers to the characteristics of the code in which a medium conveys information (symbols, signs, gestures, sounds, etc.) and the *presentational structure* or *propositional structure* within which the code is conveyed. Physical form refers to the characteristics of the technology (that is, the "hardware") that conveys the code, and the physical requirements for encoding, conveying, storing, retrieving, decoding, and using information.

2. Because of the differences in their forms, media differ in their *conditions of attendance.* These conditions can be identified by asking the following questions: To whom does a particular medium make information available? Under what circumstances does one gain access to this

information?   Does the recipient of this
information have the prerequisite skills or
knowledge to make use of this information?

3. Because of their differences in form, media
differ in their *speed of dissemination, quantity
or volume of information disseminated,* and
direction of information flow.

4. Because of the differences in physical form,
different media have different *temporal and spatial
biases.*

5. Because of the differences in symbolic form,
different media have different *sensory biases.*

6. Because of the differences in their conditions
of attendance, different media have different
political/social biases.

This Media Ecological approach is, I think, particularly
valuable for the type of investigation I am attempting to undertake in this book—identifying, describing, and delineating the
metaphysics of media—in that it illuminates (sheds light upon,
brings "out of the darkness") and makes visible certain processes (cognitive and affective) and structures (political, economic,
and social) that would otherwise remain invisible to us in the
normal course of our lives.

Furthermore, although it is not explicitly or necessarily concerned with questions of ethics, normative or otherwise,
Media Ecology lends itself very naturally to deep and probing
ethical inquiry. Uncovering and examining conditions that limit
access to a communication event to some but not to others; understanding that the way in which a medium structures information might encourage presentation of some types of information
at the expense of others; identifying "monopolies of knowledge"

that grow around dominant media; acknowledging that social, political, and economic structures influence the way our system of mass communication operates. All of these concerns are fundamentally ethical ones, and all of them may be effectively and critically addressed through Media Ecological principles and methods.

That's what I hope to do.

Chapter Two

The Contentious Nature
of Objective Reality
and the Inarguable Value of Truth

In January of 2004 I was engaged in a discussion on a discipline-related Internet discussion list regarding the role of the media ecologist in a time of war. The United States was nearly a year into what appeared even then to be a disastrous intervention in Iraq; the chief U.S. weapons inspector, David Kay, having just finished his duties and resigned, said publicly that he believed the weapons of mass destruction over which the Bush administration had committed U.S. troops to Iraq never existed. We were just beginning in January of 2004 to recognize what a truly abysmal job the assembled U.S. news media had done in delivering to our nation the documentary, physical, and historical evidence that refuted—or at the very least questioned—the Bush administration's claims that there were weapons of mass destruction in Iraq, that Saddam Hussein had reconstituted a program for the construction of nuclear weapons, that there were high-level contacts between the Iraqi government and al-Qaeda and that Saddam Hussein had been complicit in the murderous attacks of September 11, 2001. It was within this context that I made what I thought to be a fairly commonsense observation.

I suggested that "the ethical/moral obligation of media ecology—and all—scholars is the pursuit (not the illusion of possession) of truth."[1] One of my respondents—himself no fan of either the war in Iraq or the Bush administration—suggested nonetheless in his turn that my suggestion was "a tired and unproductive response"[2] to the problem of perception, objective

35

reality, and certainty in the face of an ever-increasing barrage of information. Surely, he said, we can come up with a better, more heuristic, more intellectually productive concept to impose upon the study of mass-mediated communication than the troublesome and divisive concept of "truth." Truth, after all, is an illusion, a chimera that drives men to hate and to kill. "I'll even," he continued, "just for the sake of being polemical, suggest that as media ecologists, the 'all hail truth' response is an abdication of individual responsibility and an unacknowledged dismissal of our field of inquiry."[3]

I was not persuaded by his argument five years ago and I remain unconvinced today. I invoked the apparently fearsome name of Truth not in an act of intellectual imperialism, not in an effort to impose a specific view of truth upon someone else, but out of what I saw as respect for empiricism.

"First of all," I responded, "it is (or if it isn't, it ought to be) the obligation of scholars to pursue truth . . . NOT to claim to possess it, as the 'all hail truth' remark implies. To suggest that the pursuit of truth is 'unproductive' is to say that the pursuit of something other than truth is instead productive. Fine. Productive of what? What is the end of random rumination? . . . I have no problem with anyone who wishes to pursue something other than truth. But I think rather that it is here that you find the negation of our field of inquiry."[4]

The conversation went on in a friendly yet spirited manner, and I felt at that moment that my argument, supremely logical as I saw it to be, would win the day. And yet this respondent, and others on the list, seemed to find my attachment to the "unproductive" concept of truth embarrassingly quaint. Why? The distance between us was so great, and the prevailing attitude against truth so palpable, that I found myself wondering if there had been some sort of culture-wide memo that I had missed.

Here's what I want to know: Is there or is there not such

a thing as objective reality, and is it, in fact, productive, un-productive, or counter-productive to concern ourselves with its existence? If there is no such thing, then I would have to agree with the postmodernists that it is a waste of time (a tremendous waste of time at that) to concern ourselves with it. But if reality bears an objective existence outside of our awareness or belief; if, in fact, its existence impinges on us and on others without regard to our awareness or belief in it; then I think it might behoove us to pay it some attention.

To paraphrase the bumper sticker, "stuff happens." It really does, it's outside of our control, and it doesn't matter whether we choose to believe in that particular "stuff" or deny its existence. On September 11, 2001, something happened. Something really happened. It was not, as many hoped and prayed, a figment of our imagination. It may have "felt just like a movie," but it was objectively real. Something cataclysmic and terrifying happened, and there can be no question of its reality. We know exactly what happened; we have counted the dead. Unless you're willing to countenance the (in my humble opinion) psychotic notion that nothing is "real" that we don't actually perceive through our senses, the 2,996 victims, their families, friends, and loved ones give ample evidence of the objective reality of that tragic day.

We may find room for disagreement about the causes of the event; we may find room for disagreement about what might have been or what in the future might be appropriate responses; but there can be no question, short of (again, in my humble opinion) psychotic denial, that the awful events of that day actually occurred, outside of our control and without regard to our awareness or lack of awareness. And if we ultimately find that we differ in our view of the causes or appropriate (and inappropriate) responses, I feel certain that research, study, critical thought, goodwill, and vigorous discussion will help us come to some greater understanding of the truth.

But this can happen only if we have faith in research, study, critical thought, goodwill, and vigorous discussion in the first place. This, at the end of the day, is the fatal problem of post-modernism. Postmodernism is a mindset totally devoid of faith, even in science. That is why, in many ways, September 11, 2001 should have marked the end of the postmodern era. Postmodern-istic relativism is a luxury that we, as a society, can no longer afford.

I certainly believe that objective reality, along with its neces-sary counterpart, truth, exists; and it seems logical to me that academia, of all the possible cultural institutions humans have created in two million years on earth, ought to be a good place to take this hoary old concept up and see what we can make of it. It is, after all, an institution founded on research, study, critical thought, goodwill, and vigorous discussion. Yet even (or especially?) academia resists the notion.

Or am I, perhaps, posing a straw man argument? Do post-modernists actually deny the existence of objective reality at all? Or am I taking your attention away from their real objection? Is the question to which we are seeking an answer not one of the existence of an objective reality or the existence of truth, but of the inherent inability of human perception linked with human language to either comprehend reality or express truth?

The Problem of Language

We're all familiar by now with the idea that language influ-ences our perceptions of reality. In the first half of the twenti-eth century, Edward Sapir and his student Benjamin Lee Whorf introduced the concept of linguistic determinism: the idea that different human cultures may actually experience the world differently based on the differences in their language. In this case, "reality" is very much a group phenomenon, defined and understood within the limits of a shared language. Edward Sapir saw this as a serious epistemological phenomenon, and cautioned us not to consider it too lightly: "It is quite an illusion to imagine that one adjusts to reality essentially without the use of language and that language is merely an incidental means of solving specific problems of communication or reflection. The fact of the matter is that the 'real world' is to a large extent unconsciously built up on the language habits of the group. . . . We see and hear and otherwise experience very largely as we do because the language habits of our community predispose certain choices of interpretation."[5]

Stuart Chase summed up Whorf's hypotheses in 1955 in his introduction to Whorf's classic work *Language, Thought and Reality*: "There is no one metaphysical pool of universal human thought. . . . Speakers of different languages see the cosmos differently, sometimes not by much, sometimes widely. Thinking is relative to the language learned."[6]

Furthermore, postmodernist critical thought paints an even grimmer picture of our ability not only to see the same reality, but also to talk about it in any terms that are not imposed on us against our will by an external power:

• Friedrich Wilhelm Nietzsche (not, in fact, a postmodernist, and yet he reigns as a sort of "godfather" of postmodernist philosophy) rails against a culturally imposed illusion called "reality" that "castrates"[7] the intellect and stifles the human will;

• Claude Lévi-Strauss stressed the multiplicity of interpretations that human symbol systems are prey to, as well as the ambiguous relationships between symbols in a given system, and cautioned against oppressive "normative" interpretations of language;

• Roland Barthes's existentialism spoke of the absolute freedom of the individual, of the individual's intellectual mobility and infinite potential for change and growth, and of the inherent right of individuals not to be defined or determined by others' interpretations;

• Michel Foucault's "discourse about discourses" examined the social, economic, and political forces that "legitimate" certain discourses at the expense of others, providing power to the privileged group and denying it to others;

• Jean François Lyotard—a fierce opponent of universal "grand narratives" or "metanarratives," in particular those of western Europe, and specifically of the Enlightenment—worked to undermine those narratives, claiming that in a postmodern world of social, economic, and information mobility such grand narratives lack the legitimacy to represent all people everywhere, and believed that new sets of narratives ("micronarratives") were needed to account for the diversity (and, frequently, incompatibility) of human needs and aspirations;

• Jacques Derrida's focus on (what he saw as) the repressive Western philosophical tradition of "logocentrism" sought to weaken if not remove the "metaphysics of presence" (an anti-philosophical notion in Derrida's eyes which affirms an absolute truth and ends productive discourse or investigation) of a text through the method of "deconstruction";

• Richard Rorty's pragmatism sought to free humans from the yolk of metaphysics, rejecting abstract terms like *truth, justice*, and *goodness* as being too contentious to become rallying points for human action, and urged us to find other, more useful, and more concrete terms, such as focusing on the elimination of poverty, the avoidance of cruelty, etc.

There is no doubt that each of these thinkers has a point, and together they present some good points at that. Few of intelligence would question the role of political, social, and economic power in shaping the discourse of society—*any* society. Few of goodwill would fail to acknowledge the presence (and the perpetuation?) of both privileged and exploited groups. And few with even the most tenuous grasp of reality would refuse to admit that culture-centric ideologies have been the cause of slavery, war, exploitation, and genocide, even during that time of enormous Western intellectual development which we call (without the slightest trace of irony) "the Enlightenment," and continuing to the present day.

So there is no question that speaking about "objective reality" will always be difficult: no two people will ever share the same "reality." Peoples' origins, their contexts, their needs, their desires, their aspirations, all these things stand in the way of mutual understanding. No, no two people will ever share the same reality. Or will they? Or can they?

On the surface, it doesn't seem at all unreasonable or counter-intuitive—does it?—to suggest that there might be, especially as we evolve culturally into a global community, a single objective reality that human beings, using their powers of sensory perception in tandem with their critical thinking faculties and powers of reason, might be able to agree upon. In fact, it is not at all unreasonable.

Modern empiricism was founded on the notion that humans can observe phenomena, think about them, and test their ideas through the use of meaningful abstract symbols. There is no question that no two people see the apple tree in exactly the same way. But they certainly ought to be able to agree that it is an apple tree, or—at the very least—some sort of tree and not a subway train.

Language is indeed a problem. But it is not so insurmountable a problem that it should make shared understanding of experience impossible. To see language as an insurmountable obstacle constitutes fatalistic determinism. It is our human intelligence that not only makes understanding possible, but makes it necessary to seek the truth, to see reality as clearly as possible. After all, as Daniel C. Dennett points out, "The *recognition* of the difference between appearance and reality is a human discovery."[8]

> A few other species—some primates, some cetaceans, maybe even some birds—show signs of appreciating the phenomenon of "false belief"—*getting it wrong*. They exhibit sensitivity to the errors of others, and perhaps even some sensitivity to their own errors as errors, but they lack the capacity for the reflection required to *dwell* on this possibility, and so they cannot use this sensitivity in the deliberate design of repairs or improvements of their own seeking gear or hiding gear. That sort of bridging of the gap between appearance and reality is a wrinkle that we human beings alone have mastered.[9]

Terence Deacon picks up the thought:

> Although various researchers have suggested that parallels to certain facets of language are to be found in the learned dialects of birdsong, the external reference evident in vervet monkey alarm calls or honeybee dances, and the socially transmitted sequences of sounds that make up humpback whale songs . . . these and many other examples like them only exhibit a superficial resemblance to language learning, word reference, or syntax, respectively. Even if we were to grant these parallels, no nonhuman species appears to put these facets of language together into a coordinated, rule-governed system.[10]

Is it this coordinated system, then, that accounts for the bridging of the gap that Dennett refers to? Is it language that differentiates us from those few other species? Is it a system of speech (and of thought), varying in form from culture to culture, but absolutely and objectively present in the entire species; governed by rules of word reference, grammar, and syntax; based on a logic of linear sequentiality that makes us uniquely human and allows us to carry on an active awareness not only of ourselves, but of an objective reality within which we all must live? Is it—as Socrates, Plato, and Aristotle said—the innate ability of human beings to reason?

Presentational and Propositional Structures of Thought

All human experience (unmediated by anything but the senses) comes to us through what are called *presentational structures of thought*. We are born using our presentational structures of thought. These presentational structures of thought are "hardwired" (if you will) to our senses, and all that we see, hear, feel, taste, and smell (again, if unmediated by anything but our senses) we react to—intuitively, instinctively, reflexively—as a result of our presentational structures of thought.

We humans evolved, like other advanced species, dependent on these presentational structures of thought, and it is fair to say that these structures more bind us in similarity to other species than differentiate us, in any significant way, from members of our own. When mammals emerged from their near-reptilian forbears about seventy million years ago,[11] they were endowed with certain sensory and neurological enhancements that gave them distinct advantages over their immediate ancestors—the ability to perceive colors; a larger brain with a cerebral neocortex, useful in the interpretation of sensory data as well as in spatial reasoning; and improved hearing, to name just a few.

Mammalian sensory organs and the various mechanisms of sensory perception—all delivering sensory data interpreted through presentational structures of thought—provide advantages that improve the chance of survival:

- vision, especially color and stereoptical vision, allows one to find and identify both food and threats, to differentiate edible and inedible plants, and to judge speed and distance of prey or predator;

- hearing orients an individual spatially in its environment and provides warning of dangers outside its field of vision;

- taste helps in differentiating good meat from spoiled, and edible plants from poisonous varieties;

- the sense of smell can help differentiate good food from bad; help identify members of a group and, conversely, outsiders; or warn of danger; and

- touch provides spatial orientation, warns against dangerous objects or plants, and gives information about the form and mass of objects.

When the human being emerged from the order of primates roughly sixty-nine million years after the emergence of mammals, whatever evolutionary advantages were provided by our new abilities and potentialities were accompanied by the same older abilities inherited from our mammalian ancestors. We saw things, heard things, smelled things, tasted things, and felt things, and processed those experiences through our presentational structures of thought. All of the vast sensory stimuli of nature can be thought of as infinite bits of presentationally structured information which we react to in an intuitive, instinctive, reflexive way.

All of this is to say that we inherited these presentational structures of thought directly from our evolutionary forbears with no significant differences in how they function, whether in humans or Neanderthals or australopithecines or gorillas.

However, we also evolved the ability to think in very different ways than those in which animals—including our evolutionary ancestors—think. We have developed what are called *propositional structures of thought*. Propositional structures of thought are those structures which we evolved in order to perceive, store, recall, manipulate, and share experiences through the use of abstract, meaningful symbols—that is to say language, whether spoken or written.

Propositionally structured bits of information—words—have a peculiar form unlike any other type of information encountered in nature. They have a logic that is entirely abstracted from reality, which is to say that there is nothing to the vast majority of words that is in any way similar to or imitative of reality. Words derive their meaning through cultural convention; members of a speech community adopt words through common usage based on a commonly held understanding of what they mean.[12] Words form a shared vocabulary, an inventory of useful abstract symbols, and each word has a specific use corresponding to a part of speech: noun, verb, adjective, adverb, preposition, etc.

Propositionally structured utterances—sentences, which are more than mere strings of words—have a specific grammar, and the logic of that grammar dictates the structure of the sentence and in turn influences its meaning: subject, predicate, object, dependent and independent clauses, etc.

Propositionally structured information is dependent on syntax—word order—for meaning. Not only is care needed in the choice of words, but also in how they are ordered. "The dog is sitting" is a statement and connotes presumed knowledge about some objective state of affairs. "Is the dog sitting," although constructed of the very same words (and absent any punctuation on a printed page) is most likely a question and connotes a request for information about a state of affairs. "Is dog the sitting" is not an English-language sentence at all, although if forced to, one could torture some sort of meaning out of it on nothing more than our knowledge of the English vocabulary and parts of speech.

Propositionally structured sentences are linear and sequential; whether we are hearing them as they are spoken or reading them on a page, words follow one another and "move in a straight line" from the beginning of a sentence to its end. In this time-based linear sequence we have the opportunity—and the intellectual duty—to interpret the choice of words, the grammar, and the syntactical structure to make meaning from them.

Propositionally structured utterances, as compared with the mimetic presentational data of human experience, are relatively concrete, if used with care. Sentences generally mean what their creators want them to mean if they are being honest and if they are being judicious in their use of words. It is, of course, possible to lie or to give voice to a point of view that bears no resemblance to objective reality (in fact, this is not even necessarily unusual); but it is impossible to lie or to posit a biased opinion in anything other than words. Furthermore, only propositionally structured utterances can be put to the kinds of tests for truth and logic that can support them or refute them. There is no such thing as either a true or a false image or a true or false sound. A siren is neither true nor false; neither is a ringing bell. And each picture is what it appears to be; nothing more, nothing less.

Propositionally structured information is artificial, in the sense that words are human inventions, as are all tools. They are technologies, and like all technologies, they give the impression of being "outside of nature." They are human artifacts: the work, as it were, of human hands, even though it is in fact human minds that create them. Consequently, propositional structures of thought are not innate; they must be learned.

They seem singularly unnatural even though it is paradoxical to think of the artifacts of other portions of the animal kingdom as unnatural. Is an anthill unnatural? Is a beaver's dam unnatural? No one, I think, would be so bold as to make these claims and would tend, rather, to see the anthill, the beaver's dam, the spider's web, the bird's nest, etc., as integral parts of nature.

So we should certainly look at human artifacts—houses, automobiles, clothing, words—as equally integral parts of nature. But propositionally structured information and propositional structures of thought are, indeed, unnatural in this sense: we are not born with these structures of thought, as a bird is born with an innate knowledge of nest-building, as a beaver is born to make dams, as a spider needs no instruction in web-building, as an ant naturally, without prompting, without formal education, burrows beneath mounds of dirt to make his home. We must learn to use words as we must learn to use a hammer. Nor are we born with an innate understanding of words; we are merely born with the capacity to think propositionally and to create and use words. All of this, *every single piece of it,* must be learned—and practiced.

So while the capacity for language is innate, an evolutionary advance beyond mere animal communication, specific propositional structures of thought need to be learned, while presentational structures of thought are innate. We are quite literally born experiencing the world through our presentational structures of thought. The senses delight us, both with the beauties of the world and with the ease with which we experience them; reasoning is hard, often painful work. Is objective, propositional thought—and the critical faculty of reason that it makes possible—worth all the effort when we have constructed a culture that engenders, supports, and celebrates presentational thought and a subjective, individual perception of reality? I argue that, yes, it is worth it. It is what we evolved to do. Let me explain why.

Neurological Differences in Structures of Thought

It has long been known that the brain is bicameral, divided into two chambers or hemispheres—left and right—which, while frequently complementing and possibly from time to time even duplicating each other's functions, bear individual responsibility for controlling different specific physical and mental functions. While there may be some duplication of functions across hemispheres, there is little question about what part of the brain controls our human processes of language. The outermost layer of the brain—the layer evolved most recently and therefore, arguably, most human—is the neocortex, the site of two areas strongly identified with human language: Broca's area and Wernicke's area. Broca's area, on the posterior frontal lobe of the left hemisphere, is responsible for, among other things, speech production and language processing. Wernicke's area in the posterior portion of the temporal lobe of the left hemisphere, is involved in language comprehension; making sense, in a way, of the words Broca's area generates. Both Broca's and Wernicke's areas are on the left hemisphere of the brain, linked together by a pathway of nerve fibers called the arcuate fasciculus, and, along with the Inferior Parietal Lobule, form a sort of language network (see Fig. 1). This network and its functions are not duplicated anywhere else in the brain.[13]

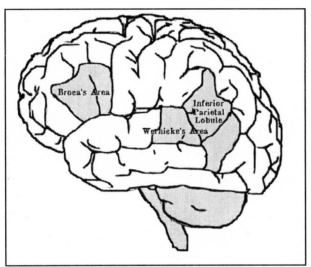

Fig. 1 Language centers in the human brain

At the very real risk of over-simplifying an extremely complex organ and its functions, it can be said reliably that the two hemispheres of the brain are differentiated and organized in the following ways:

LEFT HEMISPHERE
- Sequential thinking
- Analytical thinking
- Reason
- Verbal processes
- Logic response
- Linear thinking
- Detail orientation
- Linguistic: words, grammar, syntax, literal interpretation

RIGHT HEMISPHERE
- Simultaneous thinking
- Holistic thinking
- Intuition
- Visual processes
- Emotional reaction
- Non-linear thinking
- Pattern orientation
- Para-linguistic: intonation, contextual interpretation

However, it's important to remember that the neo-cortex layer of the human brain, the newest evolutionary part, is only one, outer-most portion of the brain and constitutes a tiny proportion of both its mass and functions: the conscious ones. There may be a whole universe of unconscious functions taking place below that cortex: intuitive, instinctive, reflexive functions. These primitive functions are all in the business of processing information—sensations, emotions, stimuli of various sorts stored in unconscious memory—most of it non-propositional and non-discursive, all of it integral to the concept of being "fully human."

That I call them "primitive functions" is only partly correct and does not reflect the true complexity of the human brain and its processes. But beneath the cerebral neocortex there are, according to a theory developed by the late Paul MacLean, two earlier-evolved segments of our brains (see fig. 2): the intermediate

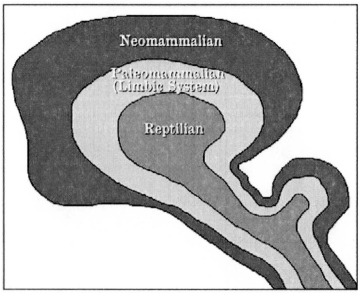

Fig. 2 Reptilian, Limbic, and Mammalian Brains
after Paul MacLean, cited in Richard E. Cytowic,
The Man Who Tasted Shapes

or paleomammalian, and the primitive or reptilian.[14] These two other areas represent earlier eras in our evolutionary development as humans.

The primitive brain consists of the brain stem itself, the medulla, the cerebellum, etc. Its concerns are of survival: aggression or avoidance ("fight or flight"). It corresponds very closely in both physiognomy and function to the reptilian brain.

Surrounding the primitive brain, the intermediate or neomammalian brain is the brain that we shared with early mammals. This segment of the brain, the limbic system, comprises the amygdala, the hippocampus, the thalamus and hypothalamus, the septum, and others.

The limbic system is the center of human emotion, and each piece of the system controls one or more aspects of our deep emotional experience: fear, desire, love, affection, friendship, aggression—both physical and sexual—pleasure, pain, and orgasm. It is the evolutionary development that allows, among other things, a smaller but smarter animal to survive in a predatory world (because of our urge to band together in cooperative groups); as well as for the survival of an infant whose development extends beyond gestation and birth (by giving his mother the urge to care for him).

The brain's complex, simultaneous, multi-layered activities actually bias us far more toward emotion than scientists, philosophers, linguists and others since the Enlightenment (or, perhaps, even since Plato) have either realized or cared to admit. In his fascinating book *The Man Who Tasted Shapes*, neurologist Richard Cytowic writes about "the primacy of emotion":

> For centuries, emotion has been looked down on as primitive, and reason held as the superior development.[15]

> The common assumption that the developed cortex makes humans unique implies that human limbic

> structures are no different from those of other mam-
> mals. If true, then human emotions are comparatively
> primitive. But exhaustive anatomic studies . . . show
> that the limbic system was not left behind by evolu-
> tion. Limbic and cortical circuits co-evolved, and so
> reason and emotion burgeoned together in tandem.[16]

I must say that I believe Cytowic poses a straw man argument here, for in no way does recognition and acknowledgment
of the profound power of propositional thought necessarily imply a belief in the inferiority of either presentational structures
of thought or of emotions. The fact is that, as Maryanne Wolf
has so eloquently explained, the reading brain is different than
even the oral brain; the act of reading uses far more parts of
our brain in both hemispheres, both conscious and unconscious,
in far more complex combinations, with far more neural activity, than speech alone demands.[17] The point is not to identify a
dominance or a primacy; the point is to recognize qualitative
differences, and to appreciate the characteristics and advantages of those different modes. There is also a second point, and
that is to acknowledge the uniqueness in all of nature of human
propositional thought, and to recognize the precarious nature
of its existence. It is a mode of thought that thrives, develops,
and sharpens when it is exercised; it becomes stilted, stunted,
blunted, and atrophied when not.

Recent studies in neuroscience, made possible by technological advances in real-time brain observation (that is, through the
use of functional magnetic resonance imaging—fMRI) provide
further evidence to support the principle of separate structures
of thought, indicate further that they take place in different portions of the brain, and suggest an urgent need to balance our
information diet. Anderson, Fite, Petrovich, and Hirsch mapped
brain activity associated with the viewing of film and video

depicting visual action and found that only certain regions of the brain were active, predominantly in the right hemisphere.[18] Bavelier, Corina, Jezzard, Padmanabhan, Clark, Karni, Prinster, Braun, Lalwani, Rauschecker, Turner, and Neville had previously shown that left hemisphere activity, specifically in Broca's and Wernicke's areas, as well as the angular gyrus, correlated strongly with reading. Furthermore, their fMRI observations indicated that this activity is dependent upon neural processes specific to the act of reading.[19]

So, notwithstanding the extraordinary complexity and flexibility of the human brain and its adaptive powers, we must still note that there are specific, innate, and even neurological differences between presentational and propositional structures of thought. Presentational thought takes place without the intermediation of words; it occurs in a specific portion of the brain, an area otherwise associated with intuition, emotion, and immediacy; it is innate and natural, requires no "curriculum," and cannot be avoided. Propositional thought is thinking through, with, and in words; its speech-specific processes occur in a discrete portion of the brain, an area otherwise associated with reason, logic, and sequential thought; it is "unnatural" and needs to be learned,[20] necessitating a curriculum that consists of learning a hierarchy of concepts and skills, from babbling, through learning simple and then more complex words, through attempts at combining words in order to make meaningful sentences, through another entire series of hierarchical concepts and skills before we move on to written propositional codes. In the absence of propositionally structured stimuli, this learning can be avoided.

When we reason, we reason in words. When we're rational, we're using our propositional structures of thought. When we're using our propositional structures of thought, we're both using and at the same time training specific areas and processes of our brains, and the more we do so, the more "natural" these learned behaviors become. By contrast, when we use our presentational structures of thought, we more "feel" than think, react than respond, participate subjectively than analyze critically.

It may seem, well, unreasonable to some to suggest this, but these two structures of thought, these two different types of thinking, these two modes, one discursive and one non-discursive, are not equal. They may be equivalent, they may be complementary, they may be (and, in fact, I suspect they are) both necessary, and necessarily used in tandem, in order to be most fully "human." But they are not equal. Propositional thought is an evolved capacity necessary to our survival. We do not reason in the absence of propositions. They are the tool we have invented—unique to the human being—in order to know, to share, to understand, and to live within a reality. And I think we have either forgotten this, or decided that it is just another modernist ploy designed to guarantee that one "privileged" group wields power, in an artificial, socially-constructed reality over another, less privileged one. This is the postmodernist complaint.

Questioning Truth

According to various currents of postmodern thought, there is no objective reality *per se*; truth, consequently, is subjective. Everyone perceives reality in a different way, or so the argument goes, and each person's perceptions are the sum of all his experiences, sensory and intellectual, mediated and unmediated. When individuals are able to agree upon the "meaning" of a particular event, that shared meaning forms the basis of what is known as the "consensus reality." The consensus reality is a group reality and is not necessarily reflective of objective reality. Being a group reality, the consensus reality of one group may come into conflict with that of another group.

This explains, especially in a world not linked by instantaneous global telecommunications, the diversity of worldviews and conceptions of reality held by different groups in different places and at different times. It also helps to explain the postmodern resistance to "privileging" one point of view or conception of reality over another, as there appears to be, at first glance, no objective tool capable of making equitable judgments about the relative quality of perceptions or interpretations, or of the value of the symbol systems or technologies available to aid in a society's construction of a consensus reality.

The Nature of Objective Reality

Consequently, there is a fashion nowadays for those schools of thought mentioned earlier—variously called postmodernist, cultural relativist, or (simply) relativist—which claim that there is no such thing as objective reality, and that theories of objective reality (science, history, etc.) are nothing more than cultural constructs. I have said that I find it difficult to dismiss them out-of-hand, dealing as they do with what I consider to be not insignificant issues of power and privilege. And yet I can't avoid the possibility that—in rejecting the notion of truth as being part and parcel of oppressive systems of thought—we have thrown the metaphysical baby out with the intellectual bathwater. "The print-made split," McLuhan explained, "between head and heart is the trauma which affects Europe"[21] and, I would add, all of Western culture, and for which postmodernist thought was intended to be a remedy, but chose not to be. The solution to a problem defined as a "man-made split between head and heart" is not, I suggest, cutting off the head; rather, it is bridging the gap, healing the wound, and putting the head and the heart back together.

During the Enlightenment, arguably the high point in the human use of language and reason, we got the sense that reality could be identified and objectified. Undoubtedly this was at least in part due to the objectification of language—facilitated and, perhaps, determined by print. Because of the propositional structure of print—like the propositional structure of writing and of speech—human perception could be put to tests of truth using empirical methods. Moreover, with the advent of print these perceptions have the advantage of being shared broadly with an interested general public who can, in their own turn, put questionable propositions to the test of truth. The result of this process of mass production and distribution of public knowledge—all structured propositionally—was the creation and growth of a self-regulating and self-correcting discourse that was not itself the repository of truth (although some were certainly happy to hold and to propagate this delusion), but a method—empiricism in the service of reason—of eliminating more and more error over time. This led, perhaps inevitably, to the idea of progress: that history was a linear process of trial and error and eventual improvement of the human condition. There was, during the Enlightenment, no less evidence of human frailty and imperfection than there had ever been in the millennia preceding it; but, for the first time, there seemed to be evidence to support a conception of human perfectibility.

Still, postmodernists are unhappy with this scenario, seeing the western European construal of the Enlightenment, of progress, and of a process of human ethical or moral perfection as no more than another grand narrative (or, in Lyotard's words, meta-narrative) like the others, meant to do nothing more than to legitimate centers of power and privilege. And so they declaim against them, and advise us to develop the same "incredulity to meta-narratives" in our own discourse as exist in postmodern discourse. Lyotard argues:

> The rule of consensus between the sender and addressee of a statement with truth-value is deemed acceptable if it is cast in terms of a possible unanimity between rational minds: this is the Enlightenment narrative, in which the hero of knowledge works toward a good ethico-political end—universal peace. . . . If a meta-narrative implying a philosophy of history is used to legitimate knowledge, questions are raised concerning the validity of institutions governing the social bond: these must be legitimated as well. Thus justice is consigned to the grand narrative in the same way as truth.[22]

But if Lyotard were here I'd need to voice this objection: I actually believe in the ends of the grand narrative you describe. I not only believe in them, I believe justice exists without regard to my or your faith in it. I believe it exists in spite of its common absence in human affairs. And I believe that the project of social justice and peace are worthy ends toward which to strive, to work, and to question. And I'm curious and disturbed as to why—although I concede readily that others have misused this narrative to achieve other, less worthy ends—you wish to bar me from invoking the narratives of peace or justice to achieve an end that is objectively good.

While giving due respect to empirical measurements of reality, Wittgenstein approaches the problem of speaking of and using abstract values as qualitative benchmarks more cynically than skeptically, with potentially damaging implications for ethical improvement:

> The correct method in philosophy would really be the following: to say nothing except what can be said, i.e., propositions of natural science—i.e., something that has nothing to do with philosophy—and then, whenever someone else wanted to say something metaphysical, to demonstrate to

him that he had failed to give a meaning to certain signs in his propositions. Although it would not be satisfying to the other person—he would not have the feeling that we were teaching him philosophy—*this* method would be the only strictly correct one. . . . What we cannot speak about we must pass over in silence.[23]

But if Wittgenstein were here I'd wish to ask him these questions: Is this the only possible and necessary course of action for us to take in an admittedly chaotic, confusing world? Moreover, is this the ethically right choice? Must we "pass over in silence" all those things which interest us but remain, for the moment, more subjective and personal than objective and observable? Why must we? I can imagine how arrogant this sounds to you: "Is he actually suggesting that we ought to speak about those things about which we are really intellectually unable to speak?"

But why shouldn't we? Hasn't all human knowledge come, ultimately, from thinking, and talking, and wondering, and asking, and arguing about things which, at a given moment, we were unable to know with any certainty? Hasn't every empirically defensible proposition of natural science shared this same ambiguous genesis? Isn't exactly this type of attitude—a lack of inhibition about taking intellectual risks—the font of all human learning?

This sounds, to me at any rate, like an unreasonable and unjustifiable demand—that I must pass over in silence all those things about which I have ideas, or theories, or intuitions, or even fantasies; things which may, at this moment, have a more solid existence in the imagination than in the physical universe; things which partake more of myth than of science. These things may indeed be merely metaphysical, and I may be unable, at this moment, to give a meaning to certain signs in my proposition. You demand that I pass over these things in silence, for to fail to do so is the hallmark of a philosophical method which is not strictly correct.

So, by a strictly correct philosophical method I am unable to speak of God. In fact, I am comfortable with that (although in principle I am still offended by your demand), for my conception of, and relationship with God is a very personal one. But I am also unable to bring up the word *truth*—even though I feel powerfully compelled to—because truth has no uniform, objective existence that can be proved empirically. And now that you mention it, I can't really talk about science to some postmodernists, because science is a social institution constructed by humans to support certain privileged points of view that justify their maintenance of power. And the same of other, noncorporeal, abstract, or transcendental ideas, values that inform our systems of ethics or morality, or around which have grown other social institutions: justice, democracy, duty, love, and the good.

I disagree with you and I don't believe I will yield to your demand, because I don't think I ought to—I don't think I need to. I don't think it's just, and I don't think it's right. To be fair, I don't think you have fully presented your case which might, in fact, justify your demand. As it stands, your demand is, to my eyes and ears, unreasonable.

Now Rorty weighs in with an appeal to our sense of pragmatism, attempting to persuade us that all this focus on truth, reality, and normative values only separates us and inhibits the real work of moral (if that is an appropriate term in this case) progress:

> The question that matters to us pragmatists is not whether a vocabulary possesses meaning or not, whether it raises real or unreal problems, but whether the resolution of that debate will have an effect in practice, whether it will be useful.[24]

> What profit can we derive from a description of a part of a culture that, instead of simply explaining its social utility, or determining the degree of consensus that obtains within it, goes on to consider its relation to reality?[25]

> Can our ordinary use of the term *true* really be described in such a way as to rid this notion of its objectivist presuppositions? If asserting that there are such presuppositions entails that discriminations between discourses can be made by reference to their ability to produce correspondence to reality, then I think that we should make no such assertion.[26]

But now I feel the need to ask of Rorty the following questions: How can you make such a statement in light of the current cultural demands to do just exactly as you wish, and in light of the consequences of those demands? We have a national, and increasingly, a global discourse that makes no such distinction between meaning and nonsense, that obsesses over unreal problems and ignores the real ones, and we are all too willing to ignore the relationship of this discourse to reality. We don't in the slightest discriminate between discourses, except to the extent that one was entertaining and the other not, that one was passionate and the other dull, that one applied to the narrow circumstances of my life and the other didn't, that one had "an impact" on us and the other "left us cold." When, outside of a philosophy class, have you heard someone invoking the authority of truth in public discourse? So I'm not sure I understand your protest and, in fact, believe that we are now living in the discursive world of your prescription. And I think we are in danger of witnessing, and participating in, a discordant, chaotic, meaningless disaster.

I am left wondering—after hearing what the postmodernists have to say, contemplating it, questioning it, and considering the consequences—why we should listen to postmodernist thinkers, or pay attention to postmodernism at all? Why should we trust (or have confidence in the authority of) anything they have to tell us? If they are warning against the evils (or uselessness) of oppressive norms, why ought we to accept the (equally oppressive) implicit norms they offer us? What authority do they invoke when they assert that there is no authority (including, logically, their own)?

Implicit Choice

Postmodernists are, in fact, in no way constrained to respect grand narratives, to interpret words or the reality they represent in any predetermined way, to surrender their liberty or autonomy, to allow others to define them, or to open themselves to exploitation. I believe they protest too much when they claim otherwise. They are free to be and to do and to say and to interpret as they wish, to create a solipsistic universe of purely personal, individualized meaning, and to insulate themselves from objective reality. And this is apparently what they—we—have chosen to do.

By the same token, I am free to judge them on the basis of their choices. I am free to make qualitative ethical and moral judgments based on the consequences of their past choices, and the natural and reasonable expectation of similar consequences for similar future choices. They may not like it; they might find it oppressive and offensive; they might think I am engaged in a futile, pathetic, unproductive, and consequently comical (or even tragicomic) pursuit. They might, in other words, find my judgments in opposition to the norms they have attempted, with some success, to establish. And so it is also very likely that they will call this point of view—a point of view focused on the pursuit of truth—oppressive and dangerous.

They have chosen to dismiss the possibility of an objective (and objectively observable) reality every bit as much as I have chosen to investigate it. They can provide no empirical evidence of the universal inexpressibility of reality (indeed, empirical measurement is itself suspect in the postmodern mind). On the contrary, the empirical record suggests that reality is eminently knowable and expressible, as evident in our sciences, mathematics, and engineering. Consequently, I think there is a moral and ethical imperative to acknowledge it and its correlative concept: truth.

The Consequences of Postmodern Relativism

One of the tragic results of the postmodern mindset is not only the loss of faith and of respect that we once had for the concept, the idea, the principle of truth, but the consequent tolerance we have developed for what Harry Frankfurt (and others) calls *bullshit*.[27] Bullshit, whether postmodernists intended it to be so or not, is the *lingua franca* of the postmodern world. The postmodern world is not a world of lies, any more than it is a world of truth. It is a world seeking, one might say, absolute liberation from absolutes, seeking certainty in randomness. It is a world where everyone and everything craves affirmation of the self, where all have come to expect that affirmation as a right, and where the "authority of truth" is a threat rather than a consolation.

The postmodernist world is one where no single idea, no single behavior, no single point of view, is inherently better than any other one. What matters about any given idea, or belief, or point of view is simply its utility, not its truthfulness: what, the postmodernist asks, can this point of view do for (or to) me? How am I affirmed (or threatened) by this idea? How am I privileged or exploited? Never do you hear the postmodernist ask the question: Is this idea true or is it false? This postmodern world, at the end of the day, is a world of bullshit, and it fits nicely with Frankfurt's descriptions both of bullshit and of the bullshitter:

> It is impossible for someone to lie unless he thinks he knows the truth. Producing bullshit requires no such conviction. A person who lies is thereby responding to the truth, and he is

to that extent respectful of it. When an honest man speaks, he says only what he believes to be true; and, for the liar, it is correspondingly indispensable that he considers his statements to be false. For the bullshitter, however, all bets are off: he is neither on the side of the true nor on the side of the false. His eye is not on the facts at all, as the eyes of the honest man and of the liar are, except insofar as they may be pertinent to his purpose in getting away with what he says. He does not care whether the things he says describe reality correctly. He just picks them out, or makes them up, to suit his purpose.[28]

The postmodern mindset may indeed have arisen from the best of intentions. As a media ecologist, I am certainly concerned about the monopolies of knowledge (and, consequently, of power) that can accrete around a dominant information form. Words have been misused in the past to gain an unfair advantage over others, to build wealth, to assume power unfairly, and to protect privilege. They have been misused in the very recent past for those purposes, and they will continue to be so misused. But creating a world of bullshit by denying the existence of objective reality, or proclaiming it unknowable, or persuading the masses that their language is insufficient to describe or understand it, or preaching that we can only have a situational, pragmatic view of it, or labeling it an "irrelevant distraction"—this stance, this attitude, this point of view does more to harm the interests of the less powerful than all the grand narratives created since the invention of writing, because it destroys the truth that belongs to all.

Frankfurt writes, "The bullshitter ignores [the demands of truth] altogether. He does not reject the authority of truth, as the liar does, and oppose himself to it. He pays no attention to it at all. By virtue of this, bullshit is a greater enemy of the truth than lies are."[29]

If, as I have suggested, it is a legitimate postmodernist defensive stance to recoil from grand narratives that have been constructed for the express purpose of maintaining a privileged group in a position of power, if their goal is to de-legitimate a privileged few and their system of hierarchical authority by legitimating the subjective views of the many, if they somehow see objective truth as oppressive or hegemonic, they might consider more thoughtfully the dangers involved. They might consider the leveling of the playing field—brought about by the emasculation of truth—to be a double-edged sword. They might consider looking closely at the administration of the federal government of the United States of America in the first eight years of the third millennium. They might be able to identify a useful and productive object lesson about the value of truth and objective reality, and about the ability of those in positions of privilege and power to use the negation of those concepts to their advantage; in other words, to *bullshit us.*

Ron Suskind, writing in the *New York Times Magazine* in 2004, recalled a conversation he had with a senior aide in the Bush administration. Suskind had been called on the carpet for an article he had written that some within the administration had found offensive or somehow biased. The official proceeded to explain what was wrong with Suskind and "people like him":

> The aide said that guys like me were "in what we call the reality-based community," which he defined as people who "believe that solutions emerge from your judicious study of discernible reality." I nodded and murmured something about enlightenment principles and empiricism. He cut me off. "That's not the way the world really works anymore," he continued. "We're an empire now, and when we act, we create our own reality. And while you're studying that reality— judiciously, as you will—we'll act again, creating other new realities, which you can study too, and that's how things will sort out. We're history's actors . . . and you, all of you, will be left to just study what we do."[30]

James Boswell, in his biography of Dr. Samuel Johnson, tells the well-known story of Johnson's critique of the subjective idealism of Bishop George Berkeley, a brilliant and influential Irish philosopher of the early-eighteenth century. Berkeley's subjective idealism suggested that matter has "no objective existence," at least no existence that can be proven outside our subjective sensory experience. To say that something exists is to say only that we perceive it; it has no probable existence outside of our perceptions. Boswell gleefully describes Johnson's pointed demurral:

> After we came out of the church, we stood talking for some time together of Bishop Berkeley's ingenious sophistry to prove the nonexistence of matter, and that every thing in the universe is merely ideal. I observed, that though we are satisfied his doctrine is not true, it is impossible to refute it. I never shall forget the alacrity with which Johnson answered, striking his foot with mighty force against a large stone, till he rebounded from it—"I refute it *thus.*"[31]

On September 11, 2001 al Qaeda played Dr. Johnson to America's Bishop Berkeley. Three jet airliners crashed into the World Trade Center in New York and the Pentagon in Washington, and a fourth plane—perhaps also heading for the capital—crashed into a field in rural Shanksville, Pennsylvania. With one hateful, devastating, fatal blow, our own postmodern version of subjective idealism should have come tumbling down, our own sense that only what we perceive is real, that what we don't perceive or can't perceive has no objective existence of its own, should have disappeared entirely. Those four planes, seventeen hijackers, several buildings, and nearly three thousand victims constitute a powerful critique of America's postmodern worldview: "I refute it thus!"

America, on the advice of its president, went shopping.[32]

Of What Use Is Objective Reality?

Allow me now to propose, for the purposes of this argument, what I am certain will be a wholly unsatisfactory—to nearly everybody—definition of objective reality: *Objective reality is that which exists, occurs, or is, whether you perceive it or not, and whether you believe in it or not.* It is, to be sure, a sloppy definition; a messy, open-ended, ambiguous definition. It is, however, one I will stand by.

And now allow me to add a correlative observation about objective reality which I am equally certain many, if not most, will dislike: *It is a moral duty, incumbent upon human beings by virtue of their intelligence and capacity for propositional thought, to pursue the fullest possible understanding of objective reality; to reject what is demonstrated to be in conflict with objective reality; and to engage in respectful but serious, critical discourse about the nature of that objective reality.*

Why, you ask? The answer is simple: Because people get hurt, fall prey to exploitation, and sometimes die when we allow ourselves to be vincibly, willfully ignorant of the objective reality of life on earth. Of what use is objective reality? Aside from the moral implications of remaining comfortably numb to the suffering of others by ignoring the reality of it, an acknowledgment of objective reality and a vigorous pursuit of truth are absolutely critical to human survival.

Here is a delicious piece of postmodern irony: in a state of nature, there is no postmodernism—no doubt about the nature of objective reality. How can there be? Postmodernism is not real, it is an intellectual choice, the self-indulgence of, ironically, a privileged group who no longer need to be concerned with either seeking or maintaining the minimum necessities of survival. It is a diversion, an amusement, a human intellectual invention, a cynical social construct, and, I hope, a momentary aberration, a result of psychic and spiritual confusion, of a glut of incoherent and decontextualized information. As such, it is also a mindset of egoistic and self-indulgent affluence, the symptom of a culture with too much time on its hands and too little to do of real use. In the final analysis, postmodernism is nothing more than another grand narrative, and as such bears all the negative marks of narratives that postmodernist philosophers like Lyotard point out to us. Postmodernism allows a privileged elite to maintain power—by denying the existence, utility, or human ability to understand and share reality—over an exploited mass who are forced to live, whether they like it or not, according to reality's immanent demands.

The postmodern mindset is a choice. It has no objective reality in and of itself; we have made it "real" subjectively by agreeing to its existence and abiding by its precepts. "That's just the way it is." "What can I do? I'm just one person." "Everyone knows that that's how things work." These are classic cop-outs of the postmodern mindset, more and more frequently heard in the last few decades than (I would wager) ever before. And they are all *false*—objectively false. We make them true by believing them. We make them true by *choosing* to believe them. And we choose to believe them because it is easier to believe them, to convince ourselves that they're true, than it is to actually do something, to go out and, to paraphrase Mohandas Gandhi, "be the change you want to see in the world." The postmodern mindset is a fearful and apathetic one.

Harry Frankfurt's description of the demanding process of developing maturity, of learning to overcome narrow, self-serving needs in order to acknowledge and engage truth might be

seen in almost Freudian terms, where we find postmodernists
suffering from an Oedipal complex, needing to kill the truth in
order to consort, without feelings of guilt, with their voluptuous
fantasies:

> We learn that we are separate beings in the world, distinct
> from what is other than ourselves, by coming up against
> obstacles to the fulfillment of our intentions—that is, by
> running into opposition to the implementation of our will.
> When certain aspects of our experience fail to submit to our
> wishes, when they are on the contrary unyielding and even
> hostile to our interests, it then becomes clear to us that they
> are not parts of ourselves. We recognize that they are not
> under our direct and immediate control; instead, it becomes
> apparent that they are independent of us. That is the origin
> of our concept of reality, which is essentially a concept of
> what limits us, of what we cannot alter or control by the
> mere movement of our will.[33]

The acknowledgment of our own objective limitations is difficult. It is far more difficult in a culture that has regulated out
of existence the concept of perceptual and interpretational limitations in the first place. We don't like to acknowledge our own
limitations. How likely are we to look kindly on others pointing
them out to us? It is much easier, far less confrontational, and
less disruptive of social decorum to simply "go with the flow"
and adopt an attitude of tolerance—*everyone's entitled to her
opinion; you have your opinion and I have mine*—than it is to
look at something, question it, think critically about it, and de-
fend an informed opinion based on objective evidence.

The *truth* is (I proclaim boldly) that the postmodern mind
is a fearful mind, a mind afraid of truth—afraid even of the
idea of truth, for to acknowledge an objective truth very often
means the necessary and consequent acknowledgment of our
own error or wrong-doing or self-indulgence. To acknowledge
the truth sometimes means that we must acknowledge our own

narcissism, egocentrism, or consumerist gluttony. To acknowledge the truth means that we must acknowledge our own imperfections and limitations. To acknowledge the truth might just mean that we admit to ourselves that our own lifestyle choices are more important to us than someone else's *life*. To acknowledge the truth means that we might have to give up our comfortable, familiar postmodernist subjectivism where there is no objective truth, where all values are oppressive, and where the personal, subjective point of view reigns supreme. We might have to admit to ourselves that, not our lifestyles, but our very lives are a lie. And who, in a postmodern world, wants to admit any of that? It's far too frightening.

Instead, to make ourselves feel better, we call it—our collective unwillingness to make this painful acknowledgment—tolerance. But the truth is that it is "better" only in the sense that it is easier and far less uncomfortable to let the truth hang cloudy around us than it is to clarify it, face up to it, and live according to its demands. That would be more frightening still. And the fearful, as Tacitus said, are not in the habit of speaking (or, we're tempted to add, hearing) the truth. Truth, as Romano Guardini pointed out to us, is power, the power to be most fully a human individual. As such, truth is the foundation of our personal sovereignty.

The ramifications of the human acknowledgment and use of this power is truly profound; mind-bogglingly liberating. It is in this sense that the truth, as the Gospel of John tells us, sets us free. He is free, said William Cowper, whom the truth makes free. It is our free choice to embrace truth, if only we'll see it, acknowledge it, and live it. And, as Socrates told us, the acknowledgment of our own limitations is the first step to wisdom. But there is an alternative to all of this, and that alternative is the postmodern denial of truth and the consequent denial of objective reality. This is the abnegation of freedom, of sovereignty, of personhood, of responsibility, and of integrity.

Those who stand for nothing, Alexander Hamilton said more than two centuries ago, will certainly fall for anything. It is those who have something to fear from the truth who rebel against it most fiercely. It is those who would rather sacrifice their own freedom—and the freedom of others—who assure us that nothing is more real than our own sensory experiences. It is those who would choose intellectual slavery over intellectual freedom and personal autonomy who are the defenders of postmodern relativism. And we have fallen for it.

Fallen for it? No, we have jumped at it, clawed at it, begged for it. Why? What is there to fear? Might it be that the fear is that of being fully human, of achieving full personhood, of being autonomous individuals, of *being responsible*—not just *for* ourselves, but *to* one another? To bullshit and to be bullshitted is, perhaps, far easier and less painful.

But still the postmodern voice calls out to us, taunting us against emotion, mocking empathy, belittling faith in transcendence, emboldening the ego and the id, and warning us not to be taken in by irrational calls to either *caritas*[34] or *veritas*:[35]

> To love man *for God's sake*—that has so far been the noblest and most remote feeling attained among men. That the love of man is just one more stupidity and brutishness if there is no ulterior intent to sanctify it; that the inclination to such love of man must receive its measure, its subtlety, its grain of salt and dash of ambergris from some higher inclination—whoever the human being may have been who first felt and "experienced" this, however much his tongue may have stumbled as it tried to express such *délicatesse,* let him remain holy and venerable for us for all time as the human being who has flown highest yet and gone astray most beautifully![36]

I believe that what some call[37] the postmodern "crisis of

meaning" is in reality a crisis of personal identity, a crisis of *being*, based on our desire to use our discourse as a shield against reality, a permanently self-referential code which necessarily makes the rest of the world irrelevant.[38] This much-desired crisis of identity has been facilitated by a glut of speed-of-light information that naturally followed the development of electronic media of communication, precisely as Marshall McLuhan told us forty years ago: "When things come at you very fast, naturally you lose touch with yourself. Anybody moving into a new world loses identity. . . . So loss of identity is something that happens in rapid change. But everybody at the speed of light tends to become a nobody."[39]

And I believe further that this crisis of personal identity, the product of this orgy of instant information, constitutes a sort of psychic orgasm, a wild abandonment of the self—as Jacques Ellul characterized it sixty years ago, a sort of psychic and spiritual suicide, "suicide in enjoyment or in despair, intellectual or moral suicide, and thus people are ready for the total suicide which is slowly preparing, and will involve the whole world, body and soul."[40]

We've embraced with some enthusiasm just this kind of nobody-ism, passive non-being, impotent relativism, and intellectual fatalism because we've bought into the self-destructive lie that our human culture is somehow no longer a part of nature,—that our tools, our homes, our material artifacts, and our wealth not only insulate us from nature, but furthermore, being products of human intelligence, have no fundamental relationship to nature whatsoever. We have certainly insulated ourselves from objective reality. We have also separated ourselves—or so we wish devoutly to believe—from nature and consequently from our own humanity.

But the truth is that we haven't. It is only our willful, conscious embrace of postmodern nobody-ism and our consequent refusal to accept the awesome responsibility of human intelligence, propositional thinking, and reason that make it feel so. We are no less a part of nature, with all our plasma-screen TVs, and iPods, and iPhones, and Xboxes, and automobiles, and sleep aids, and jet planes, and nuclear warheads, than the brook trout. And nature is waiting to administer, as it does from time to time—as it did on September 11, 2001—a reality check.

In a state of nature, neither predator nor prey can afford solipsistic indifference. In a state of nature you know who you are, you know what is real, and you learn the array of options for how to react to it, or you die. Gazelles are born and within minutes are running at great speed. Running is what they do best; it is what they were evolved to do; it is their means of survival. Propositional language and thought is the human being's means of survival, our means of adapting to a world that appears ever-changing; and it is so changing precisely because we have propositional language. But the gazelle that doubts the objective reality of the stalking lion, the ape who believes that all possible edible substances are equally nourishing, or the bird of prey who is convinced that predatory behavior is a myth meant to maintain one class of animals in a privileged position over another exploited class—without extraordinary luck, all will die.

And we who, as human beings with the unique ability to reason and share our perceptions through propositional structures of thought and language, continue to deny the existence of objective reality and its counterpart, truth—so might we all.

This is my opinion. It happens also to be the truth.

Chapter Three

Orality

εν αρχη ην ο λογος
και ο λογος ην προς τον θεον
και θεος ην ο λογος.
ουτος ην εν αρχη προς τον θεον.
παντα δι αυτου εγενετο
και χωρις αυτου εγενετο ουδε εν ο γεγονεν.

In the beginning was the Word,
and the Word was with God,
and the Word was God.
He was in the beginning with God.
All things came to be through Him,
and without Him nothing came to be.
John 1:1–3

If I am not being overly severe in my indictment of postmodernism as a virtual cancer on the intellectual life of Western culture, it is only because I believe it represents little more than a temporary aberration, a detour from an evolutionary road built upon and supported by the bed of literacy; the biological, neurological, and sociological phenomenon to whose challenges, opportunities, and advantages human beings seem to have been preordained. It is important, then, to note that we are not the first in human history to confront such an aberration, nor to rectify it. Before the advent of writing—an activity to which, again, human beings appear to have been destined—we were similarly detoured in our development of both intellect and culture. Before the advent of writing, human cultures were oral cultures.

73

Like all human cultures, like all human inventions, like all human technologies, orality presented us with certain advantages, challenges, and opportunities. In this chapter, I'd like to explore some of them.

Almost everyone who has had to endure a freshman-level Philosophy 101 course has wondered at some point why Plato expressed such open hostility to the poets in his *Republic*. It seems irrational, something we would not expect from the founder of the Academy. Why would Plato want to banish from his imagined state a class which not only entertained but also educated its citizens? What harm could come from listening to an epic, ode, or elegy? What harm could there be in a poet rhapsodizing about gods and heroes before a rapt audience? Was it that Plato was hostile to the idea of art? Was it unreasonable of the philosopher to demand,

> "We must remain firm in our conviction that hymns to the gods and praises of famous men are the only poetry which ought to be admitted into our State. For if you go beyond this and allow the honeyed muse to enter, either in epic or lyric verse, not law and the reason of mankind, which by common consent have ever been deemed best, but pleasure and pain will be the rulers in our State."[1]

Was Plato's distaste for poetry merely paranoia? Was it a blind and irrational fear of verse? What was it that Plato sensed, or felt, or saw—or *knew*—that made him fear for the health of Greek culture and social structure? Was he concerned that his countrymen would be seduced and then degraded by the very thing that had unified Greek culture and preserved a functional measure of social stability for centuries?

Something is happening here, and we get the sense as well that Plato knows that something is afoot, something important, something that has changed or will change or is changing the very soul of Greek culture and society. For the moment, we will have to leave these questions unanswered (although we will certainly come back to them) and examine the intellectual and epistemological boundaries of orality.

Orality is that peculiar mode of culture in which speech is the only, or certainly the dominant, communication medium available. In an oral culture, all learning is memorized and recited, a fact that puts significant limitations on the amount and type of information any individual can learn, retain, and use. Orality by definition precludes the existence of writing, but orality is much more than the mere absence of writing.

Before the development of formal writing systems, human beings communicated only through interpersonal interactions. The primary medium for such interactions was speech. Of course, there is more to interpersonal communication than just spoken words: there are all the nonverbal cues at work—what we call body language, the kinesthetic, proxemic, and paralinguistic registers—the understanding of which is the bane of most undergraduate communication students' existence. In such an environment, body movements, vocal rhythms, facial expressions, posture, gestures, tone of voice, speed of speaking, and so on, are mnemonic aids in the memorization of knowledge content, profoundly expressive conduits of meaning, and powerful parts of the oral consciousness.

Far more, as I have said, than a mere absence of writing, orality is a "total state of mind,"[2] a comprehensive system of communication that creates, nurtures, and depends upon the mimetic melding of mind and body, emotions and memory, that engages (*enraptures* or *enthralls* might be better verbs) the participants in communication with the "performance" of information. The body is a primary medium of communication in an oral culture,[3] and its expressive powers are put to full use, both as a means of information preservation (as rhythmic mnemonic device) and interpretation (in the sense that an audience gets powerful nonverbal cues from an oral performer acting out his message). In an oral culture, sender and receiver do not so much participate in a process of communication as they do submit[4] or surrender[5] themselves wholly to it.

To the contemporary reader, the description of such a state of affairs must come as something of a shock, or at least as a highly dubitable idea. It is difficult, here at the beginning of the third millennium, to imagine a situation where people willingly submit and surrender themselves to their culture, thereby negating their own individualism.[6] But the force of intellectual pressures brought to bear upon a culture to preserve and use their entire repertoire of knowledge, customs, mores, laws, and lore in memory over generations demanded just such a total immersion in the spoken word.

It is, in an oral culture, primarily through this sort of intense, immersive, holistic, and formulaic (in truth, almost liturgical) interpersonal interaction that the boundaries of reality are drawn. On examination, we find that those boundaries are placed farther afield than literate folk might expect. A look at scholarship into the social and psychological characteristics of orality can help us delineate these boundaries.

Orality is a curious cultural state, hard to imagine, as I've suggested, for people raised in an environment when idle thoughts can be quickly jotted down, or random family moments videotaped, and saved for future reflection. Several aspects of orality help to create its particular metaphysical framework, a framework that not only clearly delineates the epistemologically real from the epistemologically unreal, but also helps to define what is important to learn, to know, and to remember. Ear-dependent (that is to say, oral/aural) people are the centers of an aural universe. The boundaries of their universe stretch in all directions simultaneously. All aural stimuli affect us with the same nonlinear, multi-directional simultaneity. In a *visual* world, all is external, and the hand is the eye's adjunct. To allay doubt, we touch something to test its reality. But we perceive sound largely as an interior phenomenon. We are forever *apart from* the things we see; we are forever *a part of* the things we hear.[7]

Speech, interpersonal interaction, memorization, and performance are the organizing principles of orality. Group identity is intimately tied to and reinforced by the ritualistic patterns of interpersonal behaviors. This proposition goes beyond the discussion of mere content and commonality of language—in an oral culture the *performance* of oral discourse is almost always more important than what people may be talking about. This is true for two reasons: first, the rhythms, rhymes, cadences, and body movements of oral performance function as mnemonic devices to help the performer *contextualize* and *recall* information, thereby making it meaningful; and second, the event of interpersonal or public discourse always reinforces implicit connections between oral people—common language, common traditions, and common beliefs.

Anthropologist Bronislaw Malinowski called this byproduct of oral communication "the one indispensable instrument for creating ties of the moment"[8]—ties of friendship, of kinship, of fellowship—*phatic communion.*[9] All social interactions (and in so saying, let me again emphasize that we're referring here only to speech and to its parallel kinesthetic, paralinguistic, and proxemic channels, for in an oral culture all social interaction is effected interpersonally) are linked by ritualistic patterns of behavior which were learned for their mnemonic functions, but which later derived these social bonding functions.

Add to all this the fact that large-scale political administration is made more difficult—if not impossible—in the absence of a medium which will move information quickly, efficiently, and uniformly across large areas of space,[10] and we can conclude that oral societies will tend to be decentralized and tribal, interdependent and corporate.[11] Deities, belief systems, values, assumptions, and behaviors: all will be encountered as local manifestations of culture. Gods, like rituals, will be personal and tribal, and will help to define the group and give it its peculiar identity.

The experience of publicly sharing thought, while a commonplace idea to us, is a rather special event in oral culture, one to which great significance is attached. Formal speaking events are highly formulaic and ritualized, but even informal speech is not taken lightly.

There is very little time for "small talk," if in fact the concept exists at all in oral culture. Where the content of speech is less than compelling, the context of interaction becomes very important. Orality demands person-to-person interaction, and helps to bond people one to the other, providing the opportunity to actualize knowledge by sharing it. Lacking a storage medium that allows for the objective analysis of thought, oral cultures need interpersonal dialogue to "think through" any and all complex verbal concepts.[12] Knowledge thus exists as an event *in process* and as an activity manifest most clearly and powerfully in interpersonal and small-group relationships. Knowledge, it can fairly be said, is public property in an oral culture, and speech is the act by which all knowledge becomes public. Speech objectifies thought.

Of what, then, do oral folk speak? What, in an oral culture, is knowledge? What is worth knowing? Oral folk speak, ultimately, only of memorable things. Since all knowledge is memorized, knowledge by its nature must be closely tied to human experience. Alien concepts not easily assimilated into already existing contexts of knowledge will quickly be forgotten. Oral folk know few "facts" not directly connected to human experience. They learn through "close, empathetic, communal identification with the known."[13] They assess intelligence not in terms of objective, clinical "examinations," but by performance within operational contexts.[14] Just as the apprentice metal worker in an oral culture learns by watching the master and copying his actions, slowly but surely internalizing them; just as the young hunter, recently come of age, learns from his elders to stalk his prey stealthily and to wield an arrow or a spear in a manner guaranteed to deliver the kill, so do the oral poets, shamans, or historians learn their stock in trade: "by discipleship, which is a kind of apprenticeship, by listening, by repeating what they hear, by mastering proverbs and ways of combining and recombining them, by assimilating other formulary materials, by participating in a kind of corporate introspection—not by study in the strict sense."[15]

Julius Caesar, in his journals written while fighting the Gauls, noted the rigor of the oral education of the Gallic druids: "Report says that in the schools of the Druids they learn by heart a great number of verses, and therefore some persons remain twenty years under training. And they do not think it proper to commit these utterances to writing. . . . I believe that they have adopted the practice for two reasons—that they do not wish the rule to become common property, nor those who learn the rule to rely on writing and so neglect the cultivation of the memory."[16]

Furthermore, this type of education extends throughout the oral culture, for an encyclopedic array of that society's history, customs, traditions, laws, and mores are both preserved and actualized in rhythmic, formulaic speech. In Gaelic Ireland (before and for some time after the Norman invasion in 1170), the bardic branches of the Aes Dana had a hierarchy of educational achievement: "Up to twenty years of study were required to enter the filid, the profession of poetry, with the ability to recite from memory ten poems necessary to achieve the status of Tamm, fifty to achieve Doss, 175 to achieve Án Ruth, and 350 epic poems required to achieve the level of Ollamh, or professor."[17]

These "poets" (the word begins to take on a somewhat different form in an oral culture) were central to oral education because while individual skills specific to a trade or vocation might be learned on the job through apprenticeship, knowledge of one's culture and one's place within it comes only through group cultural interaction. Eric Havelock describes the ways in which the Homeric tradition, in its mythic tales of gods and heroes and mere mortals, encapsulated the structure of Athenian society, exemplifying its mores, formulas, prayers, protocols, and relationships—both hierarchical and horizontal.[18]

These tales were meant less to function as specific "instruction manuals" than as overall descriptive—and prescriptive—formulas. "This is the way in which the society does normally behave (or does not) and at the same time the way in which we, its members, who form the poet's audience, are encouraged to behave. There is no admonition: the tale remains dispassionate. But the paradigm of what is accepted practice or proper feeling is continually offered in contrast to what may be unusual or improper and excessive or rash."[19]

Orality, then, helps to create a knowledge environment, an *epistemology,* which demands that only the unchanging things of the world—things with a direct bearing on life, and a direct bearing on what lies beyond life—be dedicated to collective memory. Oral communication and the cultural modality we call orality quite simply focuses our attention on matters of life, death, survival, and eternity. In doing so, and through the specific methods of orality, the transcendent and the immanent become one.

Knowledge in an oral society is inherently precious, even sacred—that's why people have bothered to learn it, to memorize it, and to pass it down from generation to generation. Such knowledge keeps us alive, preserves our collective memories, explains who we are and where we came from, instructs us on proper behavior, and assures us that there is meaning to this thing called life, that there is (or will be in some distant, eternal realm) rest, comfort, reward, closure. We need such precious knowledge; indeed its very preciousness is what defines it to oral society as knowledge at all. A natural corollary to this idea, its "flip side" if you will, is that if some *piece* of knowledge is *not* precious (that is, it lends nothing to the life of the society), no one will bother to *learn* it (with all that verb implies).

The very concept of news so familiar to us today—information changing and being reported to us on a day-to-day or even a minute-by-minute basis—would be quite foreign to oral people. This is not to say that oral folk have no use for news, but that very little of it makes its way into the formal oral curriculum. Novelty neither blends immanent and transcendent nor lends itself to such blending; its foundation in a specific slice of time limits its meaning for an oral culture. A fire that kills many people in a neighboring village will certainly be of interest to everyone, but oral folk will assimilate the story into some preexisting myth about death and the precarious nature of life. The story itself, once told, will soon disappear.[20]

Knowledge in an oral society is also largely (though not exclusively) supernatural—animistic, totemistic, superstitious, spiritualistic, religious, with a concern for "the continued life beyond the visible one."[21] This perception of the supernatural character of much oral knowledge is supported by Walter Ong and, in a tangential way, Harold Innis. Ong points out that "the interiorizing force of the oral world relates in a special way to the sacral, to the ultimate concerns of existence."[22] Harold Innis saw in a society whose dominant medium of communication influenced a bias toward concerns over time a concomitant bias toward mythology and matters of the spiritual life.[23] Lucien Levy-Bruhl described oral folk as "hopelessly and completely immersed in a mystical frame of mind," whose "outlook is that of confused superstition, 'pre-logical,' made of mystic 'participations' and 'exclusions.'"[24] While Malinowski disagrees with much of this characterization, he concludes that although "primitive" people may have had some rudimentary understanding of protoscientific, empirical thought, they lived their lives largely in a metaphysically approachable universe,[25] a universe where immanence and transcendence are one, a seamless whole.

The metaphysical concerns of oral people—life and love, birth, death and regeneration, mortality and immortality, and the existence of some "God" or gods—are fairly universal, although different cultures have different focuses for their concerns or different manners of expressing those concerns. But all these concerns have expressed themselves through myth.

Myths are stories human beings tell to explain what is essentially unexplainable. They are, therefore, fundamentally metaphysical statements. The structural anthropologist Claude Levi-Strauss sees at the heart of myth a universal statement that differs from culture to culture not in structure, but only in surface form. Every culture has some sort of "mythscape," a collective appreciation of the fragility and preciousness of life, a communal voicing of those fears and hopes that are the expressions of the collective unconscious mind.[26] Being the expressions of language-using creatures, myths differ from culture to culture in their *symbolic form*,[27] in the images and metaphors they use to express their communal beliefs. Their metaphysical power comes from their ability to explain to an essentially pre-scientific people their origins and the origin of the universe, and to create a foundation for moral decision-making.[28] Myths differ from culture to culture, but their essential message is the same: "This is who we are; this is why we are here; this is how we are meant to live."

Myth is the psychic landscape of the oral society, the context within which all other experience takes place. Malinowski assures us that preliterate humans had the capacity for objective, quasi-empirical, "pre-scientific" thought,[29] but all such thought was still under the influence of powerful agents of *stasis*, for a culture's myths also help to preserve society in its existing form.[30]

Myth and reality, one might imagine, are easily confused in the oral mind. That is why, one might also conclude, immanence and transcendence are so intimately linked in orality. Myth is the living inventory of human knowledge, and in the oral mind all human knowledge, both transcendent and immanent, necessarily shares the same epistemological space. There is no room, nor is there an intellectual method, for separating empirically observed "facts" from eternal, transcendent "truth." While avoiding the value-laden label *primitive*, it is difficult not to conclude that orality was an early step in human cultural evolution and that, in the same way it was inevitable that we would be an animal that shares its thoughts through speech, we must have also become an animal that stores its thoughts in writing.

Chapter Four

The Metaphysics of Orality

"Lord," he said, "my servant lies at home paralyzed
and in terrible suffering."
Jesus said to him, "I will go and heal him."
The centurion replied, "Lord, I do not deserve to have
you come under my roof. But just say the word, and
my servant will be healed. For I myself am a man under authority, with soldiers under me. I tell this one,
'Go,' and he goes; and that one, 'Come,' and he comes.
I say to my servant, 'Do this,' and he does it." When
Jesus heard this, he was astonished and said to those
following him, "I tell you the truth, I have not found
anyone in Israel with such great faith."

Matthew 8:6–10

Clifford Geertz described religion as a "cultural system," a system of symbols and symbolic ritualized behaviors that shape
human emotional life, orient our behaviors toward some transcendent value, and provide a coherent picture of the order of
human existence, both material and spiritual.[1] In the broadest
sense, this is true. But a closer look at human belief systems suggests that our cultural sense of religion changes as our culture
changes. Symbol systems evolve over time, our understanding
of their meanings change, and our understanding of the agency
of ritual behaviors change. If, as I argue, a society's dominant
media of communication play an important role in both the
construction and the confusion of reality, in the restructuring of
consciousness, in helping us sort out the real from the unreal,

then the very word *religion*, when applied to oral culture, ought to be approached and used cautiously and with some flexibility.

What, after all, can be said of the metaphysical mindset of people who have left behind no written records? Little can be said with much certainty. Yet we know through other means that such ideas as God, spirits and demons, and an afterlife (or, at any rate, an "otherlife" beyond this one) were real to oral folk. We know because of ancient primary historical sources who came into contact with oral cultures (see, for example, Caesar's *The Gallic War*), because of ancient oral cultures who traveled the cultural evolutionary path to literacy, transcribing oral traditions along the way (for example, the Hebrew, Greek, Roman, Persian, Egyptian, and Chinese cultures), and we know because of modern discoveries and investigations (and, unfortunately, the consequent destruction) of what were perhaps the last existing oral cultures (for example, in Papua New Guinea, Melanesia, Samoa, and the Trobriand islands). These bits of evidence allow us to make a few reliable generalizations about the metaphysics of oral culture: words were seen to have magical (creative, and frequently, destructive) power; and the boundaries between objective and subjective experience, between magic, religion, and science, or between transcendence and immanence were not clear and concrete, but, rather, ambiguous, fluid, and changeable.

Oral Knowledge

Jack Goody has written of three modes of acquiring knowledge generally applicable to all oral cultures. The first mode, that of traditional knowledge, orients oral people to themselves and their world. It is the stuff that "everybody knows." This includes the basic assumptions of life and the values, attitudes, and behaviors that the group has defined as functionally, aesthetically, and socially acceptable. Codes of behavior, gender and social status expectations, and occupational skills (such as hunting, farming, or craft knowledge) are all examples of such traditional knowledge. These are acquired in interpersonal interaction, in participation in the social and economic life of the tribe, and by everyday experience.

The second mode, that of specialized knowledge, encompasses the ritualistic and ceremonial life of the group and the understanding of the symbolic dimension of group behavior. This, too, is acquired in participation in the rites of oral life and in interpersonal interaction, particularly with a group's elders. Havelock has described how each of these modes is addressed in oral literature, and how that oral literature was integral to the maintenance of social order.[2]

Transcendent Knowledge

But the third mode of acquiring knowledge among oral folk has nothing to do with interaction among members of the group, or participation in its rituals, or experience in the most commonly used sense of that word. There is a type of knowledge "that is not mediated by humans, either formally or informally, but comes direct from powers, spiritual forces, agencies . . . who alone seem to have the ability to reveal to man the secrets of his universe."[3] This is the knowledge that underlies, for many if not all oral cultures, all other knowledge. To call it knowledge at all is, perhaps, a mistake, for what we are looking at is a manifestation of a thought-system founded in the belief in some "otherworldly," metaphysical reality, revealed to some gifted, elite individual (a medium—a priest, medicine man, or shaman) or small group of individuals who converse directly with a figure (or figures) known as "god." It is perhaps similar to what Immanuel Kant called "pure knowledge," an intuitive understanding not founded upon any sensory experience. Or it may be akin to the human experience Karl Rahner calls the *supernatural existential*, those momentary glimpses of Divine Truth that are offered to (but not necessarily acknowledged or accepted by) all human beings by virtue of their orientation to God and his "self-communication."[4] Or, as some have suggested, it may be the result of schizophrenia or some other mental illness.[5] It is, in any case, essentially a melding (or, perhaps just as likely, confusion) of transcendent and immanent realities, a harnessing of the presentational structures of thought to the propositional, of imagination to reason, of transcendent knowledge to the immanent experience of nature. It is an experience unique to the human being.

Oral culture is a culture of *immanent transcendence* as well as *transcendent immanence*. Animism and pantheism are just two belief systems common to oral cultures that meld the spiritual with the material, that see a spiritual world as residing, inherently, in the natural world. Oral folk feel surrounded by the sacred; they live amid the mystical. Magic, spirits, and the supernatural abound. The mysteries of life that could be partly expressed by abstract, symbolic speech were too deep for the oral mind to investigate analytically and logically; that would wait for writing and its offspring: natural philosophy and theology. But those mysteries were everywhere evident. And it is in speech itself that much of the magic dwelt: "The sounds of speech—and consequently the sounds of public thought—are creative events, not things. For oral folk, words are the only means of objectifying thought and making it public. In a sense then, to speak a thought makes it 'real.' This creative power of the word is reflected in the creation story of the Old Testament, as well as in the creation myths of other cultures."[6]

Ernst Cassirer testifies to the universality of this perception of the word for oral cultures: "The original bond between the linguistic and the mythico-religious consciousness is primarily expressed in the fact that all verbal structures appear as *also* mythical entities, endowed with certain mythical powers, that the Word, in fact, becomes a sort of primary force, in which all being and doing originate. In all mythical cosmogonies, as far back as they can be traced, this supreme position of the Word is found."[7] C.K. Ogden and I.A. Richards point out to us that oral folk ascribe to words not only creative powers, but magical powers of control: "From the earliest times the Symbols which men have used to aid the process of thinking and to record their achievements have been a continuous source of wonder and illusion. The whole human race has been so impressed by the properties of words as instruments for the control of objects, that in every age it has attributed to them occult powers."[8]

Martin Heidegger ponders this fascinating power of words to give immanent form to transcendent ideas: "Where the word is missing, there is no thing. It is only the word at our disposal which endows the thing with Being. What are words, that they have such power? What are things, that they need words in order to be?"[9]

The Word and Ontological Reality

All being, in the oral mind, is linked intimately with the creative power of speech. In the account of creation found in the first book of the Old Testament, God's creative act consists essentially in the form of a fiat—a verbal command that something should exist. "Then God said: 'Let there be light,' and there was light" (Gen. 1:3). God defines the day by differentiating it from the darkness of night. "God then separated the light from the darkness. God called the light 'day,' and the darkness he called 'night.'" God then creates the earth and the heavens. "Then God said: 'Let there be a dome in the middle of the waters, to separate one body of water from the others.' And so it happened: God made the dome and it separated the water above the dome from the water below it. God called the dome 'the sky.'"[10] God continues to speak into existence the earth, the stars, and all of the earth's plants and animals.

Similarly, the New Testament Gospel of John seeks to provide provenance for the divinity of Jesus Christ by associating him with God's creative power: the *logos*; the "Word of God," the Divine Wisdom of God, the organizing principle of Creation. Unlike the Gospels of Matthew and Luke, which presented a genealogy supporting the prophetic view of a Messiah descended from the House of David, John declared that Jesus the Christ was, essentially, *sui generis*, the *Only* of His kind, descended from Himself, through Himself. "In the beginning was the Word, and the Word was with God, and the Word was God. He was in the beginning with God. All things came to be through him; and without him nothing came to be."[11]

In Islamic theology, the creative power of the word is similarly evident. "His command, when He desires a thing, is to say to it 'Be,' and it is. So glory be to Him, in whose hand is the dominion of everything, and unto whom you shall be returned."[12] In the Indian religious work the *Brihadarayaka Upanishad*, there was a primeval "self" which brought itself into existence by exclaiming, "It is I!" Similar examples abound in other religious traditions.

While names *evoke* (call to mind) the things named (as do all words), in oral culture they also *invoke* (call upon) them. Thus, in the Judeo-Christian tradition, the ineffable God of Abraham remains nameless and unapproachable, and to speak His Holy Name ("I Am") is a serious affront. So too with Islam, which offers scores of pseudonyms, mantras, or attributes[13] for Al'lah.[14] "The rule of secrecy," Cassirer reminds us, "applies first and foremost to the Holy Name; for the mention of it would immediately release all the powers inherent in the god himself."[15] Similarly, there is the New Testament account of Jesus' instruction to His disciples to call on Him when they sought His presence. "'For where two or three are gathered together in my name, there am I in the midst of them' means simply, 'Where they pronounce my name in their assembly, there I am really present.'"[16] There is a power to spoken words in oral culture that becomes diminished in literate and postliterate society. It is the power to create reality—the power to make immanent all that is both immanent and transcendent in human experience.

The Word and Existential Control

To name something is to define it, to have power over it, to control it—in both a positive and negative way. God, according to the creation myth of the Judeo-Christian tradition, implicitly gave those powers of control over creation to Adam when he told him, "Whatever the man called each of them would be its name. The man gave names to all the cattle, all the birds of the air, and all the wild animals."[17] In the antebellum United States, slave owners stripped their slaves of their native African names and gave them new names that were easier to pronounce and were frequently diminutive, familiar, or nicknames (*Buck, Jem, Joe, Annie, Abby,* or *Fannie*). White Americans, both before and after the war, called African-Americans *coons, boonies, darkies,* or *niggers,* as an acute sign of disrespect and presumed superiority, a denial of black Americans' personal sovereignty—another way of saying, "We still own you." In my own lifetime, the word *Negro* was an acceptable reference, but it was again one imposed by white America. In the 1960s, African-Americans reclaimed their personal sovereignty and took control of the issue, referring to themselves as "black," in the 1980s as "Afro-Americans," and in the 1990s as "African-Americans." Many white Americans scoffed—ostensibly over the pettiness of such sensitivity to labels, but perhaps more so in resentment that these Americans had found the temerity to name themselves, in a defiant act of self-determination.

Many cultures use curses, spells, and ridicule to sanction social behavior.[18] Corinne A. Kratz describes the curses used among the Okiek people (a primarily oral culture) in Kenya. "A formal curse . . . could be said when an evil act is done by an unknown person. For instance, a formal curse might force return of stolen property, or disarm suspected sorcery and turn it back on the perpetrator. . . . Curses wish an array of misfortunes on their victims—to be eaten by wild animals, suffer from disease and barrenness, lack peace and harmony at home, have no fire, and die that very day, sinking with the sun, moon, and stars."[19]

In Gaelic-Irish culture, one of the most serious of social sanctions was the satire. Charles Squire tells the story of Cairpre, the bard of the mythical Tuatha De Danann, who, on visiting Bress, the evil and avaricious Ri (king or chief) of the equally mythical Fomorians, is given less than a hospitable welcome. Cairpre then composed the first satire ever heard in Ireland:

> No meat on the plates,
> No milk of the cows;
> No shelter for the belated;
> No money for the minstrels;
> May Bress's cheer be what he gives to others![20]

Cairpre's satire was embarrassing enough to cause Bress to break out in a rash all over his face; a blemish of beauty serious enough to cost him the leadership of the Fomorians. While entirely mythical, this account stands as an archetype of the poetic category of satire. The idea of honor or "face" was strong enough to inhibit all but the most ill-intentioned from straying from socially acceptable behavior.[21]

Words do, indeed, have power; more power than we are likely to realize or remember in a postmodern world. Every utterance is an "outerance":[22] words objectify subjective experience, allow us to share those experiences, and make transcendent ideas immanent realities. In terms more suitable to the oral mind, *words make ideas real.* They are the basis of all meaning and consequent understanding, the foundation of all concepts, the only means of differentiating any object or idea in the universe from any other object. We postmoderns might have become rather blasé about words; primitive oral folk were entirely unable to do the same. For oral folk, words intimately link the transcendent to the immanent.

The Distinction between Transcendence and Immanence

Names are not, however, merely magical talismans or tokens of control. There is another, functional truth to the idea of words symbolizing control: they organize our objective universe and allow us to classify and systematize it. They allow us to analyze it and understand it. They allow us to generalize from it and make predictions. They are the foundation of all sciences. They are the basis of objective reality. They are tools of immanence. They put us in a position, if we choose to, to discriminate between what appears to us, immanently, through our senses, and what "appears" to us, transcendently, only through our imaginations.

As Walter Ong points out, "Without learning a vast store of names, one is simply powerless to understand, for example, chemistry and to practice chemical engineering. And so with all other intellectual knowledge."[23] The power of human propositional thought allows for the construction of bodies of knowledge, knowledge of the immanent, material universe, and provides a means for analytic thinking and greater understanding.

Nevertheless, words can be used presentationally as well as

propositionally (or expressively as well as analytically), and the power of presentational structures of thought come to dominate a mind that has no external medium through which to focus its attention on the more critical uses of language. For oral folk, words are magic, and the magic comes not just from their creative power, but from their ethereal nature. Words have an evanescent quality missing from physical objects that occupy a distinct, physical position in space and time.[24] In this way, words are a sensual link between the worlds of immanence and transcendence, and encourage the oral mind, without the benefit of any external, visual means of recording and studying them, to focus on their transient, ethereal creative power.

Magic, Science, and Religion

To speak of transcendent reality, of a "god" or of "gods," however, in the context of oral culture (as though oral culture were in itself anything like a unified, homogeneous phenomenon) is, perhaps, itself a mistake. God may have been a "person," or god may have been a power (a life force?) or a presence (in nature, perhaps). There may have been gods *or* goddesses, or a god *and* a goddess, or a pantheon of gods, gods both of good and of evil, gods of the seasons, gods of the hunt, gods of the home and of the hearth, gods of nature and of the elements, or personal gods. Gods may have been wise fathers or nurturing mothers, cosmic ancestors of the tribe, protectors of the race. Gods may have been troublesome, foolish jokers, tinkering with the lives of the people unless they were appeased by some sacrifice. Gods may have been impersonal forces found throughout creation, indwelling in all things, both animate and inanimate.

But the concept of a transcendent power is present in oral culture, an apparently necessary by-product of symbolic thought. And all concepts of "god" have one thing in common. God in some way has control of our world, of the lives and destinies of our people, and while we might (and *ought to*) offer a god praise and homage and repentance and sacrifice, *we* cannot control that god. The god remains ineffable, unpredictable, and ultimately unknowable, even though his/her presence is as immanent to us as the rising sun, or the stars at night, or the birth of a child. It is this ultimate acknowledgment of our powerlessness in the face of such mystery that is at the heart of primitive (and perhaps all) religions. It is this one characteristic of oral religions that differentiates them from the "merely supernatural"—the magical and the superstitious qualities of language.[25]

The Essence of Magic

Magic and religion (and, as Malinowski points out, science) co-exist in the oral mindset, where the immanent and the transcendent coexist. But that is not to say that we should think of magic and religion in oral cultures as equals, or even as equivalents.

> Magic is not only human in its embodiment, but also in its subject matter: it refers principally to human activities and states, hunting, gardening, fishing, love-making, disease, and death. It is not directed so much to nature as to man's relation to nature and to the human activities which affect it. Moreover, the effects of magic are usually conceived not as a product of nature influenced by the charm, but as something specially magical, something which nature cannot produce, but only the power of magic. . . . Thus the force of magic is not a universal force residing everywhere, flowing where it will or it is willed to. Magic is the one and only specific power, a force unique of its kind, residing exclusively in man, let loose only by his magical art, gushing out with his voice, conveyed by the casting forth of the rite.[26]

The human act of magic (like the human pursuit of scientific knowledge) is essentially an attempt to control. Oral folk will apply practical knowledge and observed experience to perform a repeatable task. This is an example of pre-scientific thought, itself a natural by-product of language.[27] But oral folk know (again through experience) that sometimes things just won't work the way they always have in the past, and they can't account for a reason. This is because their pre-scientific thought is just that—pre-scientific—and they have been unable to identify a specific cause for their apparently random failure. So, once the task is completed (or perhaps within the performance of the task itself), some spell is cast, some incantation is spoken, some talisman is clutched, and the workers are ensured of success (until, of course, they randomly fail).[28] There is, however, enough predictable success to make it clear why the oral mind could see magic rites as effective agents of supernatural control.

Frazer gives an example of this type of quasi-religious ritual that formed the basis for daily liturgy in ancient Egypt:

> Every night when the sun-god Ra sank down to his home in the glowing west he was assailed by hosts of demons under the leadership of the arch-fiend Apepi. All night long he fought them, and sometimes by day the powers of darkness sent up clouds even into the blue Egyptian sky to obscure his light and weaken his power. To aid the sun-god in this daily struggle, a ceremony was daily performed in his temple at Thebes. A figure of his foe Apepi, represented as a crocodile with a hideous face or a serpent with many coils, was made of wax. . . . Wrapt in a papyrus case, on which another likeness of Apepi had been drawn in green ink, the figure was then tied up with black hair, spat upon, hacked with a stone knife, and cast on the ground. There the priest trod on it with his left foot again and again, and then burned it in a fire made of a certain plant or grass. . . . The service, accompanied by the recitation of certain prescribed spells, was repeated not merely morning, noon, and night, but whenever a storm was raging, or heavy rain had set in, or black clouds were stealing across the sky to hide the sun's bright disc. The fiends of darkness, clouds, and rain felt the injuries inflicted on their images as if they had been done to themselves; they passed away, at least for a time, and the beneficent sun-god shone out triumphant once more.[29]

Early Egyptian belief in the immanence of some transcendent supernatural power is evident here. But this attempt at using that power to control their relationship to the environment indicates that magic, while immanent, is in reality something less than transcendent. It is, at the end of the day, purely utilitarian: the sun-god, Ra, the giver of life, light, and warmth, must rise again tomorrow. We must assure his ascent.

And, of course, every day Ra returned.

> Thus the analogy between the magical and the scientific conceptions of the world is close. In both of them the succession of events is perfectly regular and certain, being determined by immutable laws, the operation of which can be foreseen and calculated precisely; the elements of caprice, of chance, and of accident are banished from the course of nature. Both of them open up a seemingly boundless vista of possibilities to him who knows the causes of things and can touch the secret springs that set in motion the vast and intricate mechanism of the world. Hence the strong attraction which magic and science alike have exercised on the human mind; hence the powerful stimulus that both have given to the pursuit of knowledge.[30]

The metaphysical world of orality can be divided, therefore, into two broad symbol systems, each with its own distinct function but which, nonetheless, can be confused and therefore conjoined in the oral mind: the magical and the religious. Externally similar, both share powerful phatic elements, formulaic prayers or acts of ritual, which serve as the glue that binds people together. In the magical system, the symbolic act (be it dance, incantation, invocation of a spirit, or use of a talisman) is always the means toward some practical, desired end to follow immediately or later on. The association of some ritualistic behavior with a desired end is characteristic of pre-scientific thinking. "The principles of association are excellent in themselves, and indeed absolutely essential to the working of the human mind. Legitimately applied they yield science; illegitimately applied they yield magic, the bastard sister of science. It is therefore a truism, almost a tautology, to say that all magic is necessarily false and barren;

for were it ever to become true and fruitful, it would no longer be magic but science."[31]

Magic presumes the human ability to control the spirit world—an immanent link to a transcendent realm. The magical ritual is a mechanical act and directly causes the intervention of a supernatural power. In the religious system, however, the symbolic act is both means *and* end: within its "supernatural world of faith," a "second supernatural reality"—displaying a "pantheon of spirits and demons, the benevolent powers of totem, guardian spirit, tribal all-father, the vision of the future life"[32]—we encounter human belief for the sake of belief. Perhaps it is faith in a transcendent reality when the loss of that faith means the loss of hope.

The oral mind, the mind with which human beings were endowed, through nature, by the evolutionary gift of language, melds the transcendent with the immanent. It has to; it has no choice. It is a mind that sees the objective reality before it, but also has the ability to imagine a far more subjective, mystical reality (or realities). In the oral mind, objective sensory perception and subjective imagination are interchangeable providers of experience, and the only measure of objectivity is the extent to which those experiences are shared by a cohesive group. And any and all such sharing must be mediated by the spoken word.

With the advent of writing—the externalization of thought and experience on a physical medium—this balance of immanence and transcendence must be disturbed. A breach between transcendent and immanent experience appears, and oral cultures have a choice: to turn in upon themselves and protect the traditions of group and tribe, or to open themselves to new ways of thinking, new ideas, new beliefs based on the logic of (truly) objective experience, new orientations toward the world. It is a choice between an old, comfortable, but confining reality and a new, frightening, but expansive one.

Chapter Five

Literacy

και ο λογος σαρξ εγενετο
και εσκηνωσεν εν ημιν
και εθεασαμεθα την
δοξαν αυτου δοξαν ως μονογενους παρα πατρος
πληρης χαριτος και αληθειας.

And the Word was made flesh,
and dwelt among us,
and we beheld his glory,
the glory as of the only begotten of the Father,
full of grace and truth.

John 1:14

In a little over a millennium, from 2000 BC until about 800 BC, human beings responded to a curious urge to externalize their thoughts in writing. It is, in fact, fascinating to note that the evolution of human culture finds *all* human development of writing in this era.[1] We will investigate why this might be so at a later point.

The Development of Writing Forms

Early writing forms were frequently crudely drawn pictures meant to give a warning (much as those yellow and black traffic signs do today), or to tell a story (much as a modern comic strip might). These descriptive-representational devices[2] are non-propositional forms that represent a message within a context-bound situation. There is no semantic element involved in this type of early writing form; the picture itself tells the story solely because of its concrete, presentational structure. Thus, descriptive-representational devices are significant more because they give evidence of the human need to express thought visually than for their efficiency in doing so.

Some markings were used to signify the ownership of property, as the branding of a calf signifies a rancher's ownership,[3] or the marking on a token of exchange identifies the person to whom value has been given and from whom eventual payment is expected. These identifying-mnemonic devices are arbitrary markings meant to identify an object with its owner, as an incised "X" on a cow's rump might mean that she belongs to rancher X, or to identify the owner with some power possessed by his marking (for example, a lion painted on a shield).[4] Identifying-mnemonic devices are not meant to tell a story or describe an event, but merely to remember something or to identify an object and associate it with its owner. This type of marking had some unexpected linguistic consequences which allowed for the development of true phonetic writing systems, as we shall shortly see.

Pictographic writing forms (in which a thing or a concept was suggested by some analogous visual representation) evolved either from these early markings or entirely independent of them (as Chinese ideographs did). A pictographic marking bears some visual relationship to its referent. Therefore, "♥ " would represent heart, and "👁 " could easily stand for eye. Early pictographic systems had the disadvantage of expressing some concepts easily (things and concrete concepts, like heart and eye), but had difficulty expressing others (actions, qualities, and abstract concepts, such as truth and goodness). They suffered from the additional disadvantage of needing discrete, individual signs for each concept expressed, which made pictographic systems quite unwieldy.[5] The need to express words themselves (the sounded word, as spoken orally), rather than the things they referred to, led to the creation of logograms ("word writing").

Most logograms probably originated as pictographs—specifically, as identifying mnemonic devices. A functional shift occurs when a sign is simplified so that it ceases to look like the thing it represents, and its referent is no longer a thing but a spoken sound, an aural "word." Once we have an abstract symbol whose visual appearance bears no resemblance to its referent, we experience a psychic shift and reference a sound (such as the spoken word "lion") rather than the thing itself. This is the essence of the logogram.

Logograms developed in a number of different ways. We just looked at how identifying-mnemonic devices could shift from carrying a visual reference to an aural one. Another way is through the association of a sign with a new meaning, one which was not its original purpose, but which developed by association with the marking's referent. In a case like this, an ideogram which originally stood for the eye might also come to refer to the idea of vision or sight. Once the visual relationship is diminished, a new relationship—one between the sign and the spoken word—can emerge. A third means, the diagrammatic, is evident when a sign is arbitrarily created and agreed upon by a language group to refer to a spoken word; for example, "⌘" arbitrarily standing for the word function.

We still use logograms today, and a cursory examination of their use should give us a clue as to why further refinement of writing systems was still necessary after their development.

The standard QWERTY keyboard should give us a fair idea of the different logograms with which we are familiar. The "at" sign, for instance: @. The dollar sign: $. The percent sign: %. Then, of course, there are the ten numeric signs from 0 to 9; 1 equals one, 2 equals two, 99 equals ninety-nine, etc. Notice that, for some of these signs, the relationship is purely phonetic: @ for "at." But notice, too, that some retain a residual semantic relationship: $, which we might normally read as "dollar," we also frequently read as "money." This lingering ambiguity represented both an opportunity and a liability for cultures that adopted logographic writing forms; it allowed for the evolution of newer, different forms while at the same time making that very evolution necessary.

Through an implicit rule called the rebus principle, logograms could be combined to represent more complex phrases, facilitating multisyllabic words, thereby making it unnecessary to create a separate sign for every spoken word. "👁 ❤ U" would then be "I love you," the 👁 and the U functioning as logograms with a phonetic relationship to their referents, and the ❤ with a semantic relationship.

There is a danger to logographic writing that is directly related to the rebus principle; that is the danger of semantic ambiguity introduced by having a marking that can act as both a visual referent and a phonetic one at the same time. When will 👁 mean I and when will it mean vision or sight? When will ❤ mean heart and when will it mean love?

What is still important about this development, however, is the tacit recognition of the ability to analyze to deeper and deeper levels the phonemic structure of spoken language. It will become apparent why this deep analysis is so critically important as we near the culmination of the development of writing forms.

Syllabic Systems

In the meantime, however, different language communities in different parts of the world were continuing to develop different writing systems. Some spoken languages consist of discrete and finite sets of syllables that form different words when constructed in different combinations. To create a unique sign for a limited number of vocables results in a far more efficient writing form. A *syllabary* is just such a system; one that has broken the spoken language down to the phonemic level of the syllable, and has assigned a specific marking to each. A syllabary has a great advantage over other writing systems: it avoids the need for an unwieldy set of signs as pictographic writing demands; it avoids much of the semantic ambiguity that logograms might introduce.

Compare this with Egyptian *hieroglyphics*, which was a sort of hodgepodge writing system, having elements of pictography, logography, and logographic/syllabic writing forms. Egyptian hieroglyphic writing was an extremely complex and complicated system (very much indebted to the rebus principle), and it remained for centuries a sacred writing form, learned and used only by a highly educated, elite priesthood.

Eleven centuries before Christ, the Phoenicians assimilated a syllabary (from the proto-Semitic syllabary in use—in some form—by various Semitic peoples for centuries), which eventually spawned a Punic syllabary, an Aramaic syllabary, and, because of Phoenician naval power and influence as a Mediterranean trader, a Greek syllabary—the forerunner of the Greek alphabet.

The Alphabet

On the surface, the Greek alphabet does not appear to be the enormous breakthrough in writing that it is. The alphabet is essentially a refinement of the Phoenician syllabary, and even assimilated fully many of the same signs representing many of the same (consonantal) sounds. But a syllabary has one sign per syllable, and while it may represent the consonantal value of that syllable very effectively, it does not differentiate the vowel value. Some syllabaries (such as the Hebrew) eventually incorporated diacritical marks to indicate the vowel value. But the Greeks, presented with the Phoenician syllabary, took the phonemic analysis of their language one step further and assigned five markings to represent all vowel values of their language: a small refinement on the surface, but one with profound implications for human culture.

The alphabet has the ability to express visually any human utterance—*any* human utterance, in *any* language—in a system of only 24–27 characters (depending on cultural and linguistic adaptations). There is no need to learn and memorize an enormous number of concept signs or word signs.[6] Each character has a simple form. It is not difficult for a five- to seven-year-old child to "learn her ABCs." It is therefore the most accessible writing form developed by human intellect. Each simple character is an abstraction; it has no referent, but a sound; in the case of the alphabet, a *phoneme*, the smallest unit of a spoken language that defines meaning. There is no ambiguity in the writing system, no need to ponder whether a particular sign is functioning as a pictograph or as a logograph. And because it is a writing system founded entirely on the aural analysis of phonemes, an earlier point bears repeating: alphabetic writing is transferable to any human language.[7] Pictographic writing forms were difficult to use and time-consuming to learn. They had (and have) an inherent quality of cultural exclusivity to them. Syllabic systems are more efficient and easier to use and to learn, but there is still a problem with ambiguity in the absence of discrete markings for vowel values, and the need, on average, for roughly three to four times the number of characters as alphabetic writing. Alphabetic writing is an efficient and unambiguous system, and alphabetic literacy means that *widespread* literacy is a possibility. It is a *democratizing* script,[8] and it is certainly no accident that its development predates classical Athenian democracy by less than two centuries.

Psychologically, writing *externalizes* thought, as oral speech does, but does so in *fixed space*. The visual capture of the elusive spoken word on the page *reifies* thought, making the public "outerance" of thought not an event (as in oral culture), but an *object*. It transfers the locus of "outered" thought from an evanescent moment in time to the semipermanent world of space. It shifts (at least temporarily) the sensory focus of thought from the ear to the eye, and we begin to become aware of the linearity of thought (because of the linearity of writing), the logic of thought (because of the inherent logic of linguistic grammar), and the sequential nature of thought (because of the sequential nature of linguistic syntax, as opposed to the simultaneity of oral/aural experience).

At the same time, writing reinforces the interiority of speech by allowing (forcing?) the reflective consideration and *reconsideration* of thoughts on the basis of their linearity, their logic, and their cause/effect sequence. Marshall McLuhan suggests that "the translation of auditory into visual terms set up an inner life in man which separated him from the exterior world and, in part, from his own senses, as we know from the study of pre-literate societies."[9] Writing, Walter Ong adds, "makes possible increasingly articulate introspectivity, opening the psyche as never before, not only to the external objective world quite distinct from itself, but also to the interior self against whom the objective world is set."[10] Little wonder that Plato sensed that something extraordinary was taking place, something that he was not willing to ignore or take lightly.

Alphabetic Literacy

Literacy broadened the intellectual horizon by allowing for more creative and more critical modes of thought. Long before the invention and proliferation of functional magnetic resonance imaging (fMRI) technologies provided evidence, at least one investigator had already concluded that literacy (alphabetic literacy particularly) encourages left-hemisphere dominance, and therefore facilitates creative, critical, and analytical thought.[11] Walter Ong agrees: "The new way to store knowledge was not in mnemonic formulas, but in the written text. This freed the mind for more original, more abstract thought."[12] In addition, the visual orientation of written thoughts allowed thinking humans to pore over them, compare them with other written texts, use new or expanded intellectual techniques (such as lists, categories, and taxonomies), and build new knowledge, incrementally, on the foundations of older knowledge.[13] The systematic recording of changing, objective data undermined superstitious tendencies, and ultimately worked to undermine our faith in the immanent nature of transcendent, other-worldly "realities," by allowing us to identify patterns within phenomena, and to make predictions based on that data. Thus, literacy helps to create the skeptical mind[14] and deals a blow to transcendent experience. Scientific thought without writing is possible; *science* as a cultural activity without writing is not. With writing, science becomes an inevitability.

With the development of this new cultural activity, a cleavage occurs between immanence and transcendence; the "print-made split between head and heart," that McLuhan referred to, a breach I will refer to in the rest of this investigation as "the split." This split manifests itself slowly, however, because the spread of literacy is hampered at first by the scarcity of written texts, and even as texts become more common, many hesitate to call attention to the faltering perception of the transcendent experience.

From the development of the first Sumerian pictographic writing system in about 3500 BC until the development of movable-type alphabetic printing in AD 1452—nearly five millennia later—*all* writing was done by hand, a laborious and time-consuming job.

In the West, medieval monasteries painstakingly produced beautiful illuminated works, but these handmade manuscripts were precious works of art, as much objects of veneration as the Holy Scripture they contained. Consequently, literacy remained the exclusive domain of a relatively prosperous, educated elite, largely religious or noble, almost entirely male. A monopoly of knowledge had grown around the handwritten manuscript in medieval Europe, and it was everywhere controlled by the Church. "There was a practically universal agreement on the basic ideas by which men professed to live. Catholicism was not only the one Church but the primary inspiration of art, the main source of education, the accepted basis of all philosophy, science, political theory, and economic theory. Medieval men all knew the same absolute truth about the human drama, from the Creation to the Last Judgment. . . . Latin was the universal language of educated men."[15]

Print Literacy

It was not until the middle of the fifteenth century and the development of movable-type printing that alphabetic literacy began to have the opportunity to "find its level," to expand to the limits of its potential. The printing press was the cultural equivalent of human intellect reaching a point of critical mass, a quantum leap in the evolution of communication technologies and the spread of knowledge. Evidence of its enormous influences on culture—its transformation of a localized Florentine

Renaissance into a European Renaissance, its instrumentality in the Protestant Reformation and reorientation of Catholic practices and ecclesiastical authority, its facilitation of modern science, its role in the collapse of feudalism and the rise of both nationalism and capitalism—has been documented exhaustively elsewhere.[16] For my purposes in this chapter, it is enough to talk about how the printing press reoriented the human senses, nurturing human propositional structures of thought, and furthering the split between immanence and transcendence.

The first and most obvious effect that printing had was to take the reorientation of consciousness which writing had provided and amplify it on a mass scale. "Ear people" became "eye people," individualism trumped tribalism, skepticism impinged on both magic and religion, and people began to doubt the still-lingering assumptions which the traditions of orality had given them. J.C. Carothers notes, "It was only when the written, and still more the printed, word appeared on the scene that the stage was set for words to lose their magic powers and vulnerabilities." He goes on to explain that oral folk live "largely in a world of sound, in contrast to western Europeans who live largely in a world of vision. Sounds are in a sense dynamic things, or at least are always indicators of dynamic things—of movements, events, activities, for which man . . . must be ever on the alert. . . . Sounds lose much of this significance in western Europe, where man often develops, and must develop, a remarkable ability to disregard them."[17]

Whereas for oral folk "reality seems to reside far more in what is heard and what is said," for literate folk, he concludes, "seeing is believing."[18]

Slowly but surely, literacy also acts to destroy the tribal mindset of oral man, "freeing him from the tribal trance of resonating word magic and the web of kinship."[19] Reading is a solitary activity, perhaps even an antisocial activity. The written word is an artificial enough tool to compel us to attend closely to a text, or to risk missing or losing its meaning. Its *conditions of attendance*[20] preclude participation in any social activity while we read. Thus the onset and spread of social literacy will have the effect of creating a growing society of *individuals*.

The literate person is a wonderer and a questioner, introspective, curious, and aloof. The age of print, in time, will yield a mass society of wondering, questioning, introspective, and curious individuals. Mass wondering and mass questioning can be both an empowering and a dangerous thing. They will certainly be harbingers of change.

The Consequences of Literacy

And change there was. McLuhan notes tersely, "The Gutenberg technology retrieved antiquity and junked the Middle Ages."[21] In the aftermath of Gutenberg—the Renaissance, the rediscovery of Greek philosophy, the rise of humanism, and the weakening of traditional authority (political and religious)—there followed both a further breakdown of the dualism that had been present since the time of Augustine, and a recapitulation of the very same dualism in newer forms, in more immanent iterations. Sensuality and worldliness mark the arts of the Renaissance, while ascetic and iconoclastic Protestant reforms are recapitulations of Augustinian theology.

The split—creating something of a schizophrenic mindset in Enlightenment Europe, alternately rejecting, embracing, and celebrating transcendence—is best captured, perhaps, in this eighteenth-century Anglo-Irish poem (doggerel, really) that memorializes the art of printing:

The Art of Printing
(August 8, 1728)

Hail, Sacred Art! Thou Gift of Heaven, designed
T'impart the Charms of Wisdom to Mankind,
To call forth LEARNING from the Realms of Night,
And bid bright KNOWLEDGE rise to Publick Sight.
Th'immortal Labours of Old Greece and Rome,
By thee secured from Fate, shall ever bloom,
To farthest Times their lasting Charms display,
Nor worn by Age, nor subject to Decay.
By THEE subdued, no longer Ign'rance reigns,
Nor o'er the World her barb'rous Power maintains;
Fair SCIENCE reassumes her ancient sway;
To HER the NATIONS their glad Homage pay;
At length ev'n rude, unletter'd REALMS refine,
And the pale CRESCENT now begins to shine...
In speaking Silence the Dead Voice impart,
And sounds embody by thy WONDROUS ART?
By Sight alone to edify the ear,
To picture THOUGHT, and bid the Eyes to hear?
Live, ever Live, immortaliz'd in fame!
To kindred Skies assert THY Glorious CLAIM!
The Seeds of REASON, till by thee refin'd,
Lay huddled in the CHAOS of the MIND!
Thy honor'd SPECIES holds their just Pretence
By THEE to Triumph over Brutal Sense:
Not urge Dominion by a Lawless Might,
But sway the WHOLE CREATION in THY RIGHT!...
What darkly HIEROGLYPHICKS cou'd disclose,
By THEE enlighten'd, unmysterious, rose!
That CYRUS, CAESAR, or young AMMON fought,

We owe to THEE, to THEE that Plato thought;
Before THY ART, Tradition vainly told
Legends confus'd, and Oral Tales, of Old!...
The Generous ART, unable to withstand
The errors of the tedious COPIST'S (sic) Hand,
Unfaithful to its Trust, had almost dy'd,
Till the fam'd PRESS the failing PEN supply'd;
Scarcely sufficient to preserve its NAME
From Tyrant's Malice and Bigot's Flame;
Till What the Great PHÆNICIAN had begun,
Was finished by GERMANIA'S Godlike SON.
LEARNING revives, nor fears again t'expire,
'Midst Papal Ignorance and Gothick Fire;
Let Glad HIBERNIA Hail the NOBLE ART,
That mends the Mind and cultivates the Heart![22]

Chapter Six

The Metaphysics of Literacy

Es bin nur zwei Möglichkeiten, leben zu Ihr Leben.
Ein ist, als wenn nichts ein Wunder ist. Das andere
ist, als wenn alles ein Wunder ist.

There are only two ways to live your life.
One, as though nothing is a miracle. The other, as
though everything is a miracle.

Albert Einstein

We return now to Plato's disdain for the poets and their art. What was it that so bothered the philosopher that he would banish poetry from his idealized republic? The bards were not only the entertainers of their society, but also the repositories of knowledge as well as the educators of the people. How could Plato turn his back on an art form that had nurtured oral Greek culture for centuries—and demand like action from the entire Greek civilization? What, we might ask, was he thinking?

He was thinking, perhaps, that there was "a new kid in town," a new mindset, a new way of seeing the world, a new way of thinking, a new way of organizing life, and it was based on an entirely new technology: alphabetic writing. The mimetic arts of the oral culture were an obstacle to greater learning and understanding, and a nostalgic, even atavistic urge which threatened to stunt—if not to destroy absolutely—the growth of a greater Greek civilization. As Eric Havelock in his seminal work *Preface to Plato* tells us:

> Such enormous powers of poetic memorization could be purchased only at the cost of total loss of objectivity. Plato's target was indeed an educational procedure and a whole

> way of life. This then is the master clue to Plato's choice of
> the word *mimesis* to describe the poetic experience. It focuses
> initially not on the artist's creative act but on his power to
> make his audience identify almost pathologically and cer-
> tainly sympathetically with the content of what he is saying.
> . . . This kind of drama, this way of reliving experience in
> memory instead of analyzing it and understanding it, is for
> him "the enemy."[1]

Plato seemed to sense that alphabetic literacy opened new horizons for critical thought, the kind of critical thought he and his mentor Socrates practiced,[2] and Plato did not want to see the changes occurring in his culture slowed or reversed by the persistence of oral tradition.[3] Orality dictates a level of mimetic empathy which must, while it survives, stifle critical thought:

> The imitative poet who aims at being popular is not by na-
> ture made, nor is his art intended, to please or to affect the
> rational principle in the soul; but he will prefer the passion-
> ate and the fitful temper, which is easily imitated. . . . The
> best of us, I conceive, when we listen to a passage of Homer,
> or one of the tragedians, in which he represents some pitiful
> hero who is drawling out his sorrows in a long oration, or
> weeping, and smiting his breast—the best of us, you know,
> delight in giving way to sympathy, and are in raptures at the
> excellence of the poet who stirs our feelings most. . . . And
> the same may be said of [mimetic representations of] lust
> and anger and all the other affections, of desire and pain
> and pleasure, which are held to be inseparable from every
> action—in all of them poetry feeds and waters the passions
> instead of drying them up; she lets them rule, although they
> ought to be controlled, if mankind are ever to increase in
> happiness and virtue.[4]

So the oral, mimetic mind must go—"Out with it!" Plato decreed—and with it must go the epistemology of orality. No longer content to sacrifice critical thought, deductive reasoning, and new organizing techniques—both social and epistemologi-cal—to the demands of memory, Plato designed his good society to be one of readers.

Global Cultural Change

At the very same moment that Greek culture was making this transition and Plato was urging their adoption of new behaviors, new modes of education, and new structures of thought, humans across many parts of the earth were, for the first time, reaping the fruit of intellectual seeds sown in the preceding generations as humans experimented with systems of etched visual marks representing speech—the first systems of writing. Consequently it was the *human mind*—not just the Greek—that was undergoing this profound transformation. To a certain extent, our understanding of this transformation is speculative, but much of it is clear because it is historical.

In 1976, the late Julian Jaynes published a controversial but provocative book, *The Origins of Consciousness in the Breakdown of the Bicameral Mind.* His thesis is complex and challenging: At the moment of our evolutionary arrival as a species, humans were not conscious, at least in the sense of that word as we understand it today. Consciousness was achieved only after "breaking down" the bicameral mind.[5]

These early humans lacked speech, and therefore lacked both what we today understand as introspection and personal perspective—what we may call "the subjective I." All experience was essentially a group experience,[6] and all behavior, group behavior. With the onset of speech, according to Jaynes, bicamerality forced humans into a situation not unlike schizophrenia. Disembodied voices, originating in the right hemisphere of the bicameral brain, but perceived—by the left hemisphere—as coming from somewhere other than "the self," instructed and admonished bicameral humans on proper and improper, useful and useless, right and wrong responses to external stimuli.[7]

> During the era of the bicameral mind, we may suppose that the stress threshold for hallucinations was much, much

> lower than in either normal people or schizophrenics today. The only stress necessary was that which occurs when a change in behavior is necessary because of some novelty in a situation. Anything that could not be dealt with on the basis of habit, any conflict between work and fatigue, between attack and flight, any choice between whom to obey or what to do, anything that required any decision at all was sufficient to cause an auditory hallucination.[8]

"The gods" have their origin in this era and in the human experience of bicamerality, Jaynes insists,[9] because we naturally attributed to these auditory hallucinations—the "voices"—both an immanent closeness and a transcendent, supernatural otherness.

Jaynes's hypothesis is, as I said, a provocative one and one around which controversy continues to swirl. It is not necessary (at least I have felt no necessity) to judge the book on the basis of historical or factual accuracy—although his evidence is indeed impressive; it is enough to think about his hypothesis in the context of the other historic (and historically verifiable) changes that occurred at just about the same era of which he writes: the onset of civilization, the development of writing systems (and, therefore, the origin of the literate mind), and the rise of the "axial religions." Whether or not anything as remarkable as a breakdown of the bicameral mind occurred at this point, it is enough to note the dramatic changes in human thought and the organization of society that did take place.

It is no coincidence, Jack Goody tells us, that "major steps in the development of what we now call 'science' followed the introduction of major changes in the channels of communication in Babylonia (writing), in ancient Greece (the alphabet), and in Western Europe (printing)."[10] In its bias toward organized, linear, rational thought, writing (and then printing) helped first to standardize and spread various metaphysical "realities," and then, eventually, to undermine them. It is in the newly literate mind that the observable, objectively measurable immanent first becomes dislodged from the ethereal, personal transcendent.

The human mind, it has been said, is a direct and natural by-product, and a necessary concomitant, of language.[11] It is possible to debate whether the linguistic capabilities of the brain nurtured the human capacity for speech, or our near-human ancestors' growing facility with words hastened the brain's biological evolution. A growing body of evidence supports the argument that reading imposed upon the human brain a need to reorganize its functions, remapping neural pathways and allowing new types of thought previously impossible.[12] But such a debate is unnecessary for the purposes of the present investigation.

Suffice it to say that the power of words to organize experience, to store information, and to abstract reusable knowledge outside of day-to-day contexts made it a powerful survival tool within an evolutionary process of natural selection. The external technologies of written language amplified, extended, and standardized the advantages offered by the spoken word, and in so doing reorganized the reality known to oral culture.

The Shift from the Oral to the Literate Mind

The oral mind, with its phatic, formulaic group rituals, helped to bind people together—past, present, and future—into a tribal unity. The oral mind, with its pre-scientific, magical constructions of reality colored that reality dramatically. Transcendent truth was everywhere present; its immanence was unquestionable. The age of writing begins a subtle but ineluctable separation of the immanent and the transcendent, a recognition of that separation, and the development of methods of analyzing them. This separation marks the appearance of a new stage in human intellectual evolution and, according to some, in human evolution generally. Ong writes, "Jack Goody (1977) has convincingly shown how shifts hitherto labeled as shifts from magic to science, or from the so-called 'pre-logical' to the more and more 'rational' state of consciousness, or from Levi-Strauss's 'savage' mind to domesticated thought, can be more economically and cogently explained as shifts from orality to various stages of literacy."[13] It is at this point that, as the rational mind unleashes itself and self-reflective, critical thought becomes more common, the social idea of the supernatural changes dramatically.

History, as everyone knows, begins with writing. In a sense it is also true that religion, as a formal, human institution, begins a long ascendancy—and magic descends into a culturally defined netherworld of "evil"—with writing. When humankind had sufficiently assimilated and internalized both the skills and the structures of thought afforded by systematic writing, its very conceptions of transcendence shifted dramatically. In the last six centuries before the time of Christ, all of the world's major text-based religions and philosophies came into existence, and most remain today. It is a remarkable fact that even societies that had no contact (China and Europe, for example) began this cultural development in parallel at precisely the same time.[14] This *axial age* is the age of Confucius and Lao Tse in China; of Buddha and the *Upanishads* in India; of Zoroaster in Persia; of Elijah, Isaiah, and Jeremiah in Palestine; of "Homer," Plato, and Aristotle in Greece; of Jesus Christ and the New Testament evangelists in Palestine and Greece.[15] It is certainly true—immanently true, one might be bold enough to say—that writing is responsible for the durability (if not the validity) of these religious traditions. But could writing have inspired the radical intellectual and spiritual departures from oral religious tradition that these new traditions represented?

The new, literate religions of the axial age—all of them in

some way—represent a radical paradigm shift away from magical, naturalistic, or animistic forms, interested in control of the environment and personal and group survival by the placation of some erratic, unpredictable deity, to a more rational, more humanistic form interested in moral values, in virtues, in questions of right and wrong, good and evil, reward and punishment. They represent a shift from presentational to propositional structures of thought. They represent a shift from concerns of physical survival to those of spiritual survival—immortality. They represent at least the beginnings of a shift from a sense-based (external-world) to a reason-based (interior) religion. They represent a shift from exterior concerns of the body to interior concerns of the soul.[16] They represent a shift from unhappy dependence on the imperfect to a sometimes ecstatic hope of perfection, accepting "the negations of life, pain, sin, sorrow, misfortune, as fortifying preparations for an inner transformation which will alter man's final destiny."[17] They represent a shift from group ethos to the growth of individual conscience as "people began to realize that their own behavior could affect the fate of future generations."[18] They represent a shift from action to contemplation, from verbalization to (abstract) nominalization, from "man as doer" to "man as thinker," from the external life to the internal, from materialism to etherealism, from monistic pantheism to dualism, from immanent transcendence to immanence *and* transcendence.

By the height of the axial age, Mumford tells us, "a new type of person, meek, silent, unassertive—introverted, as we would now say—was beginning to replace the proud energetic hero as an ideal type."[19] This "new type of person," introspective, curious, self-reflective, was literate man. And rather than looking to some mystical external cause for the joys and tragedies, the opportunities and catastrophes of life, he looked inward to the spirit. Transcendent experience was no longer necessarily to be found only in the external world of immanent reality, but in the interior world of the imaginative, contemplative mind: the soul.

Reality for the literate person was no longer automatically connected to the physical world, the world of the senses, but became suddenly connected to the realm of the imagination, tempered (to some extent) by reason. "The new element in this age is that man everywhere became aware of being as a whole, of himself and his limits. . . . He raised radical questions, approached the abyss in his drive for liberation and redemption. And in consciously apprehending his limits he set himself the highest aims. He experienced *the absolute in the depth of selfhood and in the clarity of transcendence*[20](my emphasis).

This new mindset eschewed the magic, sensuality, and pre-scientism of orality, and showed the first signs of a developing dualism that saw transcendent perfection alongside the imperfection of immanent reality, supporting a view that "if I attempt to foresee tangible paradise in the form of perfection on earth, of a human paradise, I can expect nothing; but I can expect everything if I am oriented toward the profound humanity which opens up with faith in God. I can hope for nothing if I look only outward; for everything if, partaking of the primal source, I entrust myself to transcendence."[21]

Can all of this have occurred simply because of reading? Can the marshalling of propositional structures of thought have such profound consequences for human understanding? Reading in and of itself may be the kind of intellectual (psychic? spiritual?) activity inherently connected to at least one sort of transcendent experience. Literacy allows for and, in return, encourages a depth of intellectual activity that is rooted deeply both on the page and in our minds. The "deeply reasoned text" is rich with meaning, on different levels; it makes demands of us to which we must respond.[22] It stretches us beyond our normal, daily world of sensory experiences and puts us in a place of questioning, interpretation, and contemplation. It is in the nature of writing, as a propositionally structured code, to be potentially either representational or nonrepresentational, factual or nonfactual, concrete or abstract or metaphorical. And it is in the nature of the literate human mind—and the literate human mind only—to think long, hard, and deeply about what we read in order to understand it.

Literacy is, in its essence, a liturgy of thought. Sven Birkerts speaks of the written word's natural ability to nurture and encourage what he calls "vertical consciousness," the "sense of the deep and natural connectedness of things. . . . Its apotheosis is what was once called wisdom. Wisdom: the knowing not of facts but of truths about human nature and the processes of life."[23] Wisdom by its nature seeks to relate the immediate to the eternal, and is predicated on belief in "the possibility of a comprehensible whole."[24] It is in the nature of the written (and printed) word to present us with that comprehensible whole, and our experience of it comes not from the specific content of a piece of writing, but from the literary form itself: "There is a metaphysics of reading that has to do with a good deal more than any simple broadening of the mind. Rather, it involves a change of state and inner orientation, and if we contemplate the reading process in this light we can hardly get away from introducing the word *soul* (or something very like it) into the conversation."[25]

In Birkert's final analysis, what literacy and literature provide humanity with is a linear structuring of experience based on an interior depth of experience, an "existential self-formation"[26] which suggests that "life is not a sequence of lived moments, but a destiny."[27] Literacy suggests for its participants that life has a meaning, a purpose, a plot—that there is a point to life as there is a point to literature, and that we have the ability to discern it. Transcendence cannot, perhaps, any longer be a quality of immanence; both immanence and transcendence now appear to be separate dimensions of human experience.

The Objectification of Transcendence

What ultimately distinguishes writing in the evolution of religious experience is its ability to take what ought to be essentially a personal, subjective, transcendent experience and objectify it, making of it a fundamentally immanent one. Writing, by objectifying prophecy, standardizing divine revelation, and codifying moral values, effectively separated the "pagan" religions of the oral traditions from the "great" religions of the world. In fact, until text-based religions appeared, with all the hegemonic power that literacy has at its disposal, paganism *per se* did not exist; the socially-constructed concept of paganism arises only in a context within which it can be compared to textual religions.

Buddhism, Judaism, Christianity, Islam, Hindu—all religions (or quasi-religious philosophical systems) based on oral traditions fixed in space (and time) by the medium of the written word—now had the means and the motive to define and protect truth. The fixity of sacred doctrine is a powerful reference to keep the influences of paganism, heterodoxy, and heresy in check—a condition missing from the older, oral experience of religion: "We may not appreciate that this hostility toward other gods was a new religious attitude. Paganism was an essentially tolerant faith: provided that old cults were not threatened by the arrival of a new deity, there was always room for another god alongside the traditional pantheon."[28]

But a written text creates rigid doctrine out of myth, and orthodoxy out of fluid, constantly evolving oral tradition. Whereas in an oral culture myths respond to the needs of the community, in a literate culture the community must conform to the letter of doctrine. Whereas in an oral culture "truths" are fitted to respond to the exigencies of the day, in a literate culture there is only one truth. Fundamentalism, then, is the Achilles' heel of religion in a literate culture, and it is here within the literal "so it has been written, therefore, so it is" view of reality that ideas have so frequently come into conflict, and people have so frequently killed one another and died. Unlike the older, oral, pagan religious forms, change occurs in a literate religion only through schism.[29] The potential for conflict inherent in textual religion is compounded by the fact that writing also proved to be a powerful tool for spreading religious traditions beyond the confines of the tribe. Literate religions, unlike oral religions, are religions of conversion, not simply of birth or of the tribe. Like knowledge itself, they are wholly detached from the lifeworld of a particular person or a particular tribe, and so, by logical extension, are available to everyone.[30] One does not any longer have to be born into a religious tradition, as one is born into a clan or tribe. In fact, the written religious tradition embodies an implicit open invitation, based on the individual's interpretation of its meaning.

Text-based religions, therefore, were destined to transcend the boundaries of the tribe to become world religions: "A new kind of society was formed which overpassed all existing boundaries: a society of believers, united by a supernatural faith and a vision of perfection. The axial religions broke down the ancient isolation of the tribe and village, city, state, and even of empire: they marched across frontiers and summoned all men to a new life . . . . They broke down, at least in relation to God and eternity, the division between classes."[31]

Writing brings a sense of finality to the oral tradition, not in the sense that it effectively ended the communal interactions—

the phatic elements—that were once just as much a part of the metaphysical mindset as the content of myths and stories (for they certainly survived, transformed, into the era of literacy), but more so in the sense that a written text is somehow definitive.[32] "It is written" is only another way of saying "we know this to be true." This is true of writing, and it is even truer of printing, where a text can be mass-produced and distributed over vast areas and among diverse peoples.

The spread of a particular religion, like the spread of knowledge, seems inevitable in a writing culture. Add to this the fact that adherents to a religious tradition define themselves as possessors of the Truth and you have all the necessary ingredients for forceful proselytizing. Of course, many will convert quite willingly from a "folk religion" to a text-based one, because it can easily be seen as superior to the religion of one's birth: "their priests are literate and can read as well as hear God's word."[33] Gaelic Ireland, entirely oral at the time of the coming of St. Patrick, seems to have been strangely attracted to an alien literate faith. There was no "conversion by the sword" and Irish converts suffered no martyrdom for apostasy during their swift conversion to Christianity.[34] "Christianity seems to have advanced by the power of persuasion alone."[35]

With writing, transcendent truths now have the opportunity to come into contact, and into potential conflict. It becomes essential to create a specific role within the social structure to preserve and protect those truths—the role of the literate priesthood. However, to say that a priesthood (or something like it) arises only when text-based religions enter the scene would be wrong. Gaelic-Irish oral culture, for instance, had its caste of druids, as did their Celtic cousins in Gaul, who may have spent as many as twenty years memorizing and learning to perform their repertoire of sacred knowledge.[36] In that performance, the powerful phatic elements bound the people together as an interdependent group and created a unity of past, present, and future.

In a (preprint) writing culture, however, the role of the priest changes. The literate priest is still part of an elite group of society who can read. It is the priest's privilege, through his training, to have exclusive access to the word of God, and to be God's mediator to the people. It becomes an implicit, and later an explicit, assumption that the priest is the final arbiter of God's word. "In the beginning was the Word,"[37] but it is the priest who reads and interprets the word.[38] The literate priest can rightly claim, in Jesus' words, "No one comes to the Father except through me."[39] In the presence of such a unilateral claim on the metaphysical truth of salvation, the phatic elements of the oral performance of sacred knowledge must be weakened; the supernatural no longer pervades the life of the people, but rather comes to them directly (in a linear way, perhaps) from God through His mediator.

With writing, then, "religion" becomes, over time, less a human need or aspiration and more a formal social institution rooted firmly in an unchanging text. Literacy is a "profoundly conserving force"[40] that reshapes the social environment in such a way that the "institutional church," rather than being simply a set of rituals and beliefs embedded within a social context, now seeks its own continuity and protects its monopoly over sacred knowledge. While the transcendent and the immanent pervade an oral culture with the supernatural aura surrounding all aspects of life, religion—an appeal to the transcendent—becomes, in a writing culture, set apart from the other activities of daily life, the milieu of the immanent. Transcendence is experienced in a (controlled and segregated) sacred space; immanence in the profane. This situation is all the more true because other, more secular social institutions have assimilated the skills of literacy and are using them to further their goals, some of which may be in opposition to those of organized religion. "Religious literates often think that, ideally, God's reign should come to pass on Earth and the priesthood should administer His estate, an idea embodied in the medieval papacy, in the Caliphate of Islam and in the Shiite ideology of contemporary Iran."[41] Conversely, secular leaders often work just as hard to diminish the power of religion in the political arena.[42] Plato, after all, did not want to banish the poets so he could set up a theocracy, but to justify the emergence of philosopher-kings.[43]

So it is not only religion that is changed by the onset and spread of literacy, any more than it might have been that only religion held power over the thoughts of people in an oral culture. Government, commerce, and education, as well as religion—all are changed by writing. If this new literate mindset inhibited thought that allowed magic, sensuality, and pre-scientism to flourish, one might assume that it might also facilitate religious orthodoxy, empiricism, and a more skeptical, scientific perspective. And, of course, it did just that.

It is important to notice, however, the inherent paradox apparent in this new situation. Literacy opened up the possibility that the senses aided by reason offered hope of a comprehensible reality, but not the only hope that humans could expect. If the human experience of transcendence and immanence is effectively sundered by literacy, it is just as reasonable to expect that some will give greater weight to the knowledge provided by the senses than by reason or imagination alone.

The Ecological Nature of Change

In the West, the shift from oral to literate modes, we recall, might have been seen as shifts from savage life to domestic life, or from barbarity to civilization. But in the case of magic, science, and religion, the shift offered a choice based on "the split between head and heart": a shift from magic to science, or a shift from magic to religion. During the following millennium, the momentum worked toward furthering that breach. "What indeed has Athens to do with Jerusalem?" Tertullian asked, contentiously, in the third century. "What concord is there between the Academy and the Church? What between heretics and Christians?"[44] And with an uncompromising finality, he throws down the gauntlet and sets the stage for a thousand years of conflict between faith and reason: "Away with all attempts to produce a mottled Christianity of Stoic, Platonic, and dialectic composition! We want no curious disputation after possessing Christ Jesus, no inquisition after enjoying the gospel!"[45]

Some, however, tried to find some compromise.

Charting the Course of the Split: Plato

One of the first major changes wrought by literacy upon the ancient cosmology was the abandonment of monistic pantheism—the idea that all of nature, all of immanent reality, is suffused with transcendent mystery, with the divine. The axial religions (east and west), with their proto-humanistic conceptions of free will, responsibility, and moral values, exemplified the shift from an apparently objective divinity-in-nature perspective to a more introspective personal search for the divine. But the precise route that philosophers (and eventually theologians) took in order to respond to this shift and begin to reconstruct nature was the source of some controversy, dialogue, debate, and study for countless centuries.

Plato, for instance, abandoning the pantheistic monism of ancient oral life, adopted a dualist cosmology that divided reality into the thing we perceive (immanence) and its unseen and more perfect form (transcendence). "For Plato . . . nonmathematical concepts like Beauty, Goodness, and Justice shared this same reality. Some might call them mere abstractions, but Plato believed them to be 'really real'—timeless realities that bear the same relationship to the things of the sensory world that a perfect geometrical figure, say, bears to its imperfect approximation, such as an orange. How do we know a government is just without possessing some notion of genuine justice?"[46]

Furthermore, he reckoned the transcendent realm as the superior of the two—so far superior that it would be beyond mortal comprehension and would only frighten us. In his allegory of the cave, he speaks of the fate that awaits the one who sees the "real world" and brings his visions back to share with those of his comrades who still inhabit the world below: "Men would say of him that he went up and down without his eyes; and that it was better not even to think of ascending; and if anyone tried to loose another and lead him up to the light, let them only catch the offender, and they would put him to death."[47]

This dualism allowed Plato to consider the human mind (*psyche* or soul) as being separate and distinct from the physical body, having a natural and direct connection to the eternal and perfect realm of transcendent ideas. "Where can ideas come from other than some place outside nature and society: a realm of eternal Forms or Ideas? And how could such Ideas enter our minds unless those minds, or some part of them, inhabited that same realm once upon a time?"[48] Plato saw reality as existing essentially beyond the boundaries of human perceptual experience, a "realm of pure thought"[49] of which the physical world was but a pale reflection. Truth, the logos, was divine, and the measure of truth—as of reality—was the extent to which it conformed to the logos.

Charting the Course of the Split: Aristotle
Aristotle (384–322 BC), on the other hand, chose head over heart

and respectfully disagreed with his former master. He did not believe in a world of absolute, perfect concepts transcending the limits of perceptual experience. Aristotle's acknowledgment of a dualism (to the extent that he acknowledged it at all) located it distinctly within the boundaries of immanent, material reality. Plato's dichotomous realms—of transcendent forms and immanent substance, of the mind/spirit (psyche) and the body, of the eternal and the transient, of the immutable and the changing—are subsumed, in Aristotle's thinking, as two characteristics of *being*: actuality and potentiality. A being's actuality is its form (in the Platonic sense), its ontological reality. Its potentiality develops within the context of a being's material existence and is profoundly influenced by that context. All things have the potential to be what they are; in so doing, they are becoming, in so becoming, they are actual. Transcendence is not transcendent at all, Aristotle insists, but rather inherent in all things that exist.

Aristotle's reality was the world in all its material immanence; all things held within them the key to understanding. To perceive a thing is to know it, to know it is to understand it, to understand it is to question it, and to question it is to improve it. Perfection lay not in some world of Eternal Forms, beyond the reach of humans; it lay in our innate human ability to see, to think, to reason, to criticize, to improve.[50] Essentially, Aristotle's metaphysics abandoned transcendentalism entirely in favor of a materially-based reason. Aristotle believed that form or essence (actuality) and matter (potentiality) are simply two distinct aspects of existence.

God, at least in the religious sense of the word, was an unnecessary concept for Aristotle. Reason reveals, Aristotle tells us, that all being has a cause; in fact all being has four causes: a material cause, a formal cause, an efficient cause, and a final cause.[51] The material cause is that which is changed, or upon which change is imposed; the formal cause, the form or shape it will take; the efficient cause, the idea behind the change; and the final cause, the desired end for which the change is undertaken. All things are explained in terms of these causes, all things are contingent upon their cause for existence, and so there is an apparent endless chain of causality receding into the horizon of reality's past. But such an infinite regress is not possible and, logically, there must have been some first cause. This first cause Aristotle calls the "unmoved mover," and its noncontingent nature implies its necessary being.[52] It is the simple, logical fact of the existence of this first cause, this unmoved mover, this self-thinking thought, Aristotle seems to tell us, that we experience as "God."

Aristotle had confidence in the immanent, material world to reveal itself to us in a comprehensible way, in our sensory perceptions to comprehend it, and in our capacity for reason to make meaning of it. He also had confidence in Plato's transcendent world of forms to eventually reveal its essence to us and become immanent. But only after stringent observation and measurement did he feel it was appropriate to subject the physical world to the scrutiny of reason. This was both the nature of objective reality and of the consensual reality we enjoyed as members of a society, and the responsibility of beings endowed with intelligence and reason. Humans may be imperfect—prone to the passions, intemperate, or of base character—but all those imperfections could be remediated, cultivated out, and there was nothing keeping us (but ourselves) from being objective and unbiased in our observations of the world. True knowledge—as well as true being—exists in objective reality, and it is within our power to know it beyond the frailties of our subjective perceptions and interpretations.[53] It is in the nature of the universe, and everything in it, to reveal itself to us.

In the pursuit of these ends, Aristotle created a method: critical, dialectic, empirical, and syllogistic. The practical syllogism is at the heart of his method. (Here is an example of a syllogism. *Major premise:* All men are mortal. *Minor premise:* Socrates is a man. *Conclusion:* Socrates, therefore, is mortal.) But it is Aristotle's emphasis on observation of the natural world and empirical measurement as the basis for critical, syllogistic reasoning, as well as his confidence in reality's fundamentally comprehensible nature, without recourse to mysticism or transcendent ideas, that sets Aristotle apart from philosophers before or since. His systematic method shows Aristotle to be history's first example of the fully literate human.

Aristotle, applying all the available skills of propositional thinking—literacy—used not only his senses in direct observation of the world, his critical faculties in measuring and testing it, and his reason in making sense of it and finding meaning; he also used the knowledge that he and others had previously provided. He constructed what was for all intents and purposes the first research library, even buying the collections of other philosophers, and referred to the wisdom of earlier generations in his reasoning.[54] "Evidence of wide reading and frequent consultation of books meets us in his writings and in the work of his school. 'We ought to make extracts also from written works' . . . and the fact that he did so is clear from his constant citations from earlier writers: the more than thirty philosophers and poets cited in the *Metaphysics,* the stream of quotations from tragic, comic, and epic poems, from orators and rhetorical treatises in the *Rhetoric.*"[55]

The Uneasy Balance: Religion and Philosophy

In the East, Greek thought had an enormous influence on non-Christian peoples. Philo of Alexandria (20 BC–AD 50), a Hellenized Jew living in Egypt, achieved some measure of synthesis of Judaism and Greek philosophy in response to what he saw as a growing tension between them. Philo believed that beneath their surface differences, Greek philosophy and Judaic scripture recognized common realities, and believed that philosophy was important, as it could act as the "handmaiden of theology"[56] rather than as a threat to it. He took a Platonic stance that saw imperfect, immanent matter as the source of all evil, and the perfect, transcendent God as the source of all good. We can never know God's essence, for it is pure being and pure transcendence, but we can experience God's existence through His powers or energies which make immanent His activities in the world.[57] One of these energies or powers was expressed in the Stoic term *logos,* a universal reason underlying all natural law.

Philo is an early archetype of the axial-age mind navigating the hazardous straits between the doctrines of the new, formal, textual religions and the liberation of the rational intellect made possible by literacy. Indeed, much of the philosophy of the Middle Ages seeks to answer questions raised only when transcendent ideas are made immanent in writing, when thought takes on a physical form in writing and—not coincidentally—when the Logos is incarnated in Jesus Christ.

The Rise of Christianity

The coming of Christ, in a very different sense as *Logos* or Word, and the establishment of a Christian Church and a Christian canon of sacred scripture standardized Christian knowledge in very much the way we might expect it to. The transcendent truths of Divine Revelation became, for many if not most Christians, the only truths, and the only true and necessary knowledge to live one's life. The crystallization of articles of faith that is inevitable when they are written down occurred during the first few centuries of Christianity, though not without controversy. As an established faith community more and more firmly founded on written accounts of the life, death, and resurrection of Jesus Christ, Christians found it necessary to create doctrines which were themselves codified in writing, and to control the content of their faith from error, heresy, and heterodoxy. (Gnosticism was widespread during the early Christian era, and Gnostic writings rivaled orthodox Christian writings throughout the second century.) It was not until the end of the fourth century that the canon of scripture we now call the New Testament took the form in which we recognize it today.

Early Christians were jealous of their faith (as we noted briefly with Tertullian) and proud of their roles as heirs to the covenant between God and His chosen people, the Jews. Paul (originally Saul) of Tarsus, a Jewish convert to the new faith, proclaimed Christians not only as the new chosen people, but also as intellectually superior to both barbarians (pagan Romans) and Greeks (philosophers) because of the epistemological superiority of faith—transcendent experience—over reason. Only faith provides us with what we truly need to know, the eternal Word of God:

> I am not ashamed of the gospel, for it is the power of God for salvation to everyone who believes. . . . For in it the righteousness of God is revealed from faith to faith; as it is written, "but the righteous man shall live by faith." For the wrath of God is revealed from heaven against all ungodliness and unrighteousness of men who suppress the truth in unrighteousness, because that which is known about God is evident within them; for God made it evident to them. For since the creation of the world His invisible attributes, His eternal power and divine nature, have been clearly seen, being understood through what has been made, so that they are without excuse. For even though they knew God, they did not honor Him as God or give thanks, but they became futile in their speculations, and their foolish heart was darkened. Professing to be wise, they became fools, and exchanged the glory of the incorruptible God for an image in the form of corruptible man and of birds and four-footed animals and crawling creatures.[58]

Here Paul links sensual, concrete images with immanence, and puts them in a state of opposition with the ultimate reality of transcendence. In so doing, he has clearly marked the activities of philosophers, the pursuit of truth through sensory observation, dialectic logic, and reason, as inferior to the absolute truth of revelation. And further:

> It is written, "I will destroy the wisdom of the wise, and the cleverness of the clever I will set aside." Where is the wise man? Where is the scribe? Where is the debater of this age? Has not God made foolish the wisdom of the world? For since in the wisdom of God the world through its wisdom did not come to know God, God was well-pleased through the foolishness of the message preached to save those who believe. For indeed Jews ask for signs and Greeks search for wisdom; but we preach Christ crucified, to Jews a stumbling block and to Gentiles foolishness, but to those who are the called, both Jews and Greeks, Christ the power of God and the wisdom of God. Because the foolishness of God is wiser than men, and the weakness of God is stronger than men.[59]

The Survival of Aristotle in the Non-Christian World

For all of the aggressive spread of Christian evangelism and the growing neo-Platonic Christian worldview in the West, Aristotle's influence remained powerful in the East, especially in the lands that had come under the rule of his protégé, Alexander the Great. The Library of Alexandria, founded in the third century B.C. by Demetrius, a former ruler of Athens and a student of Aristotle, at the behest of the Egyptian emperor Ptolemy, is reputed to have attempted to acquire copies of all books ever written. Ptolemy and his son and successor, Ptolemy II, purchased written manuscripts from throughout the Mediterranean area, including from Rhodes and Athens, and even seized books from visitors, copied them, and returned those copies to the aggrieved owners, keeping the originals in the library.[60] At its height, the library contained more than 500,000 scrolls and codices covering mathematics, philosophy, politics and government, history, and the arts.[61]

The Ptolemys apparently learned some of the skills of classification, categorizing, and indexing from Aristotle. Strabo (63 BC–AD 24) points out that Aristotle was "the first whom we know of who collected books"[62] and suggests that Aristotle, who died before Ptolemy arose as leader at the death of Alexander, "taught the kings of Egypt how to organize their library."[63] We shall further consider the significance of Aristotle's survival in the non-Christian world in due time.

Charting the Course of the "Split between Head and Heart": Augustine

Still, despite the objective advantages of Aristotle's method and enduring influence, those portions of the world that had converted to Christianity resisted the temptations of the senses (and of literate, Aristotelian reason) for the certainty of revelation. Augustine (354–430) rejected the empirical worldview of Aristotle for something closer to the formalism of Plato. His rise to intellectual dominance came at a time when the foundations of the ancient world were crumbling; Rome was about to fall to pagan barbarians. Violence was everywhere, evil around every corner. Humans again provided ample evidence of their imperfection—their sinfulness. A conception of a realm of perfect forms to which imperfect creation should strive to conform made profound sense to Augustine, and his *City of God* wielded enormous intellectual influence over Europe for the next several centuries, while Aristotle—whose naturalistic philosophy without recourse to a perfect realm of transcendent forms made him appear, to Augustine's eyes and ears, no more than an educated pagan—would spend the next seven hundred years languishing in relative obscurity far from the Romanized West. Augustine, in fact, set the theological foundations upon which was built the European Church in the Middle Ages, even as his own African Church would soon fall to Islam.

While influenced strongly by Platonic ideas, Augustine was not a "mere philosopher," but a Christian bishop who sought to integrate the rigor of philosophical method into Christian thought, to "use pagan literary studies as a weapon in the battle against the pagans themselves."[64] Augustine believed that an unfathomable gulf separated heaven—Plato's realm of eternal forms, Christianized—and earth that could not be breached by human perception and reason alone. All that we know about the physical universe has been revealed to us by God; what He appears unwilling to reveal to us is not for us to know.

In contrast to Aristotle and his intellectual method, Augustine believed that it is only by rejecting the vain goal of understanding God's creation (immanent reality) through natural philosophy—instead surrendering ourselves wholly to the transcendent Word of God—that man must find true wisdom, peace, and happiness. It is not that Augustine had no respect for philosophy, but that he saw it as fatally flawed. It is the essence of God, the Creator, to understand creation; it is the essence of man, a mere creature, to understand only creatures. The methods of philosophy are certainly good and useful, up to a point: that point at which it reaches its necessary limits, God's divine revelation, through the Incarnation of the Word, in the Catholic faith.

The Christian must be on his guard "with respect to those who philosophize according to the elements of this world, not according to God, by whom the world itself was made; for he is warned by the precept of the apostle, and faithfully hears what has been said, 'Beware that no one deceive you through philosophy and vain deceit, according to the elements of the world.'"[65] The immutable, transcendent, and absolute truths of God's infinite love for His creation, Augustine tells us, represent the fullness of knowledge and comprise absolute existence. The material world of immanent reality, impermanent, imperfect, and constantly changing, which proceeds from the realm of transcendence and finds its fullness only there, is perceived as "through a glass darkly"[66] (the senses), and will always be one of uncertainty, poorly understood.

It is not that philosophy is evil, or useless, or even counterproductive. On the contrary, it is of signal importance in the acquisition of knowledge, and helps humans to make some sense of the information gained in the imperfect perception of imperfect objects. But it is only a beginning of knowledge, and a dangerous and incomplete beginning at that. "Being chiefly interested in the soul's orientation to God, corporeal objects appeared to [Augustine] as a starting point in the mind's ascent to God, though even in this respect the soul itself is a more adequate starting point: we should return within ourselves, where truth abides, and use the soul, the image of God, as a stepping-stone to Him."[67] Philosophy's promises of wisdom, grossly exaggerated, are empty materialism which will lead men to frustration and demoralization, or to wickedness, while God's promises are pregnant with transcendent truth. The true value of philosophy, competently and diligently practiced, is its ability to bring us closer to knowing and therefore understanding God.

> Let us see by whom men are more greatly discouraged from the study of philosophy. Is it by him who says: "Listen, my friend, philosophy is not called wisdom itself but the love of wisdom. If you devote yourself to it, you will not, indeed, be wise while you are living here in this world—for wisdom is found only with God and cannot be attained by man—but when you have applied yourself to it with sufficient diligence and have purified yourself, your soul will certainly

> enjoy wisdom after this life, that is, when you have ceased
> to be mortal." Or will you be deterred from the study of phi-
> losophy by him who says: "Come, O mortals, to philosophy.
> Great is the reward; for what is dearer to man than wis-
> dom? Come, therefore, in order that you may be wise and
> not know wisdom!"[68]

Augustine's understanding of the value of philosophy—tempered by the errors of a Manichaean youth, partially encouraged
by Platonic formalism, skeptical of and disappointed in Aristotle's positivism—led him to see and to use human perception and
the methods of rational thought in order to support ideas which
lay beyond perception and were fundamentally not (at least in
the modern sense of the word) rational. For Augustine, as Anne
Fremantle tells us, philosophy's function "was to apply its method to the exact interpretation of the data of revelation, and to
proceed along the runway as far as the wheels of human reason
could take the human machine, before it turned into the wind,
and was air-borne by faith."[69]

Unchecked curiosity, the antithesis of faith and the kind of
skeptical curiosity characteristic of a literate mind, could be a
dangerous and potentially destructive human urge. The urge
to seek truth in immanent reality was a vanity, a pretension
to worldliness. Scripture held all knowledge that was essential
for human salvation; beyond that, there was nothing else really
worth knowing. The teachings of philosophers

> are not the commandments of the gods, but the discover-
> ies of men, who, at the prompting of their own speculative
> ability, made efforts to discover the hidden laws of nature,
> and the right and wrong in ethics, and in dialectic what
> was consequent according to the rules of logic, and what
> was inconsequent and erroneous. And some of them, by
> God's help, made great discoveries; but when left to them-
> selves they were betrayed by human infirmity, and fell into
> mistakes. And that was ordered by divine providence, that
> their pride might be restrained, and that by their example it

might be pointed out that it is humility which has access to
the highest regions.[70]

Augustine's *City of God* is less a work of philosophy than
of theology—or even of polemic; in this case the subject is the
decadence and corruption of the material world, juxtaposed with
the holiness and perfection of God's Kingdom. It put into place
a worldview that would define (and be adopted as a teaching
and evangelizing tool by) the Catholic Church through much of
the Middle Ages, a dualistic view that held immanent creation,
represented by concerns of the flesh, at a careful distance, and
yearned for a transcendent world of perfection, not terribly unlike Plato's realm of eternal forms, represented by the soul. Ultimately, for Augustine, philosophy and theology were two un-
equal dimensions of the same activity, for if the philosopher is
a lover of wisdom he must also be a lover of God who is all wisdom and from whom all wisdom flows.[71] This worldview, and the
Church that adopted it, would dominate and shape the European
social, cultural, and political structure for the next millennium.

Charting the Course of the Split: Boethius

In contrast to Augustine, Marcus Anicius Severinus Boethius
(476–524) offered a more humanistic counterpoint to the early Middle Ages, which is to say that he valued and encouraged
human intellectual forays into the realms of immanence while
accepting—on faith—the doctrines of the Christian Church. For
this reason he sought to preserve and make available for future generations the fruit of classical Greek learning. Perhaps
as a direct result of the Augustinian strain of dualism suffusing
Catholic Christianity, the Western horizons of classical learning
were receding. "With the decline of the old educated aristocracy
(in the early sixth century) and a widening cultural rift dividing
the Greek East from the Latin West . . . the Latins were forgetting

their Greek. Since all educated Romans had studied the writings of Plato, Aristotle, and other Greek thinkers in their original language, there had been no need to translate these works into Latin. The loss of literacy in Greek was therefore a potential catastrophe for Western society."[72]

Boethius made a goal for himself—one, however, that he was unable to achieve—of translating the entire works of Plato and Aristotle into Latin with the aim of showing that they were not incompatible[73] (a subtle and somewhat pointed reference, perhaps, to Augustine's rigid neo-Platonist dualism, for Boethius had formulated a principle which would remain a subtext, a controversial yet necessary one, throughout the Middle Ages: *fidem rationemque coniunge*[74]—"the compatibility of faith and reason"). While he fell far short of this goal during his lifetime, he was nonetheless able to translate, and comment upon, Porphyry's *Introduction to the Categories of Aristotle*, six of Aristotle's works on logic known as the *Organon* (Boethius's translation being the only works of the great philosopher a medieval scholar was ever likely to encounter), writing commentary about two of them, a commentary on Cicero's *Topics* and commentaries on several of Cicero's treatises on logic, as well as several commentaries on Aristotle, a number of original works of Christian apologetics, and "several short texts on subjects basic to the classical curriculum—arithmetic, music, and astronomy."[75]

Boethius also composed the work for which he is probably best known, a defense of classical learning in a time of reaction against worldliness, *The Consolation of Philosophy*, an attempt to demonstrate (contrary to the austere Augustinian strain that had begun to suffuse Christianity) that one could be both a believer in transcendent reality (that is, a devout Christian) and an inquisitive observer of immanence (a natural philosopher). In it, he relates a dreamlike vision where he encounters his muse and great love:

> When I looked at her closely, I saw that she was Philosophy, my nurse, in whose house I had lived from my youth. "Mistress of all virtues," I said, "why have you come, leaving the arc of heaven, to this lonely desert of our exile? Are you a prisoner, too, charged as I am with false accusation? She answered, "How could I desert my child, and not share with you the burden of sorrow you carry, a burden caused by hatred of my name? Philosophy has never thought it right to leave the innocent man alone on his journey. Should I fear to face my accusers, as though their enmity were something new? Do you suppose that this is the first time wisdom has been attacked and endangered by wicked men?"[76]

With Boethius, a new phase of Christian thought reveals itself, one which seeks both to affirm the transcendent truths of revelation and to justify the rigors of human intellect—the observation and measurement of immanent reality through the use of the senses, and the processes of interpreting and understanding that reality through the use of reason.

Boethius's melding of philosophy with theology, of faith with reason, marks the beginning of the period known as Scholasticism. Looked at skeptically, one can see the phenomenon of Scholasticism as an attempt to do nothing more than to rationalize faith—the construction of propositional arguments hoping to prove the improbable and understand the unknowable through reason. Looked at from another point of view, the perspective from which this book is written, Scholasticism can be seen fundamentally as an attempt to return to transcendence the equal measure of urgency it once shared with immanence. From a media ecological point of view, Scholasticism was an attempt to integrate the text (revealed truth) with human reason in an effort to halt or, perhaps, to repair, or, at the very least, to reconcile "the split between head and heart" brought on by literacy.

The Ascendancy of the Christian Church

But such reconciliation was difficult in the face of active Christian resistance as Christianity became "mainstream" and was proclaimed the established religion of the Roman Empire. Claim to transcendent authority or some special knowledge of ultimate reality implied considerable power in the material world. A monopoly of (transcendent) knowledge based on scripture was unwilling to yield to the demands of reason. Constantine I (288–337) became the first Roman Emperor to convert to Christianity, and in 325 he called for a council to be convened in Nicea to standardize and codify Christian orthodoxy. In 380, Theodosius in the Eastern Empire and Gratian in the West each gave official recognition to Christianity. The ascendancy of the new religion appeared complete when, in 529, the Emperor Justinian, in pursuit of a policy of eradicating paganism, closed the Platonic Academy of Athens (which Boethius had himself attended just decades earlier), thereby ensuring a Christian advantage in future scholarship,[77] and almost guaranteeing a non-Christian monopoly on Aristotelian thought in the coming centuries.

Charting the Course of the Split: John Scotus Eriugena

Nevertheless, the work of the Scholastics had begun—and it continued. John Scotus Eriugena (ca. 810–77) propounded a system which some observers consider to be a relapse into monistic pantheism (transcendence suffusing the immanent).[78] In his *De Divisione Naturae,* he segmented nature conceptually into four categories: that which creates and is not created; that which is created and itself creates; that which is created and does not create; and that which neither creates nor is created.[79] In this way, God (that which creates and is not created) might be seen merely as a species of nature (a singularly unique one to be sure) and transcendence might be seen similarly to inhere in immanence. In Eriugena's system, God is not only beginning and end, but present at all times in all of creation, both from within and from without, a solution to the problem of conflicts between transcendence and immanence, between faith and reason, and between the spiritual and material worlds that satisfied, in fact, neither side of the divide. This is not the rational empiricism of Aristotle, devoid of reference to transcendence; nor is it the dualism of Plato, imperfect material immanence aspiring to the perfection of the forms. This is, within a Christian context, a dangerous (from the point of orthodoxy) blending of spirit and matter, of the divine and the mundane, of absolute, eternal, and universal transcendence and immanence anchored in time and space.

> God Himself is the maker of all things, and is made in all things; when He is sought above all things, He is not found in any essence, for He is not yet being, but when He is understood in all things, nothing subsists in some save him alone. Nor is He one thing and not another thing, but He is all things. . . . [But] man is the unity of all creatures. He is intellect, reason, sense, life and body, and there is no nature besides these except God. All things are made in the divine mind, but they may be made in other minds also. . . . As all things are derived originally from God, by various intermediate steps, so are all things resolved ultimately into God by the same intermediate steps. Thus, God is the beginning, the middle and the end of all things, beginning because all things are from Him by participation in his essence, middle because all things live and move and have their being in him, end because all things have their perfection and the end of their motion in him. Diffusion is goodness: reunion is love. God as cause of things is supreme goodness, and as end of all things is supreme love. . . . God as goodness and God as love, the first cause of all things and the final end of all things, are the same. The fact that they are identical is the fundamental law of nature.[80]

Charting the Course of the Split: Roscellinus

Roscellinus (variously known as Roscelin de Compiègne or Roscellinus Compendiensis, 1050–1125) took the split between head and heart to another level, and anticipated postmodern thinking in his linguistic criticism of the language of transcendence. The first of a new category of philosophers known as nominalists, Roscellinus claimed that only "things" are real; abstract categories into which we sort and classify those things are not. This throws the very conception of transcendence into question. Plato's realm of ideal forms is seen now as having reality only in the imagination. Contrary to Plato's opinion, Roscellinus tells us that the realm of forms is not only *not* the true reality, it is not at all real.

Roscellinus did not question the existence of God (ultimate being and ultimate transcendence) *per se*, but did question the way the Church, consistent with Augustinian thought, spoke of God. Roscellinus was more in line with the Aristotelian view that if we are to understand a thing, it is the thing itself that must cede its secrets to us through its immanent, material being. We must not look to transcendent universals; these are mere words, meaningless and confusing when used to speak of the ineffable.

Roscellinus's nominalism got him into some trouble with the Church. Examining the Catholic dogma of the Trinity, he reasoned that it was only our human habits of thought and of speech that kept us from thinking of the "three persons" of God as three separate persons. Otherwise, he argued, God the Father and God the Holy Spirit must have been incarnated with the Son. Church leaders condemned Roscellinus for tritheism (belief that there were three Gods), and he recanted, at least temporarily. But his notion that categories of transcendent being existed only in the human imagination survived.

Roscellinus's critical, analytical mind and explicit concentration on the role of language in the process of human understanding typifies the split which had occurred between the hearts and minds of the educated classes following the spread of writing. His thinking anticipates both the modern and postmodern in its attention to semantic detail: "[Roscellinus] bequeathed to modern philosophy two great principles: first, that abstractions must not be reified, and second, that the power of the human soul and the secret of its development are largely in language."[81]

Charting the Course of the Split: Anselm

Anselm (1033–1109), on the other hand, was a realist, which is to say he affirmed the Platonic notion that transcendent ideas or forms were real and existed without regard to the physical world, or to our ability to comprehend them. Furthermore, in order even to understand things, knowledge of the abstract, transcendent universals is not enough; more important is that one first believes in them. Anselm changed the entire relationship between faith and reason, and buried Aristotelian empiricism even more deeply in the Christian European mindset. Where oral folk saw transcendence and immanence inextricably bound together; where Plato saw two separate realms, of perfect idea and imperfect being; where Aristotle gave prominence to physical reality, believing that physical reality would yield all knowledge to a curious, perceptive, and reasoning mind, Anselm followed the Augustinian tack of acknowledging both the transcendent and the immanent as separate realms of experience needing reasoned investigation, but insisted that faith must precede reason. For how can a person understand that in which he does not believe? "I do not seek to understand," he writes in his *Proslogium, (Discourse on the Existence of God)*, "that I may believe, but I believe in order to understand. For this I also believe, that unless I believed, I should not understand."[82] This anticipates something Marshall McLuhan is purported to have uttered: "If I hadn't believed it, I never would have seen it!"

In fact, Anselm would have appreciated McLuhan's meaningful wordplay and frowned upon the supposed intellectual limitations placed upon us by language, as implied by Roscellinus and other nominalists. He believed that there was a richness to human language and a depth to the human intellect that allowed us to see the truths in even improperly structured propositions, and (consciously or unconsciously) referencing Aristotle, taught that the truth of a proposition is determined by its correspondence to reality. Rather than reproaching those who engage in "improper utterances," Anselm only demands that those utterances be directly translatable into some other meaningful proposition, illustrated here in a dialogue between teacher and student:

> TEACHER: Now there's one last point I want you to learn; namely, that we sometimes say "ought" and "ought not" improperly. For example, I use "ought" improperly when I say I ought to be loved by you. For if I truly ought, then I have an obligation to fulfill, and so I wouldn't fulfill my obligation if I were not loved by you.
>
> STUDENT: It follows.
>
> TEACHER: Where the word is missing, there is no thing. It is only the word at our disposal which endows the thing with Being. What are words, that they have such power? What are things, that they need words in order to be? But if I ought to be loved by *you,* then love should not be demanded from *me,* but from you.
>
> STUDENT: I must agree.
>
> TEACHER: So when I say I ought to be loved by you, it does not mean that I have some obligation, but that you ought to love me. Likewise, if I say that I ought not to be loved by you, then the only thing I mean is that you ought not to love me.
> This same mode of speaking also occurs in conjunction with notions of ability and inability. For instance, we say, "Hector could be overpowered by Achilles" or "Achilles could not be overpowered by Hector." But there is no ability in Hector, who is conquered, but only in Achilles, who conquers him. And there is no inability in Achilles, who cannot be overpowered, but only in Hector, who cannot overpower him.[83]

Anselm continues the Scholastic drive to reconcile the split between head and heart brought on by literacy. Like Augustine, he is a Platonist in seeing a dual reality consisting of realms of transcendence and immanence. Like Augustine, he gives primacy to the demands of the heart (transcendence) over those of the head (immanence). Like Boethius, he can legitimately be called a philosopher as well as a theologian, for his concern for the influence of language in the process of understanding is more Aristotelian than Augustinian. But unlike Roscellinus and other nominalists, he thought that the transcendent forms—the abstract, universal concepts that exist and which inform immanent reality—were real.

"The Split" in the Jewish and Islamic Worlds

Meanwhile, in the non-Christian world a similar debate as that which had been roiling Christendom raged over the very same split between head and heart. In the first centuries of the Christian era, even before the coming of the prophet Muhammad and Islam, the influence of Aristotle had been widely felt in the East—in Asia Minor, Egypt and North Africa, and the Arab lands, as we noted earlier. As early as the sixth century, Syrian Christians translated the works of Plato, Aristotle, and other Greek philosophers into Arabic. In Persia, Aristotle and Porphyry were translated into Persian. By the eighth century, Syrian scholars were at work in Baghdad, and by the ninth century a school of translators was established there.[84] Baghdad and Cairo, and in the West, Cordoba in Spain, became the preeminent centers of intellectual activity in the medieval world at a time when Europe and Christendom were mired in a fairly sterile environment of Augustinian neo-Platonism.[85]

Islamic philosophy was, it must be said, Islamic in the same sense that medieval European philosophy can be said to be Christian. There is, at each foundation, a worldview, an ideology, an eschatology, and a metaphysics flowing from the cultural traditions of two different peoples that sets apart and colors their actions, even as their motivations have a common human foundation. They are the different articulations of a common thought, the "surface-structure" differences of universal "deep-structure" urges. And the differences at the surface are trivial compared with the similarities beneath.

Like the Nestorians (Syrian Christians who believed that Christ had two distinct and separate natures, one human and one divine, making it not only possible but necessary, consequently, to speak of two different Christs), Muslims found and developed their faith in an environment that was familiar with both Plato's and Zoroaster's dualism (the "world of order beset by chaos"). They found it in an oral, tribal environment that traditionally emphasized group over individual identity. However, they also found it in an environment that was beginning to value the immanence of newfound wealth over the questionable utility of transcendent tradition. "By the end of the sixth century AD [Mecca] had gained control of most of the trade from the Yemen to Syria—an important route by which the West got Indian luxury goods as well as South Arabian frankincense."[86]

The Quraysh—the ruling tribe of Mecca, and the tribe of which Muhammad was a member—appeared to be in danger of losing their traditional communal values to a "rampant and ruthless capitalism."[87] Muhammad feared that the time-honored idea of *muruwah* ("personal courage, patience in suffering, and dedication to one's tribe") was being threatened by an overarching emphasis on profit and competition. "In the old nomadic days the tribe had had to come first and the individual second: each one of its members knew that they all depended upon one another for survival. Consequently they had a duty to take care of the poor and vulnerable people of their ethnic group. Now individualism had replaced the communal ideal and competition had become the norm. Individuals were starting to build personal fortunes and took no heed of the weaker Qurayshis."[88]

It was within this social framework that Muhammad struggled three times with the Angel Gabriel on Mount Hira in AD 610, and finally reluctantly agreed to be the conduit for Al'lah's holy word. "Recite in the name of thy Sustainer, who has created—created man out of a germ cell! Recite—for thy Sustainer is Most Bountiful, One who has taught [man] the use of the pen—taught him what he did not know![89]

This Qur'an ("the recitation") was a revelation to the Arab people in their own language from a god they already worshipped as the great God among a pantheon of lesser gods. It was revealed to Muhammad in a series of painful trances over the space of twenty-two years. Unable to either read or write, Muhammad recited the words that came to him from Al'lah, and they were memorized by others and eventually written down. The first complete collection of these twenty-two years of revelation was compiled twenty years after Muhammad's death. As the title suggests, these revelations were meant to be read aloud to, and in the language of, a people who had been waiting for their own version of the transcendent word of God; only they hadn't realized it until Muhammad brought it to them.

Al'lah, the God of the Qur'an, is pure transcendence, unknowable in and of Himself. He is ineffable, inscrutable, and it is possible to speak of Him only indirectly, in parables, and to understand him equally indirectly, through signs. Consequently, the Qur'an urges observation of the world and the use of reason in coming to terms with Al'lah's messages.[90]

In the century after the Prophet's death, Islam spread across much of the known world, throughout the Arab lands, southeastern Europe, western Asia, India, and across North Africa. Following close behind was Arabic philosophy, non-Christian points of view, and Aristotle.

It is in this context that we begin to see, in the ninth century, attempts at reconciling Islam with the demands of philosophical inquiry. And in the Islamic world, unlike in European Christendom, philosophical inquiry meant looking to the works of the one called simply "the Philosopher." These attempts at reconciliation were called *falsafah*, and those who engaged in them *faylasufs*.

Philosophy beyond Christendom: Avicenna

Avicenna (Abu Ali al-Husain ibn Abdallah ibn Sina, 980–1037) was a Persian teacher, physician, statesman, theologian, and faylasuf. He skillfully wove together elements of Islamic theology, Platonic dualism, and Aristotelian materialism in his attempts at reconciling faith and reason.

God, Avicenna said, is absolute unity and absolute transcendence. God is both necessary Being and absolute goodness. Being absolute goodness, He is the eternal act of creation. It follows logically then that God, in His goodness and necessity, has no choice but to create.[91] But God is also pure reason, and being so, can contemplate only pure reason itself and not contingent reality.[92] One of the first things God creates, then, is intelligence—the agent of creation of all that is not absolute Being. Intelligence, then, can be seen as both existence and its agency, while we look upon God as pure essence. This allows for the Qur'anic doctrine of the unity of God as a form of Islamic iteration of the Aristotelian conception of being as both actuality and potentiality.

Averroes

In Cordoba, Spain, Averroes (Abu al-Walid ibn Ahmad ibn Rushd, 1126–98), another Muslim faylasuf, looked upon Aristotle as "the completer of human science, the model of human perfection, and the author of a system which is the supreme truth."[93] He argued that falsafah, not theology, was the highest form of spiritual activity. He argued this on several grounds: that there was a "twofold truth," wherein the truths of faith and the truths of reason need not be held to the same measure;[94] that philosophical truth was the highest truth, and it could only be interpreted by what the Qur'an called "those who are well grounded in knowledge";[95] that the faylasuf had a better vantage point to observe and study the truth objectively, standing as he did outside the phatic boundaries of liturgy and ritual and thereby enriching the religious experience;[96] and that religion itself was necessary more to bring moral values—and social stability—to the masses than to enlighten them.[97]

At the same time, he counseled his disciples to keep their knowledge—and their superiority—to themselves. For one thing, he saw falsafah as an esoteric activity that by its very nature inflamed the passions of theologians; better to share the knowledge only where it will be appreciated. For another thing, falsafah was not for everybody. It was to be reserved for an intellectual elite who would not be confused or led astray and whose faith would not be weakened by the power of scientific knowledge. For the mass of people, however, Averroes was astounded by how effective divine revelation (such as that contained in the Qur'an) could be at making moral individuals out of a barbaric rabble.[98]

To Averroes, absolute truth was to be found in reason, not in revelation; and more specifically, he advised, it is to the method and philosophy of Aristotle that we should look in our pursuit of truth. Much of what passed for knowledge in theology—transcendent "truths"—could never be proved by reason. So don't try to prove them by reason. Accept them, or not, on faith. But for the answers to questions about immanent, material phenomena, look instead to Aristotelian method—observation and reason—to discern the natural laws that underlie the natural world.

Moses Maimonides

Averroes' disciple and countryman, Moses Maimonides (1135–1204), may have echoed Augustine in his claim that reason is best used in contemplation of God,[99] but his proofs for the existence of God come directly from Aristotle, including the proofs as first mover, as necessary being, and as first cause.[100] But Maimonides kept a respectful Judaic intellectual distance from Yahweh, who remained inscrutable, indescribable, and impossible to fully comprehend through reason alone.

Maimonides made use of the *via negativa* in speaking of God as a way of avoiding the temptation to remake God in our image. The proper way to speak of God is to talk about what He is not: not powerless, not ignorant, not imperfect, and so on. Furthermore, we can only make these determinations about God's actions, as observed in nature and in natural law, and not His essence, which is infinitely beyond our grasp.[101]

The Rehabilitation of Aristotle

Peter Abelard (1079–1142) was among the first Christian scholars to resurrect, in a Christian context, a dimension of Aristotelian materialism in teaching that the transcendent world was inherent in, and integral to, the world of material reality. Abelard—a nominalist, like Roscellinus—was also something of a philosophical minimalist, preferring simple explanations where previous philosophers had set up elaborate metaphysical systems. Transcendent universals were unnecessary to explain being; everything necessary for being was contained in being itself. If Aristotle is a man, no universal transcendent form, *man,* needs to exist, abstracted from reality. *Man* is a word referring to a concept which can be defined by certain characteristics, all of which are inherent in the particular thing, man. Whatever transcendence may exist in this state of affairs dwells, in other words, in the immanent. Abelard's was an exercise not so much concerned with fusing the transcendent with the immanent, of combining faith with reason, but with seeing the complexity of the relationship between the two.

In this way, Peter Abelard could not and did not reject outright the transcendent truths implicit in the Christian faith. In fact, his very embrace of those truths is one of the explanations for his nominalism. Words, he believed, can become ritualized and mechanistic and allow us to miss the deeper meaning of the inherent truths they represent. The meaning of a sacrament, for instance, lay not in a recitation of empty words, but in a true and deep faith that creates a foundation for those words. Reality, for Abelard, was at least in part a function of human intention.

Ultimately, Abelard embraced the split between head and heart. In embracing it, he favored the head, but as adjunct and aide to the heart: "I do not wish to be a philosopher to the point of resisting Paul; I will not be an Aristotelian to the point of rejecting Christ."[102]

It is obvious that the fundamental intellectual problem of Medieval Europe remained the precarious balance between transcendence and immanence that the written word had upset. The engagement of the senses with the propositional mind that writing encouraged put significant stress upon and inevitably undermined the imagistic presentational structures of thought that supported so much of what human beings experienced as transcendence. In order to maintain this balance, or at the very least, to maintain the appearance of balance, it became necessary once again to make transcendence immanent, to objectify subjective experience, to rationalize faith. Many medieval scholars resisted this temptation (although, given the monopoly of written knowledge controlled by the Church, such resistance is understandable, for this was often a difficult and always a dangerous thing to do).

The Dominican Friar, Thomas Aquinas (1225–74) demonstrated that human perception and reason deserved recognition, along with Divine Revelation, as important sources of faith. Furthermore, he insisted that ultimate transcendence—God—could be experienced and understood in much the same way that we experience material reality. Transcendence, Aquinas taught, could legitimately be the subject of human reason.

The world of Aquinas was one that saw, thanks in no small part to the work of Islamic scholars like Averroes, an enormous expansion of human knowledge through the employment of Aristotelian method: sensory observation combined with critical reason. This empirical rationalism posed a threat to the Church's entire worldview. Natural philosophy was more and more yielding insights into the physical world that were at odds with Divine Revelation.

To understand the threat was only common sense. Aquinas' philosophy was one of uncommon sense. It had to be, at least partially as a result of the renaissance of Aristotelian thinking that Islamic scholars such as Avicenna and Averroes had made inevitable. Aquinas adhered as much as possible to the still-dominant dualistic neo-Platonism of Augustine, taking care to distance himself and his ideas, as Augustine did, from those of "pagan" philosophers. "Whenever Augustine, who was imbued with the doctrines of the Platonists, found in their writings anything consistent with the faith, he adopted it; and whatever he found contrary to faith, he amended."[103]

Yet Aquinas' approach was, at the same time, at least partially Aristotelian. He set out to demonstrate, among other things, that God was knowable through reason, that the ultimate transcendence could be apprehended and comprehended through the same processes that humans used to know immanent reality. Knowledge and being are intimately related. "In so far as a thing is, it is knowable, and in this resides its ontological truth."[104] As it was to Aristotle, transcendence for Aquinas was inherent in the immanent, and all creation "bears the very stamp of God's nature."[105]

In his *Summa Theologica*, Aquinas set out five proofs for the existence of God from natural philosophy. It is an exquisite argument, yet one that was destined to be ridiculed by scientists and philosophers in the coming modern era. These are his five proofs:

• **The proof from motion.** In the physical world, many things are in motion, and their motion is evidence of some mover. A thing cannot cause its own movement, but must be acted upon by another. But this potentially infinitely recursive process demands the presence of some prime mover—one that moves but is not itself moved.

• **The proof from efficient cause.** There is no logical basis to expect anything to be its own efficient cause; there must always be some agent that precedes the phenomenon. If we are not to fall into the trap (an impossibility to Aquinas) of infinite regression, this assumes the existence of some first efficient cause, whom we call God.

• **The proof from necessity.** All things in physical experience have a cyclical existence: they have the potential both to be and not to be. They will come into existence, and they will pass from existence. It is inevitable, then, that at some point nothing existed. Since nothing can come into existence by itself (nothing can move itself, nothing can be its own efficient cause), it becomes necessary to have a being who is prime mover and first efficient cause, whose own necessity is inherent but provides other beings with their necessity.

• **The proof from gradation.** Things bear different relationships to other things, and we judge them according to those relationships. Beings are more or less good, more or less true, and more or less beautiful. But there must be some absolute quality, a perfection against which all such judgments are made and which is the cause of all these qualities; that perfection is God.

• **The proof from intelligent design.** Things lacking human intelligence act, they act predictably, and they act toward some end. This could not be the result of mere chance, but rather indicates a *telos* or purpose in their design which implies an intelligence which directs their action.[106]

True being, therefore, is transcendent because God is the fullness of all being, the perfection of all being, and that from which all being flows. At the same time, human beings can work to actualize their potential—to *fully be*—and in this sense share in God's transcendent nature. Natural philosophy—enquiry into the nature and working of the material world—is not to be feared, therefore, as a threat to faith. Immanent reality is God's creation and we do God honor by studying His work.

Aquinas responded to the challenges to the Church posed by the

> resurgence of Aristotelian thinking with brilliance and creativity, yet only temporarily slowed the momentum of a widening breach between faith and reason. His *Summa Theologica* "was indeed a marvelous synthesis of 'science and sanctity,' wrought with remarkable zest, patience, and acumen, unsurpassed in the history of thought for its combination of imaginative breadth, intellectual rigor, and loving care in detail; but its equilibrium was even more delicate and precarious than that of the Gothic cathedrals. Later schoolmen pointed out basic inconsistencies, and with the

rise of science the whole foundation of the elaborate structure was undermined."[107]

Charting the Course of the Split: John Duns Scotus

The Franciscan monk John Duns Scotus (1265–1308) provided the first gentle subversion of the Thomistic foundation by suggesting that Aquinas's system diminished God's transcendent nature, made God too subject to His creation, and intellectually too approachable—more immanent than transcendent. God is infinite being, not necessary being, for who is to impose such necessity upon God? Since God is absolute being, His actuality must be superior to His potential; therefore all of His immanent works that we look upon and call nature must be subordinated to the transcendent wisdom through which God exercises His will.[108] In this way, Duns Scotus shifted the metaphysical balance back toward transcendence once again.

Church Reaction

The Church itself rebelled against the increasingly tight focus on immanence as manifest in the growing power of rationalism—and its hostility to transcendence. In 1277, Etienne Tempier, Bishop of Paris, drew up a list condemning 219 propositions coming either directly from Aristotelian philosophy or via Averroes' interpretations of the philosopher.[109] Tempier considered these propositions (and Pope John XXI agreed) to be irreconcilable with Christian doctrine. These included the following propositions: "there is no higher life than philosophical life (prop. 40)"; "nothing should be believed, save only that which is either self-evident, or can be deduced from self-evident propositions (prop. 37)"; and "Christian Revelation is an obstacle to learning (prop. 175)."[110]

As though lampooning the Church's reactionism to empiric reasoning, John of Jaudun, in the early fourteenth century, wrote laudatory commentaries on Aristotle, stopping just short of heretical denial of Church teaching at the last moment. He then undertook a comically lugubrious—and transparently sarcastic—confession of his absolute, unshakable faith in whatever article of Christian doctrine he had just nearly demolished.

> I believe and I firmly maintain that the substance of the soul is endowed with natural faculties whose activities are independent from all bodily organs. . . . Such faculties belong in a higher order than that of corporeal matter and far exceed its capacities. . . . And although the soul be united with matter, it nevertheless exercises an (intellectual) activity in which corporeal matter takes no part. All those properties of the soul belong to it truly, simply, and absolutely, according to our own faith. And also that an immaterial soul can suffer from a material fire, and be reunited with its own body, after death, by order of the same God Who created it.
>
> On the other side, I would not undertake to demonstrate all that, but I think that such things should be believed by simple faith, as well as many others that are to be believed without demonstrative reasons, on the authority of Holy Writ and of miracles. Besides, this is why there is some merit in believing, for the theologians teach us, that there is no merit in believing that which reason can demonstrate.[111]

Arguing the impossibility of the Augustinian concept of creation *ex nihilo,* John nonetheless affirms it—making certain to assure his reader that no philosopher ever dreamed up such an unlikely explanation for the origins of the physical world and everything in it: "And no wonder, for it is impossible to reach the notion of creation from the consideration of empirical facts; nor is it possible to justify it by arguments borrowed from sensible experience. And this is why the Ancients, who used to draw their knowledge from rational arguments verified by sensible experience, never succeeded in conceiving such a mode of production. . . . Let it be added, that creation very seldom happens; there has never been but one, and that was a very long time ago."[112]

Charting the Course of the Split: William of Occam

A significant new threat to the foundations of Scholasticism—far greater than that of satire—came from William of Occam (or Ockham, ca. 1300–49), a Franciscan studying and teaching at Oxford and eventually teaching in Paris. Many, if not most, transcendent ideas are irrational, said William. Like Averroes, Occam believed that reason can neither comprehend nor prove transcendent truths, no matter how probable we believe them to be.[113]

Like Roscellinus, William was a nominalist and denied the existence of universals, believing that transcendent ideas can be counterproductive or even destructive, as we can know them only as expressed through words—they have no other reality. Like Abelard, he was also a philosophical minimalist and believed that the shortest intellectual distance between two points is a straight line: Do away with unnecessary theories and assumptions.

Occam's razor was the name given to the principle that the best possible solution to an intellectual problem is the simplest one. In this way, questions regarding the immanent world ought to be addressed through empirical methods, and questions of transcendent reality through theology.

Charting the Course of the Split: Meister Eckhart

Meanwhile, Meister Eckhart (1260–1327) suggested a third way, and a way which further undermined the system established by his Dominican brother, Thomas Aquinas. Eckhart believed in the transcendent world of forms, and taught that the world of immanent, material experience is a shadow, a mere reflection of the "real" world of transcendence. One might say that this marks him as a realist and more in the tradition of Augustine than Aquinas, but Eckhart took this realism further, arriving at the point of *mysticism,* emphasizing the Divine unity from which the material world is a "breaking away"—and therefore essentially evil.[114] His answer, then, was to escape from the immanent world as much as possible and to dwell, as closely as one might, with God in the world of transcendence.

Print Deepens the Breach, Widens the Split

During the Medieval Era, as we have noted, the fundamental intellectual problem of the day was the precarious balance between transcendence and immanence that the written word had upset. On the one hand, neo-Platonists like Augustine had argued that transcendent reality was the "real" reality, and humans could not be expected to understand reality outside of the personal experience of Divine Revelation (very rare) and the mediated Divine Revelation we call sacred scripture (far more common to those wise enough to believe). Some Aristotelians, like Aquinas, tried to maintain a balance between faith and reason. Revelation, if it can be adequately captured in writing, might also be present in nature itself; here wisdom belongs to those who pursue it. Others, like Occam, believed that there must henceforth be two vocabularies, one for transcendent reality and theology, the other for immanent reality and science.

The breach that constituted the split between head and heart remained and was never repaired. Conflicting worldviews saw far too much at stake to surrender their positions too easily. As the fifteenth century brought us to the threshold of the age of print literacy, the sympathies of the defenders of transcendence were summed up well by Thomas á Kempis (1380–1471): "If thou knewest the whole Bible, and the sayings of all the philosophers, what should all this profit thee without the love and grace of God? *Vanity of vanities, all is vanity,* save to love God, and Him only to serve. That is the highest wisdom, to cast the world behind us, and to reach forward to the heavenly kingdom."[115]

While writing helped to create religion as a formal social institution and set the stage for the medieval struggle between faith, reason, and those who wished to maintain a connection between the two, the rise and rapid spread of print literacy after the middle of the fifteenth century began to undermine its metaphysical foundations. The monopoly of knowledge founded upon manuscript literacy—and fiercely protected by the Church—began to crumble in the face of an assault by the printing press and its fruit. As objective knowledge grew and spread with print literacy, print helped to begin a "wholesale attack on man's senses and common sense."[116]

Charting the Course of the Split: Martin Luther

In 1517, Martin Luther (1483–1546) posted on the door of the Wittenburg Cathedral his "95 Theses" against the selling of indulgences, both challenging the authority of the pope and the institutional Church and denying a fundamental doctrine of salvation. Martin Luther—considered a heretic leader of a schismatic movement by the institutional Church—became, to his supporters, the standard-bearer for a reformation of that Church. The engine of the Reformation was the printing press. "Between 1517 and 1520, Luther's thirty publications probably sold well over 300,000 copies. . . . Lutheranism was from the first the child of the printed book and through this vehicle Luther was to make exact, standardized and ineradicable impressions on the mind of Europe. For the first time in human history a great reading public judged the validity of revolutionary ideas through a mass medium which used the vernacular languages."[117]

But having been born in 1483, Luther was already a second-generation child of the print revolution, and his heretical—or certainly heterodox—ideas were themselves influenced by the explosion of information available as a result of print technology.[118]

Luther's ideas were as much a product of the new epistemology of print literacy as the Reformation was a product of Luther's ideas.

With Luther, the question is not of whether we might have faith or believe in some sort of transcendent experience; the question was one of the nature of the transcendent itself. With the Lutheran rejection of papal infallibility and clerical necessity, it became possible (indeed, necessary) for each person to experience the transcendent truths of revelation through the agency of the printed book.

Charting the Course of the Split: Francis Bacon

The split between head and heart was destined to become broader and far deeper as the age of print progressed. Francis Bacon (1561–1626) began the formal dismantling of Aristotelian science and the method that supported it syllogistic formal logic. This was the continuation of a campaign begun, without much success but with enormous academic sympathy, by Peter Ramus in 1536.[119] In so doing, Bacon also helped to undermine the foundations of both Scholasticism and Thomism, leaving medieval theology an intellectual orphan in the shadow of the rapidly developing institutions of science and Protestantism. It was the growing opinion of this new age that philosophy and theology had become conflated under Scholasticism and remained so throughout the medieval era. This marriage of philosophy and theology was not only incapable of sufficiently addressing the mysteries of immanent reality, it was equally incapable of addressing the mysteries of the transcendent world.

Science would do better: "For the heathens themselves conclude as much in that excellent and divine fable of the golden chain: That men and gods were not able to draw Jupiter down to the earth; but contrariwise, Jupiter was able to draw them up to heaven. So as we ought not to attempt to draw down or submit the mysteries of God to our reason; but contrariwise to raise and advance our reason to the divine truth."[120]

Bacon devised a new method for enquiry into the natural world that he believed would lead to new discoveries about the universe and man's place in it, to new knowledge about the world, and to new understanding of the human experience. This was the method of inductive reasoning. This method involved the empirical observation and measurement of material phenomena with a goal of isolating specific regularities—facts—about them. Having identified these regularities, we can compare them with facts about other phenomena and evaluate the relationship between them. This allows us to identify and test causal relationships among things.

Charting the Course of the Split: Galileo

Galileo Galilei (1564–1642) was, like Bacon and Luther, the product of a culture of widespread print literacy. That is to say, he was not alone in his attitude that revealed truth might be giving way to an entirely different kind of truth: a truth based on rigorous observation, measurement, testing, and inductive reasoning.

One of the things he believed Aristotle had gotten wrong was the great Philosopher's contention that the Earth was the center of the universe. The astronomical works of Nicolaus Copernicus reordered the earth-centered cosmos into a heliocentric one and implicitly challenged the biblical notion of divine creation, thereby—in the eyes of the Church—"marginalizing, even trivializing"[121] human beings. Even though he was born and raised Catholic (his entire family were third-order members of the Dominicans), his *De Revolutionibus Orbium Coelestrium* (1543) was published, just before his death, under Protestant auspices.[122]

It was immediately placed on the Church's index of proscribed books.[123]

In 1613, Galileo used a telescope he had invented to provide evidence that Copernicus' interpretations of his observations were correct. He was called before the Inquisition and made to retract his claims, and was yet imprisoned until his death, nine years later.

So as the sixteenth century gave way to the seventeenth, firmly rooted in the age of print literacy, the sympathies of the defenders of immanence are summed up well by the (perhaps apocryphal) last words of Galileo: "Eppur si muove!" "Still, it (the earth) moves."

Charting the Course of the Split: Thomas Hobbes

Thomas Hobbes (1588–1679) was, like Aristotle, a materialist. But the resemblance does not extend much further than that. All of the universe, Hobbes said, and everything in it—including God—has corporeal existence and is in constant motion. Bodies in constant motion throughout the universe exert an influence on one another. This influence either generates or extinguishes an "accident" in another body—the accident of motion, the accident of rest, and so on.

Similarly, Hobbes envisioned a very materialistic epistemology. Perception was the interaction between external objects and the senses which set off "accidents" of thought between the "brain and the heart."[124] There is no room, in Hobbes' philosophy, for *a priori* knowledge informing experience or an individual's view of reality. "The cause of Sense, is the Externall Body, or Object, which presseth the organ proper to each sense, either immediately, as in the Tast [sic] and Touch; or mediately, as in Seeing, Hearing, and Smelling; which pressure, by the mediation of Nerves, and other strings, and membranes of the body continues inward to the Brain and Heart, causeth there a resistance, or counter-pressure, or endeavour of the heart, to deliver it self: which endeavour because Outward, seemeth to be some matter without."[125]

These accidents—human thought and reason—might take place in the form of words, or they might not. They might take place instead in the form of images or memories of sensations. And, in fact, Hobbes seems to give more credence to the memories of sensations than he does to the words in the processes of reason, for he finds fault with what he calls "insignificant speech."[126] One such example of insignificant speech becomes apparent, Hobbes tells us, when humans begin to use "signs" (words) to speak and reason not about things, but about abstractions, emotions, intentions, and transcendence—that is, nonrepresentational speech. In all, Hobbes provides four examples of "insignificant" or misused speech:

> First, when men register their thoughts wrong, by the inconstancy of the signification of their words; by which they register for their conceptions, that which they never conceived; and so deceive themselves. Secondly, when they use words metaphorically; that is, in other sense than that they are ordained for; and thereby deceive others. Thirdly, when by words they declare that to be their will which it is not. Fourthly, when they use them to grieve one another: for seeing nature hath armed living creatures, some with teeth, some with horns, and some with hands to grieve an enemy, it is but an abuse of speech to grieve him with the tongue, unless it be one whom wee [sic] are obliged to govern; and then it is not to grieve, but to correct and amend.[127]

Hobbes' thinking resembles that of the nominalists in this regard and, like them, anticipates the postmodern mistrust of language as a medium through which to engage and comprehend reality. Unlike Anselm, Hobbes' reality is one of immanence and his method demands a concentrated focus on immanent reality, to the point of putting faith in sensations and the memory of sensations as much as (if not more than) in words.

Charting the Course of the Split: Rene Descartes

Rene Descartes (1596–1650) believed that there is a duality to reality; it is divided into mind and matter. Like Hobbes, Descartes too saw the universe as being made up of bodies (matter) in motion. Again, like Hobbes, he saw change as being related to or caused by bodies in motion. But the motion of bodies is regulated by distinct, unchanging, and very mechanistic laws, laws that could be identified, objectified, and used to understand the universe.[128] It was important to Descartes to have such a set of identifiable, knowable, understandable laws, laws that—even though they might explain phenomena popularly considered to be transcendent—were derived from immanent experience. Certainty, Descartes believed, had been the Achilles' heel of Scholasticism, and too often had been sacrificed for the primacy of authority. His method, therefore, was to reduce all human experience to a fundamental level of certainty, and to work upwards from there. Doubt was integral to his method— not for its own sake or the sake of skepticism, but as an important means of achieving certainty. Consequently, for Descartes, this imposed a necessary focus on immanent and sensory reality, as opposed to a transcendent or spiritual one, as the locus of his "first principles."

Charting the Course of the Split: John Locke

John Locke (1632–1704) was among the first Enlightenment Deists. Deism was an essentially rational system more indebted to the senses and immanent reality than to the imagination and transcendence. Locke did not reject the possibility of divine revelation; but he insisted on reason as its judge.[129]

For Locke, there was no *a priori* knowledge, no intuitive knowledge, and no transcendent knowledge upon which a rational system could be based. All was perception, experience, and reason.

Neither Locke nor Deists in general denied the existence of God (or other transcendent ideas); he merely insisted that in the pursuit of knowledge one must be forced to confront immanent reality and satisfy the demands of human reason. The immanent world is the only world we can ever actually know (in an empirical sense) and is the source of all ideas. With Locke, the transcendent and mysterious within humankind (the soul, the spirit, the imagination) recedes into the background, and all that is immanent (the body, the mind, reason) takes on new significance.

A new spirit began to suffuse European civilization, one that sees man as the pinnacle of creation, with the power, the will, the freedom, and the intelligence (if we use these gifts wisely) to expand human knowledge and improve the world: the spirit of humanism.

Charting the Course of the Split: George Berkeley

We have already mentioned George Berkeley (1685–1753) in our earlier discussion of reality. Berkeley, an Anglican Bishop and a deeply religious man, rebelled against the materialism that the seventeenth-century focus on immanence had so strongly emphasized. Alarmed at the spread of atheism, repelled by the humanism that relegated God to a position of irrelevance, Berkeley saw materialism as its root and believed it could be abolished if matter were diminished in importance in the human mind.[130] Berkeley's *subjective idealism* maintained that nothing is real except our perceptions. Sensation is the only source of our ideas, and it is the only thing we can have absolute certainty about. He also insisted that those sensations which become our perceptions do not come to us from the material world, but from the mind of God.[131] Within such an intellectual framework, the immanent world shrinks in significance, and the milieu of the transcendent—the mind, soul, or, to use the Greek term, *psyche*—ascended to a far greater prominence than at any time since the end of the era of Scholasticism.

Charting the Course of the Split: David Hume

David Hume (1711–76) introduced a radical skepticism into human thought, agreeing with Berkeley that the only reality that exists for human beings is that which they perceive. For Hume, both transcendence and immanence are irrelevant; it is only our own internal experience of sensations that matter. All other ideas are speculation—necessary and frequently appropriate speculation, to be sure, but speculation all the same. Transcendent ideas in particular are suspect, but still often necessary, at least in the functional sense. We fear death and our own mortality, desire happiness, wonder about the meaning of existence, and construct stories that address these impulses: immortality, perfection in a realm beyond the mortal world, divine justice, God, and so on.

It is pointless, to Hume, even to question the source of our sensations; is it the immanent world, as John Locke suggested? Is it God, as Berkeley insisted? We can't know. All we have are our impressions and the ideas that they support. For Hume, sensory experience is everything. Neither the immanent world nor the transcendent realm can offer us much solace. We are alone within ourselves.

Charting the Course of the Split: Immanuel Kant

Immanuel Kant (1724–1804) sought to integrate more fully what had been the warring intellectual powers of rational judgment and empirical observation. Rationalists, following the tradition of Plato, believed that the whole of reality was comprehensible through the use of human reason. Rationalists identified transcendent universal ideas about which humans could have a great deal of certainty, but whose practical utility was of questionable value.

Empiricists, following the tradition of Aristotle, argued that a comprehensible reality could only be experienced through the senses. Empiricists identified knowledge that was useful, but about which—because of variations in human cognition, understanding, and behavior—one could not claim a great deal of certainty.

Kant breaks human thought down into two functions which correspond to empiricism and rationalism: sensibility and understanding.[132] Sensory experience is experience of the particular; reason, the agent of understanding, is the experience of concepts, which include the universals. There are things we know through reason, Kant argued, that we know *a priori*, prior to sensory observation. These *a priori* judgments—"pure" thought, without foundation in sensory experience[133]—can be applied both to knowledge gained through sensory experience (particulars) or to concepts that transcend the boundaries of the senses, such as space and time.

We have an intuitive understanding of space and time that cannot be explained by our powers of empirical observation. "What objects may be in themselves . . . remains completely unknown to us. We know nothing but our mode of perceiving them—a mode which is peculiar to us, and not necessarily shared in by every being, though, certainly, by every human being. With this alone have we any concern. Space and time are its pure forms, and sensation in general its matter. The former alone can we know *a priori,* that is, prior to all actual perception; and such knowledge is therefore called pure intuition."[134]

Kant's recognition of universals bears a resemblance to Plato's ideal forms. But his framing of them as *a priori* judgments intuitively arrived at through the power of human intellect—

pure reason—brings them squarely back into the material realm of immanence.

Charting the Course of the Split: Hegel

In the thought of the German idealist Georg Wilhelm Friedrich Hegel (1770–1831), we encounter what appears at first sight to be another attempt to buttress the sagging foundations of transcendence, and even to return it to equal prominence with immanence. But in the final analysis, the attention he gives to transcendence is not of the sort to place it beyond human comprehension—making it, for all intents and purposes, very immanent indeed. Hegel did not see this to be a problem. Indeed, his view of reality is one that embraces, rather than runs in fear from, contradiction and paradox.

Like Kant, Hegel believed in an absolute reality that is knowable through reason. Unlike Kant, he argued that reality was reason—the conscious act of thought. The totality of existence was reason, and that totality could be comprehended only through reason. He argued that consciousness constituted both the milieu of the immanent—through reason—and the seat of the transcendent. Such a conception of reality is going to be fraught with oppositions and antitheses.

Hegel maintained that the fundamental purpose of philosophy is "overcoming oppositions and divisions,"[135] not unreasonably inferred to be between the warring demands of immanence and transcendence. In this way, his philosophy resembles the Scholasticism of the Middle Ages. There is a dependence on a conception of reality that emphasizes the total dominance of the universal and the absolute ("the one") over the mutable, the determinate, and the contingent ("the many").

But then Hegel continues by describing the speculative and

intuitive method of philosophy necessary in order even to attempt to comprehend reality.

The absolute is being itself. Consciousness is being itself. Rather than some transcendent abstraction, reality is the manifestation of conscious being. Philosophy needs to look at reality not merely in terms of substance, but as a subject whose object is itself.[136] This seems to echo Aristotle's idea of God (absolute transcendence) as prime mover or self-thinking thought. But Aristotle's God is self-sufficient and necessary, and Hegel sees absolute consciousness as a dialectic process, constantly moving forward, creating history, actualizing itself.[137] This absolute consciousness in an eternal process of actualization Hegel called "spirit."

Hegel's insistence on a unitary absolute, a universal spirit which is not only the essence of consciousness, but is also present in all human consciousness, justifies the coming age of ideologies and paves the way for the solipsistic worldviews which both support them and provide solace to those who seek an escape from them. Hegel's thought constituted a *Zeitgeist*—a spirit of the times—that was, in the final analysis, profoundly materialistic and centered upon the ideology of progress.

Recapitulation: Writing, Print, and Reality

The profound changes that took place in this initial era of print leading up to the Enlightenment are self-evident—changes in learning, in science, in politics and political theory, in approaches to knowledge, and in the relationship between the transcendent and the immanent. Tycho Brahe, Johannes Kepler, Galileo Galilei, Isaac Newton, and John Locke proposed that knowledge comes only from experience and sensation, questioned the legitimacy of the divine right of kings (implicitly questioning the right of religious leaders to endorse secular leaders), championed religious tolerance, and posited the sovereignty of the human person. Jean-Jacques Rousseau, Charles Montesquieu and John Locke argued, respectively, for popular sovereignty, for a separation of executive, legislative, and judicial powers of government, and for the right—even, sometimes, the obligation—of citizens to revolt against corrupt or illegitimate authority. Martin Luther and Galileo challenged the authority of the Church in the interpretation of both transcendent and immanent truths. Berkeley and Hume suggested that even immanent reality is ultimately unknowable; all we can know—all that is real—are our sensory impressions of reality.

Hegel, along with Friedrich Engels and Karl Marx, argued that human history was an inexorable march of material progress toward perfection. Humans began to imagine themselves as moving steadily toward an era "which, in itself vastly superior to any age of the past, need be burdened by no fear of decline or catastrophe but, trusting in the boundless resources of science, might surely defy fate."[138] The idea of progress is very much an ideology, concerned with material relationships of human political, social, and economic institutions and the technologies that support them; it is in their ideological orientation that we see their strongly immanent nature.

Writing, Walter Ong has told us, introduced an "alienation within the human lifeworld," one that has "restructured consciousness, affecting men's and women's presence to the world and to themselves and creating new interior distances within the psyche."[139] The printing press took this alienation and amplified it, extending it to mass proportions. With printing and the beginnings of mass literacy, the distance between objective reality and metaphysical reality increased enormously, immanence and transcendence sustaining a breach that has proven difficult if not impossible to bridge. In this way, literacy and the modern age contained—and eventually have sowed—the seeds of their own postmodern destruction. And with the electric simultaneity and instantaneity of postmodernism, the literacy-inspired rift between transcendence and immanence disappears because, as we shall see, transcendence itself all but disappears.

Chapter Seven

Electric Culture

We have not received the spirit of the world but the Spirit who is from God, that we may understand what God has freely given to us. This is what we speak, not in words taught us by human wisdom but in words taught by the Spirit, expressing spiritual truths in spiritual words.

1 Corinthians 2:12–14

Our contemporaries only see the presentations that are given them by the press, the radio, propaganda, and publicity. The man of the present day does not believe in his own experiences, in his own judgment, in his own thought: he leaves all that to what he sees in print or hears on the radio. . . . What he himself has seen does not count, if it has not been officially interpreted, if there is not a crowd of people who share his opinion.

Jacques Ellul
The Presence of the Kingdom

In the 1830s, a professor of art at New York University named Samuel Finley Breese Morse perfected an electronic telegraphy system and a code that allowed messages to be sent over great distances at (roughly) the speed of light. This was the opening salvo in the coming electronic communication revolution. Soon to join the battle were the telephone, the radiotelegraph, the radio, television, and an entire catalog of digital-age media too numerous to mention. As Morse asked, when testing his invention on a line strung between Washington and Baltimore on May 24, 1844, "What hath God wrought?" It is a question to which many still seek answers.

Electrification of communication techniques has had profound implications for human civilization. It resulted not only in the radical acceleration and increase in information, the ease of access to information, and the connection of peoples in far-flung corners of the world (the first trans-Atlantic cable between the United States and Europe was laid in 1865), but also in the disembodiment of information. For the first time in human history, information no longer needed to be scratched, engraved, or written on some physical object. Rather than moving, on paper or papyrus, at the speed of a man, a camel, a horse, or a locomotive, it was now able to move, via electric currents, at roughly the speed of light.

The End of the "Metaphysics of Presence"
With electricity, physical presence is no longer necessary (not even the limited sense of presence found in the form of a handwritten letter) to effect interpersonal communication. When all or even most of our daily interpersonal interactions are consummated through some electronic intermediary, when it is no longer necessary to "be with" someone to speak with them, what becomes of the phatic elements of human communication?

"We have reached," Neil Postman cautions us, "a critical mass . . . in that electronic media have decisively and irreversibly changed the character of our symbolic environment. We are now a culture whose information, ideas, and epistemology are given form by television, not by the printed word. . . . Print is now merely a residual epistemology, and it will remain so, aided to some extent by the computer, and newspapers and magazines that are made to look like television screens."[1]

Electric media have a strong bias toward the senses, particularly the senses of hearing and vision. But to say that (for instance) television people are ear people is not to say that they are just like oral folk to whom the spoken word had power. Nor is it to say that they are like literate people because of their emphasis on the eye, because written words and visual images are very different symbol systems and present information to us in radically different ways.[2] The profoundly presentational structure of visual images and nonverbal sounds so characteristic of electric media limit the nature and intellectual depth of the discourse that makes use of those images and sounds. This is not to say that there is no depth to the visual image; but the depth is presentational, not propositional.

Television is so intensely visual that it has a difficult time dealing with any subject matter that is not itself inherently visual.[3] We process images much more on an *affective* or emotional level, however, than on a *cognitive* or rational level. We can feel something about an image, about a sound, about a piece of music, but we can't make many critical judgments about it—at least not on our initial encounter. We will either like it, or not like it; it will appeal to us, or it won't. And if we never even see it, we have reason to doubt its existence.

The Irrelevance of Time and Space

We have reason to doubt—because we cease to experience—the existence of space in electric culture. Electricity obliterates space. This means that distances between communicators become invisible, irrelevant; but it also means that once-restricted information gains a general audience. Walls fall, frames shatter, and boundaries disintegrate. "To have information from an environment is to be partially 'in' that environment."[4] Authority, dependent on tight control of information, on symbolic ritual, on "sacred space," disintegrates.[5] Traditional boundaries, for better and for worse, are destroyed. The globe shrinks, becomes a village; we all know one another's business. We live in a permanent "here."

There are no secrets in an electric world. With the rise of electric media as the powerful tools they are for opening windows on the world, the social concept of childhood, dependent for its origins upon specialized knowledge and secrecy, begins to disappear. Television is an aggressive deliverer of content without regard to the audience that receives it, and Joshua Meyerowitz notes that while "children were once shielded from certain topics such as sex, money, death, crime, and drugs,"[6] such vulgar and tawdry concerns are the very lifeblood of television. Television "exposes many adult secrets to children and also reveals the 'secret of secrecy'"[7]—the foundation, in a literate milieu, of the social category of childhood. "Children are a group of people who do not know certain things that adults know. In the Middle Ages there were no children because there existed no means for adults to know exclusive information. In the Age of Gutenberg, such a means developed. In the Age of Television, it is dissolved."[8] We have reason to doubt—because we cease to experience—the existence of past and future in electric culture. Along with obliterating space, electric media make all time *now*. The electric world is a world of spaceless simultaneity. What happens anywhere in the world (or in space), we know here and *now*. Electricity absorbs and eradicates the idea of the past, the concept of history. In their place we get "an ever-new and ever-renewable present";[9] we live in a permanent *now*, an uncomfortable situation with which we cope by retreating further into the only predictable milieu we know—the postmodern world of our own subjective sensory experiences. McLuhan tells us, "This global-village world of ours is entirely the result of the force of telegraphic, teletyped communication—information that is moving at a relatively instantaneous rate. This increasingly terrifies ordinary people in the community. The general atmosphere in which they live is one in which total global information presses upon them daily as a continuous environment bringing with it all the dangers in decision making."[10]

The Ascendancy of the Senses and Presentational Thought
Combine this characteristic with the powerful bias toward the senses and the affective rather than the cognitive processes, and you might be inclined to forecast the onset of a chaotic spell, a period of unpredictability, turmoil, and constant change, an era of multiple perspectives in competition, of old ways of seeing and old ways of thinking threatened. You just might be able to perceive old social structures begin to topple.

Institutional authority was once supported, first, by the logic of writing and then by the mass logic of print. Text-based institutions have a vested interest in controlling (preserving, protecting, and interpreting) information. In an electric age, the authority of every social institution, and the functionaries who comprise it, is questionable and threatened. Meyerowitz argues, "From the doctor's knowledge of the body to the divine monarch's channel to God, high status is protected through special and exclusive access to information. Once authorities 'give away' their information, their expertness and status may dissolve. High status that is not (or is no longer) based on special access to information is generally revolted against."[11]

Visual electronic media like television create an *illusion of objectivity*. They allow us to think that what we are seeing is real ("seeing is believing"), and leave us to make our own value judgments about that reality. In this sense, electric media appear to bring us into a state of harmony with the skepticism and analytic qualities of writing. But electric media such as television are not real, but mimetic. They mimic the human lifeworld and present information to us in a holistic, simultaneous, nonlinear, nonrational, and nondiscursive way. In this sense, they are an atavism, a throwback to the intensely engaged, subjective, and emotional mindset of mimetic orality (a "secondary orality"[12]) that Plato argued so strenuously against in *The Republic*. There is a powerful phatic element to television, but rather than bonding in an interpersonal or group association, we now bond to the television experience itself—the image.

The sensual, material immanence of our image of reality remaps our neural pathways and destroys what is left of transcendence. We become oral people, but only to a point. Walter Ong describes the new condition: "With telephone, radio, television and various kinds of sound tape, electronic technology has brought us into the age of 'secondary orality.' This new orality has a striking resemblance to the old in its participatory mystique, its fostering of a communal sense, its concentration on the present moment, and even its use of formulas."[13] Ong observes, "Abstractly sequential, classificatory, explanatory examination of phenomena or of stated truths is impossible without writing and reading. Human beings in primary oral cultures, those untouched by writing in any form, learn a great deal and possess and practice great wisdom, but they do not 'study.'"[14]

The Consequences of Electricity

The ubiquity of electric media makes the argument for the rise of a secondary cultural orality all the more compelling. The average American household contains—as of 1999—2.9 televisions, 1.8 VCRs, 3.1 radios, 2.1 CD players, 1.4 video game systems, and a computer.[15] The average American child is engaging more and more media at a much earlier age which serve to structure her thought in a powerfully presentational way. Eighty-three percent of American children *under the age of six* use "screen media" (television, computer, video games) on a daily basis;[16] on average, for two hours each day. Thirty-six percent of children *under the age of six* watch television in their own room.[17] Fifty-six percent of boys and thirty-six percent of girls between the ages of four and six play video games on a regular basis, on average for more than an hour each day.[18]

Meanwhile, standardized test scores have fallen continuously since the 1960s, even in spite of a process of "re-centering" the data. In 1966, the average verbal score for all students was 543 and the combined verbal and math score for all students was 1059 (both uncorrected by re-centering). Thomas Sowell reports that SAT scores fell continuously from 980 in 1963 to 900 in 1990.[19] They hit a low of 499 for verbal that year. Nor can the decline be blamed, as some would like, on the more diverse group of students who now take the exams than did so in the 1960s. More than 115,000 students scored greater than 600 on the verbal SAT in 1972, but only about 70,000 scored higher than 600 in 1980.[20] By 2001 they had improved (slightly) to 506 on the verbal,[21] nearly forty points lower than in 1966. This phenomenon runs consistently throughout American culture; it is not restricted by geography or social class, and is as true of students in the top schools of the country as of those entering more local, less prestigious schools.[22]

Fewer than half of all American adults now read literature. The number and proportion of Americans who have read any book has declined even more precipitously.[23] This decline in reading correlates strongly with a parallel decline in civic engagement.[24] This decline, coupled with electric culture's emphasis on immanence (and the concomitant disappearance of transcendence), has taken a toll on Americans' views of their fundamental rights. In a 2007 study by the John S. and James L. Knight Foundation, 73 percent of U.S. high school students said they don't know how they feel about the First Amendment, or that they take it for granted, and they were more likely than older Americans to support censorship.[25] A 2006 study by the McCormick Tribune Freedom Museum found that 22 percent of Americans could name all five Simpson family members, while only one-tenth of one percent could name all five First Amendment freedoms.[26]

But an electric media-saturated culture is not, in and of itself, the problem; falling standardized test scores is not the worst-case scenario for our future; a disengaged American polity with no sense of the importance of transcendent ideas is only the tip of an iceberg that threatens the intellectual and cultural development of human civilization on a global scale.

It is rather the specter—as a result of all I've just mentioned—of a diminished capacity for rational, propositional thought that is the real danger, and that ultimately engenders and supports all these other problems. It is the susceptibility to gossip, innuendo, insinuation, and other forms of bullshit that is the real danger. That is what ought really to concern us. The recent studies (mentioned in an earlier chapter) into the neural activity directly related to reading and viewing visual media suggests strongly that propositional structures of thought are "mapped" early on in human life by and through the activities of reading, writing, and speaking with others. The more time dedicated to nonpropositional media of various sorts, the less time there is either to train a child in the habits of literacy or to "train" his or her synapses to fire across the correct neural pathways to make the child literate, both in the intellectual sense and the behavioral sense.

This situation could not be taking place at a worse time, because as image-based communication forms diminish the power of our propositional structures of thought, thereby changing what we mean by the word reason (in both its noun and verb forms), appeals to action based on emotion have come to dominate our mass information environment. This is the moment of critical mass that Neil Postman has referred to.[27]

Space-biased Media, Space-biased Information

Harold Innis has described the power of space-biased media to focus our attention on the imperatives of immanence. Information that moves quickly and efficiently through space will bias our attention on the types of information whose value lies in its speedy mobility. Information that moves quickly gives those who use it a strategic advantage over those who do not have access to it. This space-biased information is useful in the administration of large-scale organizations, whether political, economic, or military. Space-biased information facilitates empire in the broadest sense of the word.

Electric media are profoundly space-biased media; indeed, it is difficult to imagine moving information any more quickly than the speed of light. Since the middle of the nineteenth century, we have watched a procession of electronic media introduced in order to wage wars, to regulate commerce, to administer laws, and—above all else—to expand trade and sell things:

- In 1840, Volney R. Palmer founded the first advertising agency in Philadelphia.[28]
- In 1848, the Associated Press was founded.[29]
- In 1858, the telegraph was used in the Crimean War;[30] less than a decade later, it was used by the Union forces during the U.S. Civil War.[31]
- In 1867, the telegraph was used as the foundation for the stock ticker.[32]
- In 1882, the Wirephoto was developed.[33]
- In 1889, a card tabulating machine was used in analyzing data from the eleventh U.S. Census.[34]
- In 1890, the first recording studio was opened in New York.[35]
- In 1891, the first telephone line connected London and Paris.[36]
- In 1892, Thomas Edison invented the Kinetoscope.[37]
- In 1896, Marconi perfected the wireless (radio) telegraph.[38]

- In 1897, General Electric created the first corporate publicity department.[39]
- By 1899, the social phenomenon of conspicuous consumption was officially acknowledged by Thorstein Veblen in his book, *Theory of the Leisure Class.*[40]
- By 1900, there were over one million telephones,[41] more than eight thousand registered automobiles,[42] and 24 million electric lightbulbs in the United States.[43]
- In 1902, the U.S. Navy equipped its vessels with radio-telephones.[44]
- In 1906, the first classical music performance was broadcast on radio.[45]
- In 1907, E.W. Scripps founded the United Press International (UPI) newswire service.[46]
- In 1908, Henry Ford began the mass manufacture of a car affordable for mass consumption, the Model T.[47]
- In 1920, KDKA (Pittsburgh) broadcasted the first regularly scheduled radio programming.[48]
- In 1921, the first franchise chain for the sale of mass-produced hamburgers—White Castle—opened in Chicago.[49]
- In 1922, the first radio advertisement was sold on the first commercial radio station in the United States, WEAF in New York.[50]
- In 1923, A.C. Neilsen was founded;[51] Young and Rubicam was founded;[52] Edward Bernays wrote the how-to book on manipulating the mass mind, *Crystallizing Public Opinion.*
- In 1924, there were more than 1,400 radio stations and 2.5 million radios in the United States;[53] in the first radio political campaign, Calvin Coolidge spent $120,000 on radio advertising, and won.[54]
- In 1926, General Electric and Westinghouse formed the

Radio Corporation of America (RCA), which initiated NBC—the National Broadcasting Company.[55]

- In 1928, Edward Bernays wrote his other how-to book on manipulating the mass mind, *Propaganda;* television was invented.[56]

- In 1929, Chrysler automobiles were the first to be equipped with radios.[57]

- In 1934, 60 percent of all American households had radio, representing 43 percent of all radios in the world.[58]

- In 1936, in a major propaganda coup for Adolf Hitler, the Berlin Olympics were broadcast live to the world by radio, and televised via closed circuit to the people of Berlin.[59]

- In 1939, television was introduced to the people of the United States at the New York World's Fair.

- In 1940, 80 percent of American homes had radio;[60] CBS demonstrated a color television system in New York.[61]

- In 1946, in the United States 6,500 television sets were sold,[62] and more than two hundred new "niche" magazines were launched.[63]

- In 1949, U.S. network television broadcasting began.[64]

- In 1950, A.C. Nielsen began tracking TV viewing,[65] and the credit card (Diner's Club) was introduced.[66]

- In 1951, there were 1.5 million television sets in the United States.[67]

- In 1954, there were television sets in 29 million American homes.[68]

- In 1960, there were television sets in 60 million American homes.[69]

- In 1962, the American Telstar satellite enabled the first live trans-Atlantic television transmission.[70]

Information, persuasion, and entertainment are the three functions of mass media that undergraduate communication majors learn in the typical "Communication 101" class. The technological innovations just listed fulfill all those functions. Information for the administration of government and industry; persuasive messages that create artificial needs in a marketplace; diversions from the emptiness of a material world bereft of a felt transcendence: these are what our electric media offer us.

The Death of Transcendence

We have, through the monopoly of space-biased knowledge created by the dominance of electric media in the last century-and-a-half, created an empire of capitalism, of consumption, of control, of the capitulation of conscience. Our electric media have "made it not only possible but imperative that the masses should live lives of comfort and leisure" because "the future of business lay in its ability to manufacture customers as well as products."[71]

A whole new epistemology was created, one which says simply that what is worth knowing is that which relates directly to me and the satisfaction of needs artificially created for me by an information industry linked directly and intimately to the mechanisms of production and distribution. "The American economy, having reached the point where its technology was capable of satisfying basic material needs, now relied on the creation of new consumer demands—on convincing people to buy goods of which they are unaware of any need until the 'need' is forcibly brought to their attention by the mass media."[72]

"Mass production demands the education of the masses," said Edward A. Filene, scion of the Boston department store empire, in 1919. "The masses must learn to behave like human beings in a mass production world."[73] What is important to know, in other words, is nothing more than what one needs to be a productive worker and a canny, efficient consumer of mass-produced commodities. Is this what accounts for "relevance" in the postmodern mind? Is it nothing more than, in a culture of constant change and uncertainty, the predictable, dependable familiarity of consumption? Has the comfortable immanence of *"that's just the way it is"* prosperity replaced the uncomfortable transcendence of *"I dream things that never were and ask 'why not?'"* idealism? Is this what has become of our moral imagination? Can it be that our only purpose in life is to stay alive in order to participate willfully and play our role, with all the false enthusiasm we can muster, in the unending cycle of highly efficient production, artificially created demand, and profligate consumption? "When techniques make possible the production of all kinds of things, if we give people their freedom, it will be used to produce things that are absurd, empty, and useless. A remarkable truth thus comes to light: Producing is regarded as good in itself. No matter what is produced!"[74]

But not only does electric culture exhibit a powerful space-bias and, consequently, focus our attention disproportionately on the immanent, transitory, and trivial at the expense of the transcendent. The space-biased media that constitute electric culture are themselves fundamentally inimical in form to transcendent experience, transcendent thought, and transcendent truth.

It is the time-biased media, Innis tells us, those media which, because of their physical form, store information much more efficiently and effectively than they transmit it, which are the milieu of transcendent knowledge. One does not unnecessarily, automatically, thoughtlessly dedicate unchanging, eternal truth to a medium that is ill-suited to store it. Rather, one is more likely to choose a medium that will store such information, unchanging, immutable, and true, forever. Similarly, we intuitively allow our information environment to dictate what we mean by the word *information* depending upon what sort of medium is predominant in our culture. In a profoundly space-biased environment, we will look at space-biased information and say, "I need to know that, and I need to know it now." We will look at time-biased information and say, "Are we still talking about that? It's not relevant!"

In an earlier chapter, I suggested that my description of orality could come as something of a shock to the contemporary reader. I suggested further that it might be difficult, here at the beginning of the third millennium, to imagine such a situation where people willingly submit and surrender themselves to their culture, thereby negating their own individualism. But have we not done the very same thing today?

In a space-biased culture such as the one in which we twenty-first-century, consumerist, postmodern, materialist, affluent, technologically developed Westerners live, we surrender our individualism by failing—or *refusing*—to ask certain questions. Questions of God, of transcendence, and of timeless, eternal truth—all sound quaint and naïve. Those who ask the questions appear silly, superstitious, credulous, and even reactionary.

Such are the occupational hazards of the harvester of transcendent truths laboring in the vineyards of immanent experience. One might be inclined to advise any who fit that description to "get used to it," because "that's just the way it is," and "you'll never change it, because you're just one person; just go about your business."

Can this be what human beings were meant to do? Can this be what human beings were meant to be?

Chapter Eight

The Metaphysics of Electric Culture

The only thing that matters is the state of our soul, and that's very hard because I'm in the entertainment business, which is completely based on illusion and physical things. Any success I have is a manifestation of God.

Madonna

Is Belief in God Good, Bad or Irrelevant?: A Professor and a Punk Rocker Discuss Science, Religion, Naturalism & Christianity

title of a recent book

Thank God I'm an atheist.

anonymous graffito

Electricity changes everything. "Civilization gives the barbarian or tribal man an eye for an ear and is now at odds with the electronic world."[1] The propositional mind normalized by print recedes into the distance in the face of a new orality. "The electric service environment of simultaneous information, as was first exemplified by the telegraph, provided a new social ground favorable to the rediscovery of oral culture."[2] "With telephone, radio, television, and various kinds of sound tape, electronic technology has brought us into the age of 'secondary orality.' This new orality has striking resemblances to the old in its participatory mystique, its fostering of a communal sense, its concentration on the present moment, and even its use of formulas."[3]

With electricity, a mimetic, secondary orality emerges; the entire world accelerates; the quantity of information available increases explosively; divergent points of view proliferate;

certainty becomes, at best, a pipe dream or, at worst, an arrogant attempt to impose intellectual control; we shift our attention slowly, perhaps, but ineluctably away from print and propositional structures of thought; and information loses its corporeal existence.

Explosive increases in information become difficult, if not impossible to manage and comprehend, without the storage and categorical abilities of print. Standardized form, a child of the literate mind, disappears. An epidemic chaos arises. Information overload burdens us. Boredom ensues. We detach ourselves from all but that information most relevant to us. We consume, because consumption is one of the few things that makes any sense. Nothing will ever be the same again.

Fixed point of view, another of the many children of the literate mind, begins to yield to a constant rotation of new and different points of view. Radical subjectivism trumps objectivism over and over. Truth becomes, to many, a naïve delusion and to many more a dangerous obsession. Cubism and other abstract art forms arise in the visual arts; absurdity and surrealism suffuse the literary works of Lewis Carroll, James Joyce, Franz Kafka, and T.S. Eliot.[4] Electricity changes everything.

The age of electricity sees the end of the human delusion of transcendent experience in the popular mind. Theology—and for that matter, philosophy, to the extent that it concerns itself with transcendent truths—becomes arcane, specialized knowledge. God becomes a fairy tale; intellectual curiosity becomes an affliction, not an advantage. From now on, we live in an age of pure material immanence, a permanent now, a simultaneous world where all things are before us and within our grasp. And our only role is to pursue them, acquire them, and consume them.

Does Transcendence Survive?

But if as a function of language—symbolic thought—an experience of the transcendent is inherent in the human experience (a notion suggested, but certainly not guaranteed, by the workings of presentational structures of thought), what is there to worry about? We will certainly not lose the idea of "God," but rather we will simply find new and different ways to experience and express it. That is a reassuring argument. But if particular media *do* engender particular metaphysical frameworks through which we shape and interpret reality, it is perhaps too optimistic. We may not have lost our sense of the transcendent, in some form or another, to be sure. But if we haven't, then, like so many things in our world of profligate material consumption, "it sure ain't what it used to be."

No: Transcendence is Dead

By the nineteenth century, the fissure between transcendence and immanence was only too apparent. Friedrich Nietzsche in *Der Froelische Wissenschaft* declared that "God is dead," and that "all of us are his murderers."[5] "Where has God gone? I shall tell you. We have killed him—you and I. We are all his murderers. . . . God is dead. That which was holiest and mightiest of all that the world has yet possessed has bled to death under our knives. There has never been a greater deed."[6]

The transcendent could no longer function as *telos* in human life, as a motivation for, and the end of, human thoughts, attitudes, and deeds. We no longer believe, Nietzsche was saying, in any transcendent realm beyond immanent, material reality. Objective reality, as a concept, as a universal experience, becomes confusing, unclear, and frightening; the immanent world is a subjective world subject to the vagaries of individual experience and interpretation.

In the early twentieth-century, Sigmund Freud labeled religion a "universal obsessional neurosis"[7]—one that could be remedied only through psychoanalysis—and he questioned "the future of an illusion" (God). "Ignorance is ignorance," he wrote:

> Where questions of religion are concerned, people are guilty of every possible sort of dishonesty and intellectual misdemeanor. . . . They give the name of "God" to some vague abstraction which they have created for themselves; having done so they can pose before the world as deists . . . notwithstanding that their God is now nothing more than an insubstantial shadow and no longer the mighty personality of religious doctrines. . . . To assess the truth-value of religious doctrines does not lie within the scope of the present enquiry. It is enough for us that we have recognized them as being, in their psychological nature, illusions."[8]

The German theologian Hans Kung considers the logical—and inevitable—implications of Freud's analysis: "If Freud's own analysis of religious ideas is correct—that is, that religion fulfills the 'oldest, strongest, most urgent wish of humanity' ('illusory,' to be sure, in his opinion) —and if 'the secret of their strength is the strength of these wishes,' then their repression must have consequences. And the consequences could be highly destructive."[9]

Maybe: Do We Still Believe in Transcendent Experiences?
So, have we repressed these wishes? While most Americans give lip service to God (90 percent believe in God according to a Harris poll),[10] we simultaneously seem to agree that we are living in a time of increasing nihilism, materialism, crime, violence, and degradation of moral values. Has all of this chaos come from the 4 percent of Americans who admit they don't believe in God? Or has the meaning of the phrase "I believe in God" changed?

Consider the following: While 90 percent of Americans say they believe in God, only 36 percent attend religious services once a month or more frequently.[11] This is a very strange measurement of belief. About one-third of Americans believe that astrology is scientific.[12] Half of all Americans believe in the reality of UFOs—unidentified flying objects presumably carrying extraterrestrials to earth.[13] And 80 percent of Americans believe that the government of the United States is hiding evidence of those extraterrestrials.[14] If 90 percent of us claim to believe in God even while many of the same embrace other, more preposterous (to me, at any rate) ideas, does this not signify a deep need—emotional, spiritual, neuro-biological—to connect or reconnect with some sort of transcendent reality?

Yet we seem unable to connect with real transcendence; we seem to be attracted to the artifacts of "material transcendence": space aliens, stars in alignment, forces of nature, magic, witchcraft, pseudoscience. We can see the postmodern mind at work: oppressive religious traditions (like Christianity, for instance) are replaced by more personal, more liberating belief systems like Wicca, Buddhism, Taoism, and neo-paganism. Science refolds itself into magic and religion as Western forms of medicine are replaced by holistic medicine, herbal medicine, and Eastern treatment methods such as acupuncture and the use of crystals. The Judeo-Christian-Islamic tradition of a spirit world—once the home of angels and demons—is expanded to include fairies, nymphs, and space aliens. One could be excused for seeing something like a return to monistic pantheism in the embrace of such "new age" beliefs.

If, as Walter Ong has suggested, electronic culture places us in a condition of secondary orality—similar to the primary orality of the past, but lacking the spontaneity and un-self-consciousness—then we are living in an age of self-conscious, mass-produced, and very immanent transcendence. We have developed a metaphysics of secondary orality.

We Consume, and Are Consumed

Much of the "new age" ideology cited above is attributable to the information explosion associated with electronic media. Consider *these* facts: 98.2 percent of all U.S. households have *at least* one television set,[15] and 82 percent have two or more.[16] The average U.S. home receives 118 television channels.[17] The average U.S. home has the television turned on for 8 hours and 14 minutes each day[18] (7 hours and 12 minutes in 2001). The average American watches television for four hours and 35 minutes during that same day.[19] American teens spend an estimated 3,518 hours a year—or nearly five months—consuming media: 65 days watching television, 41 days listening to the radio, and a week on the Internet.[20] The average American youth spends 900 hours per year in school.[21] More than one hundred television channels, twenty-four hours per day, a seemingly infinite number of Web sites of all types, all spewing information of questionable provenance without any authoritative reference will put pseudoscience on an equal footing with science. At the same time, traditional belief systems languish precisely *because* they are traditional. There is a peculiar and interesting postmodern paradox at work here: mass-produced, mass-mediated pseudo-transcendence trumps the social sharing of personal, subjective transcendent ideas.

The phatic communion that has historically characterized oral culture, and which survived in a residual form in literate culture, survives in an electric culture, if at all, in a perversely changed way. Our most common human interactions, our minute-by-minute connections to the real world are, more and more and to a greater and greater degree, mediated by some electronic device. How are we to make the human connections so peculiar to our species when the bulk of our experiences and interactions take place at great distances, distances of both space and time?

While the illusion of objectivity fostered by electronic media (particularly visual media) can make evolution and scientific creationism appear to be equivalent ideas (even to the point that we might refer to creationism as a theory), or even to arise from equivalent thought processes, it cannot bring back the abstract experience of transcendence to a sense-saturated world. Television, as the archetypal twentieth-century medium, is inimical to spirituality, and unfriendly to religion in any form. It cannot constitute a "sacred space," saturated as it is with the images of commercialism, of secularism, of profane events.[22] The televised ritual "flattens" it into "pure spectacle."[23]

Catherine Bell writes, "Instead of a theatrical ethos of a staged performance highlighting a single and exemplary moment in time, televised rites tend to create an emotional process that viewers feel compelled to see through to the end. . . . By transposing reality into a spectacle . . . the mass media perform the functional equivalent of what traditional myth and ritual used to do when they imbued reality with a sense of the sacred."[24] Transcendent reality cannot become television content without somehow becoming part of the immanent context—entertainment, enchantment, mimetic empathy—and losing its very transcendence.

Indeed, Jacques Ellul tells us, echoing Paul Tillich, that the experience of electronic communication in and of itself is something mystical and fascinating:

> People deify the technical device. It is universal and spectacular; it defies any attempts to master it; it performs what would usually be called miracles; to a large extent it is incomprehensible. It is thus God.[25] . . . Like God it is everywhere, it is watched everywhere, it speaks everywhere. It is a practical god in a human dimension, much less mysterious

than our older God. By way of advertising it has a revelation for humanity. Christianity should see that it has lost the two messianic messages that are at its heart, the one regarding the Savior, the other regarding the world to come.[26]

Electric Culture: Our Ultimate Concern

The very immanent experience of being connected electrically to the world—television watching is most definitely included—becomes, in Paul Tillich's words, our "ultimate concern,"[27] our most personal mode of psychic and spiritual connection to nature and to others, and replaces true transcendent experience. "Everything that makes religion an historic, profound, and sacred human activity," Neil Postman insists, "is stripped away: there is no ritual, no dogma, no tradition, no theology, and above all, no sense of spiritual transcendence."[28] This 1999 "people" column from *Salon* illustrates the point:

> Two words you may never have expected to hear uttered in succession: Claymation Jesus. But soon, you'll be able to see Claymation Jesus in action. Ralph Fiennes will give voice to the gummy version of the Christian savior—joined by Miranda Richardson as Mary Magdalene —in the Mel Gibson-funded, stop-action, 3-D and digitally animated, "The Miracle Worker," set to air on Easter Sunday Y2K. . . . "It sounds funny—a Claymation life of Jesus," ABC TV exec Jeff Bader recently admitted to the press. "But we screened it and it was spectacular. We were mesmerized by the look of it. It is so different." Now, now . . . you can just keep all those sacrilegious quips about clay feet to yourself.[29]

If immanence is defined as the quality of "operating within a domain of reality or realm of discourse," then Americans in the twenty-first century locate Jesus residing in roughly the same domain of reality or realm of discourse as Batman, Scooby-Doo, Hellboy, or Hannibal Lecter.

In ushering in our "information revolution," television and other electric media have helped to decontextualize experience—physical *and* metaphysical—and robbed us of living, breathing touchstones of transcendent reality. They have greatly undermined our understanding of the immanence of God and, most importantly, the experience of transcendence—*the love of God*—that we experience in our relationships with others. Hans Kung poses a question and presents us with a challenge:

> "The characteristic neurosis of our times is probably no longer repressed sexuality (what is there left to be repressed?) but rather the *lack of orientation, lack of norms, want of meaning, and emptiness* suffered by countless people. Isn't the whole critical development in modern times—right up to the problem of susceptibility, even among the young, to alcohol, drugs, and criminality on the one hand, and to practical nihilism, terroristic anarchism, and suicide on the other—isn't this development related to the severing of our ethical-religious conviction, norms, and communities?"[30]

Isn't the severing of our ethical-religious convictions, norms, and communities related to the disjoint we feel as a result of the ascendancy of immanence and the loss of transcendence? Isn't this severing related to the loss of a feeling of "bonded-ness"—*phatic communion*—with others? Have we perhaps robbed ourselves (deliberately or unwittingly) of the opportunities to rejoin the transcendent with the immanent, and have we also willingly used instruments of mass communication to participate in a sort of global "noncommunication?"

The etymological roots of the word communication (Latin *communicare,* "to share" or "to make common") suggest that there is no communication that is not mutual. The human creature is unique among all creatures in having evolved a capacity for sharing abstract concepts and ideas through the use of shared meaningful symbols. In a sense (beyond the merely truistic), human beings are the only creatures capable of human communication. We human beings are the only creatures who can actually engage in a process of sharing with others, through the use of meaningful symbols, our innermost thoughts, feelings, and beliefs.

But there is no law in the universe—transcendent or otherwise—that forces us to actually do so.

Chapter Nine

In the Dark:
The Survival of Ignorance
in an Age of Information

America is a hurricane, and the only people who do not hear
the sound are those fortunate if incredibly stupid and smug
White Protestants who live in the center, in the serene eye
of the big wind.

Norman Mailer

We shall have no better conditions in the future if we are
satisfied with all those which we have at present.

Thomas Edison

To each his sufferings: all are men,
Condemned alike to groan,
The tender for another's pain;
The unfeeling for his own.
Yet ah! why should they know their fate?
Since sorrow never comes too late,
And happiness too swiftly flies.
Thought would destroy their paradise.
No more; where ignorance is bliss,
'Tis folly to be wise.

Thomas Gray
from "Ode on a Distant Prospect of Eton College"

I reach now the moment in the unfolding exposition of my argument when I make an appeal to the reader, like Havelock's
Plato to his countrymen—but with opposite intent—to do what
so many in our culture say and believe is both idealistic and unproductive: resist the temptations of a new mode of culture, and
cling, as tightly as possible, to the old. But whereas Plato was
urging Athenians to banish the mimetic, mnemonic epistemology of oral poetry and adopt the new mindset of propositional lit-

eracy, a mindset that cleared the psychic clutter of memory and freed the mind for more creative, more critical modes of thought, I wish to urge you, the reader, to banish the new. For the new cultural mindset is much like what Plato warned the Athenians against in *The Republic*,—a mindset and epistemology based on a medium which provides us with a mimetic analog of the human lifeworld, and the old one I wish for us to preserve is the very literacy Plato wished to spread.

Literacy, as Plato foretold, brought us out of the darkness of oral superstition and ignorance. To lose literacy, at least as the dominant epistemology of our culture, might indeed mean our return to that darkness. I am hopeful that it is not too late. The signs, however, are not encouraging. The honeyed muse of electric culture is singing our song, and we've all stopped to listen— entranced—to her blissful tune.

Ignorance is . . . Bliss?

"What we don't know won't hurt us." This old saying begs a burning question about democracy, mass communication, and the free-market capitalist conception of information as a salable commodity. It is a question with both an ethical and a moral dimension, and it has been resisted in the postmodern era by the hyperempirical objectivity of academia which casts a cold eye upon values based on unchanging truths. I propose that, in a time of war, in the face of growing global anti-Americanism, it is time to face the following questions without flinching: Do objective reality and truth exist or not? And if so, do they matter? I propose further that it is the media ecologist who is in the best position to ask these questions and, if possible, to answer them.

Neil Postman, in the keynote address to the first Media Ecology Association convention, said that media ecology "exists to further our insights into how we stand as human beings, how we are doing morally in the journey we are taking."[1] He said further that he didn't "see any point in studying media unless one does so within a moral or ethical context. I am not alone in believing this. Some of the most important media scholars—Lewis Mumford and Jacques Ellul, for example—could scarcely write a word about technology without conveying a sense of either its humanistic or antihumanistic consequences."[2]

I agree with Postman, and I believe that academics who subjugate their values to the demands of empiricism—or the pragmatic demands of a global marketplace—are every bit as guilty of bias as those who abandon objectivity to suit their values. For the role of media ecology—the role of media studies generally and, in fact, the role of all education—ought to be, as Postman concludes (with tongue in cheek, perhaps, but, then again, perhaps not) "to further our insights into how we stand as human beings, how we are doing morally in the journey we are taking. There may be some of you who think of yourselves as media ecologists who disagree with what I have just said. If that is the case, you are wrong."[3]

And so it appears necessary (to me, at any rate) to question whether our Information Age—ushered in a century-and-a-half ago by the harnessing of electrical power—lives up to its label.

The Paradox of the Information Age

By this point in this book you have probably noticed while reading that there's no actual original theory in it. In the process of researching, thinking about, and writing this book I have discovered no new data, no new ideas. I have not been looking for any new ideas or new theory. This was not my task.

Rather, what I have tried to do, as a media ecologist and therefore as a communication generalist, is to synthesize various ideas, data, and theories that have been at our fingertips for years in order to shed light on why we believe the things we believe, and don't believe the things we don't. Based on this synthesis, my observations of the world we're living in today, a postmodern world, a world of promiscuous information delivered by profligate mass media, strongly suggest this thesis: With all the information at our disposal, with all the vast resources of mass communication technologies available to us, we are ignorant of our world—in both its immanent and transcendent dimensions—and happy and complacent in our ignorance. We are guilty of an ignorance easily dispelled—a supremely vincible ignorance. And if this is so, I believe we ought to be ashamed. Furthermore, those of us who consider ourselves to be people of spiritual or religious values must consider the possibility, raised at the beginning of this work, that our ignorance, unremediated, is an occasion of sin. When was the last time you heard someone make that kind of claim in our postmodern culture?

This is the bad news I referred to in the Introduction to this book. A popular television show of recent years used this tag line: "The truth is out there." At the risk of lending credibility to another trivial artifact of electric culture, I'm forced to say those words get one thing right: the truth is out there. The extent to which we don't see it, or won't see it, is a measure of our human imperfection. To live in a world where we don't have to see the ugly realities of life is to live in a world of fantasy. Similarly, to live in a world where we see truth only in so far as a certain idea might appeal to our own individual interests, appetites, biases, or subjective beliefs, is equally fantastic. Such a fantasy world may make us feel more secure, more comfortable, more personally affirmed, but it does nothing to help anyone else who happens to be stuck living in the real world. And, in truth, it's not helping us either.

But are we really ignorant? And are we really to blame?

In a mass culture such as ours, we depend on our electronic media of mass communication to be our eyes and ears our "window on the world." More than that (as both Marshall McLuhan and Pierre Teilhard de Chardin, each in his own way, pointed out), the network of transoceanic and transcontinental cables and the vast system of satellites floating miles above the earth, linking the world together through radio, television, telephone, and computers can function as a sort of global central nervous system, a "noosphere," a "liberation of consciousness,"[4] moving all of humanity closer and closer to becoming a single global organism. This would be, if it were true, entirely consistent with Enlightenment-era rationalism's concept of human progress and the perfectibility of the human person—through the agency of technological progress.

But, on the contrary, I see no such human progress occurring. I suggest that as a result of our technological "progress," our eyes and ears have closed rather than opened, and deliberately so, consciously so. I suggest that for all the millions and billions of dollars spent every year on expanding the communication potential of the human species, for all of the hundreds of channels of broadcast and cable programming, for the hundreds of thousands of radio outlets worldwide, for the amazing rise of cellular technology, for all that it appears that human beings are more closely linked to each other and to the world than ever before, we in fact learn and know very little of the world, and have used our communication technologies—deliberately—to cut ourselves off from it. We "walk in the darkness, and do not know where we are going because the darkness has blinded our eyes."[5] Worse still, we appear happy to remain in the dark.

How can this be? We live, after all, in the much-vaunted Information Age, an age where we seem, by all appearances, to be in tune with everything that is going on around us. We are "all connected"[6]—or so the old telephone company advertisement told us. We wake every morning to a litany of disasters, scandals, crimes, and controversies. We know what the weather will be like for the next five days in New York, Chicago, and Phoenix. We know whether our stocks have made or lost money in the last two hours and whether our favorite ball team won last night. We believe that we have more information at our fingertips than any people in the history of humankind have had at their disposal, and we're right. And we believe we have enough information to make responsible, ethical choices in our lives—and we're wrong.

The Ascendancy of Ignorance

So much of what we know today seems meaningless. It seems to matter so little to the realities of life. Robberies. Car chases. O.J. Simpson. Monica Lewinsky. Greta Van Sustern's facelift. Katie Couric and Jay Leno "trading places." Rosie O'Donnell's feud with Barbara Walters. Brittany Spears's missing undies. Lindsay Lohan's latest visit to a rehabilitation clinic. Michael Vick's conviction for killing dogs. Even stories about public health menaces like the West Nile virus, SARS, swine flu, and Monkey pox seem to be presented in such a way that we will be more fascinated by them than informed.

It's not that these stories are uninteresting or unimportant (to someone), but that point is not entirely indefensible, either. The problem is that we learn from these stories nothing of what is going on in the world, issues and events which have a direct bearing on our lives and the lives of people elsewhere, a fact that often becomes apparent only after the fact, often when it is too late to take remedial action.

Consequently, when we are then attacked brutally and mercilessly for no apparent reason; when innocent Americans are killed for no apparent reason; when violence rears its grotesque head for no apparent reason, we are understandably shocked and ask, "Why do they hate us?" In our ignorance of the world, there seems no reasonable explanation for such events other than pure evil—and no responsible way to fight against them other than war.

But perhaps we've missed something. Perhaps, as in Aristotle's example of the person acting in ignorance, we are ignorant of the particulars of a situation even as we have knowledge of the universal values or principles at play. Plato says this type of ignorance attenuates the blame we might bear for any bad consequences of our actions. But do we have to be ignorant? If our ignorance is vincible—easily dispelled through due diligence—is Aristotle's quick dismissal of blame at all appropriate?

Ignorance is Not the Inevitable Result of Electric Culture
Henry Perkinson, in *Getting Better: Television and Moral Progress*, illustrates the many ways in which television acts as a window on the world, revealing to us the good, the bad, and the ugly of the human experience. When we watch televised violence we recoil from it, because that is in our nature. When we see injustice portrayed on television we are outraged and want to see justice prevail. Television portrays the world as it really is, and we can use this external eye to objectively evaluate the state of the world and to improve it.[7]

The civil rights movement of the 1950s and 1960s was helped by the emergence of television. Images of men, women, and children in peaceful protest being beaten with truncheons, attacked with dogs, and swept off their feet and blasted with fire hoses, brought home to America the injustices of inequality. The powerful, emotional images entering our homes night after night sparked our sympathy for Americans of African descent and changed our minds about accepting the status quo of Jim Crow segregation.

We "saw the light."

The nightly broadcast of the Vietnam War in the 1960s and 1970s was probably largely responsible for the collapse of American popular support for the war. Images of U.S. Marines lighting the thatched roofs of a village with lighters, of General Nguyễn Ngọc Loan blowing the brains out of a Viet Cong spy on a Saigon street, of napalm strikes in which South Vietnamese civilians—including children—were mistaken for North Vietnamese troops, and here at home the death of four American college students at Kent State University in Ohio, took a collective toll on the American conscience, undermining public support for what many were beginning to see as a misguided—if not illegal—war.

Again, we "saw the light."

Yet Ignorance Reigns

But today, far from being a window on the world, television seems to be—in American culture at least—a mirror. But does the mirror reflect our true image or, like the wicked stepmother's, does it show us only an image of ourselves that we wish to see?

The narcissistic power of material consumption seems to accompany an urge to attend more closely to ourselves than to the outside world. Our mass media outlets are very good at selling things to us. Advertising is a $330 billion industry in the United States alone[8]—up from $200 billion in 1999. But advertisers are only good at selling us, it seems, the things and ideas that we want to buy. Our news tends to be sensational and entertaining, and we see little of the real world. Neil Postman, in his classic critique of television culture *Amusing Ourselves to Death*, calls Americans "the best entertained and quite likely the least well-informed people in the Western world."[9] Viewers, according to Postman, are fed an endless diet of disinformation: "misplaced, irrelevant, fragmented or superficial information—information that creates the illusion of knowing something but which in fact leads one away from knowing."[10]

Television news, according to Postman, presents us "not only with fragmented news, but news without context, without consequences, without value, and therefore without essential seriousness; that is to say, news as pure entertainment."[11] Much of this is the result of the deregulation of the television industry under the Communications Act of 1984 and the emasculation of the FCC under (Ronald Reagan appointee) Mark Fowler, a man who believed that television had no greater responsibility to the public than any other home appliance, because TV was just "a toaster with pictures."[12]

The Reagan Legacy: Information as Salable Commodity
In a paradigm-shifting 1982 article, Fowler redefined the idea of public service within the context of market forces, gave us a clear vision of the role of television in a competitive global society, and a preview of what a deregulated media environment would look like: "The perception of broadcasters as community trustees should be replaced by a view of broadcasters as marketplace participants. . . . Instead of defining public demand . . . the commission should rely on the broadcasters' ability to determine the wants of their audience through the normal mechanisms of the marketplace. The public's interest, then, defines the public interest."[13]

Thanks to the Communications Act of 1984 (and subsequent acts) the present economic structure of television—dependent on advertising revenues for operation, owned by large and wealthy corporations (many of them multinational or even foreign-owned), competing for viewers in an ever-tightening market, unburdened by the requirement to operate in the public interest—ensures that we will consume programming that supports, rather than challenges, the status quo.[14]

Gone are the days of Fred Friendly, Edward R. Murrow, and "Harvest of Shame." The documentary news units of the three major networks before deregulation—ABC, CBS, and NBC— are gone for nearly two decades now. One of my first assignments as a young videotape editor for NBC News was working on one of their last news documentaries, a profile of Mehmet Ali Agca called "The Man Who Shot the Pope." That was in 1982. Instead, documentary filmmaking has gone independent, and has largely shifted to cable outlets.

Why aren't we angry about that? Why aren't we angry about the diminution of meaningful information and meaningful discourse in our lives? Postman asks us, "What if there are no cries of anguish to be heard? Who is prepared to take arms against a sea of amusements? To whom do we complain, and when, and in what tone of voice, when serious discourse dissolves into giggles? What is the antidote to a culture's being drained by laughter?"[15]

Jacques Ellul, French sociologist, theologian, and media theorist, raises the stakes of the discussion even higher, elevating it to a moral plane. He sees the role of modern media of mass communication as distracting us from the essential evil of our technological society, a society that strips us of our humanity, that separates person from person, that isolates us from our brothers and sisters and from ourselves. Furthermore, by delivering to us enormous quantities of "facts," mass media encourage us to believe, through a sort of intellectual sleight of hand, that we know reality. But we don't; nor do we want to.

Ellul writes, "In the sphere of the intellectual life, the major fact of our day is a sort of refusal, unconscious but widespread, to become aware of reality. Man does not want to see himself in the real situation which the world constitutes for him. . . . The dramatic characteristic of this epoch, in this sphere, is that man no longer grasps anything but shadows. He believes in these shadows, he lives in them, and dies for them. Reality disappears, the reality of man for himself, and the reality of the facts which surround him."[16] What, then, is the nature of these shadows? And why do they so obscure our view of reality?

The Structure of Electric Culture

Television is a medium of pictures and sounds, of lights and colors and music and movement. It structures information presentationally as opposed to the propositional structure of speech and writing.[17] That is to say that it recreates or presents to us a mimetic reality, an analog of the human lifeworld. Its content is far more concrete and sensorally understandable than the abstracted experience of, say, reading a book.

Unlike speech or writing, it cannot be stopped or questioned, pored over or studied. It cannot be parsed, criticized grammatically, or put to a test of linear logic. It simply is what it appears to be, nothing more and nothing less. Therefore, critical thought about the televised image is difficult. On an emotional level, we might either like it or hate it. That is the nature of presentationally structured information and of presentational structures of thought. But when we see something, we tend to believe it. In fact, as noted earlier, "seeing is believing" is a fairly accurate principle to explain our culture.

A logical corollary to this principle, however, is that not seeing is not believing. We tend not to believe in those things with which we don't come into contact. Immanence is the milieu of television; transcendence is not. To be sure, Americans give lip service to belief in transcendent ideas, such as God (for instance), but how much of this is testament to the ability of ideas (in the shallowest sense of the word) to survive in the presence of a residue of orality?

Is it not fair, however, to question the depth of our personal as well as cultural commitment to those ideas? Let's consider, once again, these statistics: 90 percent of Americans say they believe in God,[18] yet only 36 percent attend religious services once a month or more often.[19] Lest we feel too comforted still by that 90-percent figure, let's remember that 31 percent of Americans believe that astrology is real (43 percent of those between the ages of 25 and 29),[20] 56 percent believe in the reality of UFOs,[21] and—in at least one poll reported on the Internet—80 percent believe that the U.S. government is hiding evidence of extraterrestrials.[22]

Television, by focusing our attention so powerfully on our senses, has cut us off from that piece of our psyche[23] that allows us to comprehend the incomprehensible and has done tremendous damage to our collective experience of transcendence. Television is so profoundly visual that it has a difficult time dealing with any subject matter that is not itself inherently visual.[24] The sensual, material immanence of our image of reality destroys transcendence. "The Light shines in the darkness, and the darkness did not comprehend it."[25]

So what is it, on balance, that we do believe in? We believe in those things that are immanent to us in our world. In the world that television creates for us, those things seem to be crime, show business, and the consumption of material goods.

The Culture of Immanence

Our awareness of crime (our belief in it, if you will) seems to exist disproportionately to its commission. Throughout the 1990s, violent crime rates dropped 6 percent from a decade earlier, and homicides dropped 13 percent. Yet, in a series of ABC News/*Washington Post* polls during the same period, six times more Americans (30 percent) named crime as America's biggest problem in 1993 than did in 1992.[26] In fact, according to a 1997 study published by the Center for Media and Public Affairs, during the 1990s the reporting of crime eclipsed the reporting of all other stories, totaling some 14,289 stories, more reports than were aired on the war in Bosnia, the 1992 and 1996 presidential campaigns, the plight of post-Soviet Russia, and the Israeli-Palestinian conflict combined.[27]

The number of stories dedicated to show business has risen dramatically, too, since the early 1990s. More entertainment stories (868) were aired between 1992 and 1997 than were aired on such important topics as the environment (561) and education (464).[28]

And while stories on crime, disasters, and war dominate our information environment, accounting for some 40 percent of all news coverage,[29] precious little reporting on international political and economic stories is done—stories that are not disconnected from our increasingly global economic system. Such reporting might help us to understand the relationships between peoples and nations that cause wars, and could motivate us to take political action to intervene diplomatically or economically before wars break out. But in the *"Tower of Babble"* that we call the Information Age, a critical and objective view of the world and our place within it is replaced by a chaotic, discordant onslaught of meaningless "facts."

The Need for Faith in Objectivity

Even though wars are big on television, not all wars infiltrate our consciousness. Where the United States or its (economic?) allies or (economic?) interests are not involved, war does not seem to exist for us. The Conflict Data Project of Department of Peace and Conflict Research at Uppsala University in Sweden, along with the Conditions of War and Peace Programme at the

International Peace Research Institute, Oslo, report that on average nine minor armed conflicts (where the number of deaths does not exceed one thousand during the course of the conflict), twelve intermediate armed conflicts (where the number of deaths exceeds one thousand, but is fewer than that in any given year), and thirteen wars (with more than a thousand deaths a year) have been going on somewhere in the world since 1946.[30]

In the year 2000, according to the World Health Organization, war took the lives of 168,000 Africans, 65,000 Asians, 39,000 Middle-Easterners, 37,000 Europeans, and 2,000 Central and South Americans.[31] At the same time, American arms manufacturers were making it possible for war to be the booming business that it is. Forty-three of the top one hundred arms-producing companies in the world, with sales totaling well over one-half trillion dollars ($598,960,000,000.00) in 2006, are American companies. Nearly $217 billion ($216,730,000,000.00) of that amount comes from the American manufacture and sale of weapons (up from $93 billion in 1999), more than one-third of the profit from all sales (including consumer goods) of the other sixty companies combined (the equivalent of $642 billion, comprising the sales of corporations from Italy, $102 billion; France, $91.6 billion; Germany, $66 billion; Britain, $65 billion; a western European consortium of companies, $53.6 billion; all other countries, including Japan, Sweden, Russia, Israel, India, Singapore, Canada, Spain, South Korea, Switzerland, Australia, the Netherlands, Finland, $264 billion).[32] Is this not something Americans should know about?

Meanwhile, those in the less technologically developed world who are not dying in warfare are likely to be dying of disease or starvation. While the life expectancy of the average American was about 77 years in 2002 (up from 75 years in 2001), it was 66 for the Indonesian, 64 for the Russian, 42 for the Afghan (down from 45 years in 2001—has "liberation" helped?), 40 for the Zambian, and 38 for the Zimbabwean.[33] While an American baby has a 99.4 percent chance of survival after birth, the infant mortality rate is 2 percent for the Russian, 10 percent for the Ethiopian, almost 15 percent for the Afghan, and nearly 20 percent for the Angolan.[34]

And while much of the developing world believes that we care little for their welfare, many more question our motivations even less kindly. They believe we are more interested in exploiting their natural resources for our benefit and exploiting their people for their cheap labor.

Among the violations of the fair-labor conventions of the International Labor Organization between 1996 and 2000, were many committed on behalf of American companies. Here are some examples:

• Factories in the Northern Mariana Islands (a U.S. commonwealth) that produce clothing for Abercrombie & Fitch, Cutter & Buck, Donna Karan, the GAP, J. Crew, Levi Strauss, Liz Claiborne, Nordstrom, Ralph Lauren Polo, Target, Dress Barn, and Tommy Hilfiger demand contracts of their workers which waive basic human rights, including the right to join a union; demand twelve-hour workdays seven days a week; and subject workers to "lockdowns" in the factory.

• Factories in China producing clothing and shoes for Adidas, Disney, Fila, Nike, Ralph Lauren, and Reebok employ forced labor in prison camps; demand their employees work 12–16 hours a day, seven days a week; employ child labor; and demand forced overtime; (Chinese workers for Nestle have been subjected to electric shock to maintain productivity.)

• Factories in Indonesia manufacturing clothing and shoes for Adidas, the GAP, and Nike subject workers to forced overtime at a poverty wage.

• Factories in El Salvador producing clothing and shoes for

Adidas, Ann Taylor, the GAP, Liz Claiborne, and Nike pay their female employees about $30 a week for a sixty- to eighty-hour week; subject their female workers to forced pregnancy tests; fire their female workers if they become pregnant; and force some employees to work overtime without pay, up to eleven hours a day.

• Factories in Haiti producing clothing and toys for the Walt Disney company pay their workers an average of $2.40 per day, and charge them for transportation ($.66 per day), breakfast (cornmeal and fruit juice for $.53 per day), and lunch (rice and beans for $.66 per day).

• Factories in Russia producing clothing for the GAP pay their employees $0.11 per hour.[35]

If terrorism is evil—and it is—we are looking at terror's recruiting grounds.

But, apparently, not one of these events, conditions, or stories qualifies as news! We are kept in the dark about such ugly, painful realities, but delivered "facts" on a daily basis about O.J., "Monica-gate," Britney's shaved head, Lindsay's addictions, and Rosie's tantrums. "What we don't know can't hurt us." But if we are, on the whole, ignorant of the brutal realities of the world, we know on another level that there is suffering out there. We know there is poverty. We know there is exploitation. We know it. And we ignore it.

In the 1980s, Lester C. Thurow argued that true economic and social equality demanded a fundamental restructuring of the economy. The "zero-sum" concept reflects a growing global ecological understanding that we cannot have great wealth as a nation without taking it from someone else. The game of capitalism, as currently played, is a zero-sum game. Corporations amass wealth at the expense of other corporations. National economies flourish at the expense of other national economies.

Productivity—and profit—comes at the expense of workers. Competition rather than cooperation is at the center of the zero-sum conception of free-market capitalism as we currently play the game. Competition, however, does not have to be at the center of capitalism.

It might be a disturbing thesis to Americans in a post-communist world, a world of global, unregulated, laissez-faire, free-market capitalism triumphant, but it is possible that the only solution to economic inequality, environmental damage, and political conflict is the active management of national economies and the modest redistribution of income. That is not a suggestion I choose to put forward in this book. I am, frankly, not sure we're ready as a nation to accept the reality (admittedly, a subjective one) of this idea. In fact, I rather doubt it. Nevertheless, I do think it's time we found the courage to think and talk about it, rather than keeping the idea and its discussion locked in the dark.

To at least a certain extent, Adam Smith was fooling himself, and we know it. We've known it (at least) since the time of Marx. Communism is dead, and rightly so, for communism denied the essential freedom, dignity, and intelligence of the human person. But an economic system without strict regulation also denies the essential imperfection of the human person. Greed exists. Envy exists. Hatred exists. Egoistic self-centeredness exists. Not just in the hearts and minds of our "enemies," but in ours as well. They are part of our reality, whether we want to acknowledge their existence or not.

I think I probably need, at this point, to assert as strongly as possible my faith in three great American myths or, in postmodernist terms, metanarratives: the myth of American goodness (as inherent in our Americanism), the myth of American generosity, and the myth of capitalism (as solution to problems of social injustice). These myths work themselves through our conscious rational minds in a manner something like this: "We're good people and a good nation. We give so much to other nations. Our wealth and our goodness allow us to be generous. We are unusually generous people. Everyone wants to be like us. Everyone wants to come to America."

Joseph Campbell reminds us that myths are not fables or fairy tales. They are not untrue.[36] Indeed, a story cannot become a myth if it doesn't have the ring of truth to it. Myths are explanatory stories—stories that tell us something about ourselves. So the reader would be wrong to infer an assertion here that Americans are not good and generous, or that capitalism itself could not adequately address problems of social injustice anywhere in the world.

These basic American myths are true. But, bowing momentarily to postmodern thought, it seems evident that these myths or metanarratives are true only until we come to believe in them to such an extent that we can no longer see that there are exceptions to them all around us. And the so-called Information Age has made it very easy for us to do just that. In a sense, we wash our hands of the reality of life outside the United States by focusing on things—truths?—in the abstract. We dismiss any sense of a present global responsibility by reminding ourselves of what we have done and have been in the past.

We tend to neglect—no, to ignore with impunity—much of the poverty, disease, deprivation, and death of the third world (objectively real, whether we're aware of it all or not) while at the same time we expect them to provide the raw materials and fuel that run our economy and give us the wealth we enjoy on a daily basis—a prosperity that enables us to ignore them entirely! This cynicism is typical of postmodern culture, where we believe in nothing, yet mouth empty shibboleths; a culture that gives (very vocal and emphatic) lip service to the idea of "the sanctity of life"—an idea that clearly means "the sanctity of my life."

And then, when cold hard reality—as it eventually always does—administers harsh shock therapy, we have the audacity as a nation to ask, "Why do they hate us?" Could it not be because, by all outward appearances, we hate them? Well, we don't hate them. Nor, for that matter, do we love them, or even care about them. We hardly know they exist. And that, I suggest, is the real problem.

The Moment When Everything Was Supposed to Change

On September 12, 2001, I told all my students in all my classes that, "from this moment forward, apathy is no longer permissible." Apathy and ignorance about the rest of the world was part of the pre-9/11 mentality. It would no longer do. I felt certain that these brutal attacks, as horrible as they were, would bring about a transformation, profound and necessary, that could only improve us, make us stronger, help us to see the suffering of others with greater empathy.

For a while, it seemed that might be the case. I was reminded of William Butler Yeats's great poem, "Easter 1916," about the transformative power of suffering and the belief in and commitment to an ideal. In it, the Nobel Prize winner (Literature, 1923) speaks of normal people, unassuming people, everyday people, the Irish people of the early part of the twentieth century, people who were so inured to colonial subjugation that it seemed normal to them; the very same people about whom Eamon De Valera, following the failed uprising, had said, "Oh, if only you had come out with your knives and forks,"[37] the Irish nation would have had its great victory. The Irish people were apathetic and generally comfortable with their relative prosperity; moreover, they were worldly enough to know the power of the British Empire and its armed forces. Anticipating postmodern Americans' complacency and presumed impotence, the Irish people looked upon foreign rule stoically: "That's just the way it is." "It will never change." "I'm just one person. What can I do?"

Yeats captures something of their character and of the awesome transformation they underwent in the days following the uprising:

> I have met them at close of day
> Coming with vivid faces
> From counter or desk among grey
> Eighteenth-century houses.
> I have passed with a nod of the head
> Or polite, meaningless words,
> Or have lingered a while and said
> Polite, meaningless words,
> And thought before I had done
> Of a mocking tale or a gibe
> To please a companion
> Around the fire at the club,
> Being certain that they and I
> But lived where motley is worn:
> All changed, changed utterly:
> A terrible beauty is born.[38]

It took the awesome tragedy of the Easter Uprising, and especially the executions that followed, to galvanize the Irish people to stand up against illegitimate authority. The American people were ready on September 12, 2001, I believe, to look squarely in the face of global poverty and suffering and to resolve to do something about it. For one brief, grievously painful moment we all believed in something once again, something bigger than our own vain desires. We felt the world's pain, and we wanted to make it better. This helps to explain our collective willingness to invade a country about which we knew very little objectively, but about which we believed we had a lot of damning intelligence—all of which turned out to be false.

The United States of America has been suffering a crisis of

leadership predicated upon an equally disturbing crisis of imagination. This crisis of leadership is not partisan; it affects both Republicans and Democrats. We have sacrificed all that is noble in our history—the transcendent Enlightenment values upon which we were founded, our respect for education, our generosity of spirit toward immigrants—to a global capitalist bottom line. I am reminded of another Yeats poem, "September 1913," in which he described the bourgeois malaise that would only be broken by catastrophe:

> What need you, being come to sense,
> But fumble in the greasy till
> And add the halfpence to the pence
> And prayer to shivering prayer, until
> You have dried the marrow from the bone?
> For men were born to pray and save:
> Romantic Ireland's dead and gone,
> It's with O'Leary in the grave.[39]

Idealistic America is dead and gone, it's in the grave with Franklin Delano Roosevelt, Jack and Bobby Kennedy, and the Rev. Dr. Martin Luther King, Jr. But if idealistic America is dead and gone, it is *we* who have killed it and buried it, or at the very least, looked on in presumed impotence, washing our hands of any complicity in its death.

The Immortality of Transcendence

In April of 2002, the former Prime Minister of Pakistan Benazir Bhutto, speaking at the Joseph F. Maher Leadership Forum at Molloy College, called the United States "a beacon of democracy in a world of tyranny." Bhutto's visit was, it should be noted, part of a world public relations tour to garner global support for her Pakistan People's Party against the dictatorial rule of General Pervez Musharraf (in the course of my writing this book, Ms. Bhutto was assassinated following her return to her homeland to contest Musharraf's dictatorial rule; Musharraf's government barred an objective, international forensics investigation into the murder; elements of the Taliban and al-Qaeda have found a safe haven in Pakistan's western frontiers, and Musharraf, until finally forced from office, remained an American "ally"—a very postmodern sort of ally to be sure). But despite its political motivation, I want to believe that her assertion was sincere, and I want to believe it is true.

By some measurements, it is unquestionably true. The transcendent ideas upon which our nation was founded—liberty, equality, freedom of expression, freedom of the press—make it true, at least in principle. But we can't ignore these ideas and pretend, if they are threatened, that they'll just go on without our protection. We must be awake to the world and awake to ourselves to make certain that the beacon of democracy never dims. We must not allow the light of truth to be extinguished.

But what are we to do? If, as I have suggested, our ignorance is of the vincible variety and can be remediated, where do we go to find the information we need to make the best ethical choices? Even the late pontiff, His Holiness Pope John Paul II, told us that we are working at a distinct disadvantage. Speaking a few years back to the Pontifical Council for Culture at the Vatican, he echoed Jacques Ellul when he spoke of a disjoint between the Church and the contemporary world. The transmission of truth, he said, is difficult "mainly because our contemporaries are immersed in cultural contexts that are often alien to an inner spiritual dimension, in situations in which a materialist outlook prevails. One cannot escape the fact that, more than in any other historical period, there is a breakdown in the process of handing on moral and religious values between generations."[40]

Former Czech President Vaclav Havel, speaking at Independence Hall in Philadelphia on July 4, 1994, told Americans:

Today we find ourselves in a paradoxical situation. We enjoy all the achievements of modern civilization that have made our physical existence on this earth easier in so many important ways. Yet we do not know exactly what to do with ourselves, where to turn. The world of our experiences seems chaotic, disconnected, confusing. There appear to be no integrating forces, no unified meaning, no true inner understanding of phenomena in our experience of the world. Experts can explain anything in the objective world to us, yet we understand our own lives less and less. In short, we live in the postmodern world, where everything is possible and almost nothing is certain.[41]

Real Human Communication

In order to try to address these difficulties, I would at this point like to go out on a limb and stray a bit from the media ecological realm and into an area where I claim no real authority but have some ideas: theology. I can assure you that I do this with more than a little trepidation, yet I am encouraged by the advice of Dr. Monika Hellwig who, in the February 15, 2000 edition of *The Observer*, the student newspaper of the University of Notre Dame and St. Mary's College, urged Catholic intellectuals to cross disciplines in their studies and work. The goal of education, she noted, ought to be a "lifetime engagement in search of the reign of God,"[42] and empowerment to engage the world is more likely within a broader, multi-disciplinary perspective. In that spirit I would like to offer to you what I call a "trinitarian" conception of communication.

The Trinitarian conception of Deity sees three persons in one God: the Father, the Son, and the Holy Spirit. God the Father is creator of "all that is seen and unseen," who "so loved the world that he gave His only begotten Son";[43] God the Son is the *Logos*, the Word Incarnate, fully human and fully divine; and God the Holy Spirit is the loving relationship between Creator and all creation.

A trinitarian conception of communication would need to recreate or resemble this model. Unlike the traditional and well-known model of communication which includes a sender, a receiver, a message, and a medium, a trinitarian conception of communication would situate in dynamic relationship a creator (the sender of the message), the message itself (a creation of the sender, and necessarily being of the same essence—that is, a truthful expression of the sender), a receiver, and a context: a sincere and genuine love and concern on the part of the creator/sender for his/her audience.

At the risk of sounding arrogant, I'd like to suggest that real human communication occurs *only* when such sincere and genuine love and concern exist between participants in the communication act, whether interpersonal, group, or mass communication. Anything else may be "communication" in a lesser form—the maintenance of control or orientation, for example, or the initiation of a stimulus/response chain that helps us fulfill our needs (for even animals can communicate for those purposes); but these other forms should not be thought of as real human communication. Only love yields real human communication.

I see this trinitarian conception of communication reflected in many social institutions—in marriage and in the family, for instance. I see it in friendship. I see it in the social institutions of religion and education. You probably see or have seen, as I have, powerful evidence of it in the schools where you teach or study or have studied in the past.

But also, from time to time, I see it absent from all these institutions; I see some motivation other than mutual care and concern—some motivation other than love—taking over. At such times, I believe, we are in jeopardy; our very humanity, perhaps, is in jeopardy.

Lack of faith in the abstract concept of truth in our

communication yields inaccuracy and incompleteness and results in chaos. Subjective self-interest in communication yields deliberate distraction from the truth and results in manipulation. Egoistic self-interest yields half truths and lies and falsehood and results in totalitarian control. Emphasis on efficiency in communication within and throughout an institution, rather than on shared meaning among the individuals who constitute it, yields rigid formalism and results in cynicism, demoralization, and hopelessness. Only a shared context of mutual respect, care, and concern for the other results in true human communication. And I further suggest to you that when our societal systems of mass communication assume profit rather than the common good as their motivation, there is no love, and there is no real human communication.

Marshall McLuhan—the legendary media philosopher and prophet of the age of electronic communication who is now enjoying something of a renaissance in the academic circles of communication study—is probably best remembered for his intriguing and somewhat mysterious aphorism, "The medium is the message." McLuhan scholars still argue over the meaning of this phrase.

Whatever McLuhan's specific intentions, I like to think that this aphorism can be applied to the trinitarian conception of communication. The medium (Christ) *is* the message (the *Logos:* the Word, truth, the divine wisdom or meaning of God). Furthermore, this truth or meaning of God is made clear in the message of Christ, God's self-communication with his creation: the loving act of creation. Life itself. Love itself. In Christ, medium and message come together and are one, creating a cosmic ecology of love, if only we have the eyes to see, the ears to hear, and the good will to believe in ourselves and in others. This is not virtual reality. This is *virtuous* reality.

At the same time that McLuhan was teaching and writing at St. Michael's College at the University of Toronto, a great American was teaching the world about communication from within a trinitarian framework. He was trying to get Americans to step out of the darkness of racial bigotry and comfortable complacency and into the light of love. The Rev. Dr. Martin Luther King, Jr., in a sermon delivered at the National Cathedral in Washington, D.C. in 1968, posed a warning and a challenge to us:

> Through our scientific and technological genius, we have made of this world a neighborhood, and yet we have not had the ethical commitment to make of it a brotherhood. But somehow, and in some way, we have got to do this. We must all learn to live together as brothers or we will all perish together as fools. . . . And whatever affects one directly, affects all indirectly. For some strange reason I can never be what I ought to be until you are what you ought to be. And you can never be what you ought to be until I am what I ought to be. This is the way God's universe is made; this is the way it is structured. . . . John Donne caught it years ago and placed it in graphic terms: "No man is an island entire of itself. Every man is a piece of the continent, a part of the main. . . . Any man's death diminishes me because I am involved in mankind; therefore never send to know for whom the bell tolls; it tolls for thee." . . . We are challenged to rid our nation and the world of poverty.[44]

Or, I might add, *not* to do so. We are radically free and intelligent creatures, and the choice is entirely ours. What are our commitments? What are our values? What do we believe in?

If we do eventually choose to take up that challenge, however, we must—in the first place—be aware of the world, be engaged in it, be more open to the reality of the event than we are to its "instant replay." We must turn away from the honeyed muse of electric culture, as Plato urged the Athenians to do from their mimetic epistemology. We must somehow learn to turn off the computer, turn off the Playstation, turn off the CD player, the iPod, the DVD player, the VCR; as painful as it may be, we must learn to turn off the television. Turn off that eerie blue glow that each evening threatens to envelop our homes in darkness. Turn off the allure of material consumption, the temptations of physical comfort, the distractions of the technological society, and turn on the light in our hearts and our minds.

At the same time, we must demand the truth from those in positions of authority in our social institutions. We must never sit by complacently or deferentially when legitimate authority practices disinformation, whether that takes the form of disseminating false evidence to justify war, hiding sexual abuse by priests, or ignoring and obfuscating the likely consequences of the global expansion of manufacturing and trade.

By using the gifts God gave us—our intelligence, our capacity for language, our propositional structures of thought, our reason—and by having faith in the power of the word and the goodwill of others to communicate with us, we can change the ways we relate to the world, and we can change the world. We can lift up poorer people and nations, and make a safer world. For where there is real human communication—where there is love—there can be no terror.

The challenge is really a choice, and in reality our only choice. We must rein in our appetite for the exteriorization of experience so characteristic of electric, mimetic, presentationally structured information (our secondary orality), and rediscover an interior life of contemplation through propositionally structured information—the stuff of books, thoughts, poems, and prayers. We must rebuild and renew our relationships with one another and with the real world of which we are only a small but still powerful part. We must rediscover the transcendent that is a part of each of us. We must begin to reclaim our psychic connections to reality—most importantly, to the value, the sacredness, and the reality of others, even when they are not immanent to us. Or we must choose to remain, as we are now, in the dark.

The truth is out there. Will we choose to see it?

An Explanation of the Media Ecological Principles[1]

Edward T. Hall observes in *The Silent Language* that the study of human communication is inextricably linked to the study of culture, and the study of culture to communication.

For the better part of this century, a growing number of researchers and theorists in different fields have reinforced the view that communication is profoundly implicated in all processes of culture. Anthropologists (Hall, Malinowski), historians (White, Eisenstein), psychologists (Watzlawick, Beavins-Bavelas, Jackson), linguists (Goody), economists (Innis), and others have created a growing body of literature which has become the core curriculum for a new field of study: media ecology.

Media ecology is essentially the study of information environments. A central concern of media ecology is to examine how the structure of a medium effects the information that it conveys, and how the structure of such information shapes our thought processes. As such, media ecology can be seen as a branch of philosophy, a philosophy of communication, whose concern is to investigate the epistemologies created and fostered by different media.

How does the structure of a medium effect the information that it conveys, and how can the structure of information shape our thought processes? This is a difficult question and a good starting point, as there are many ways these things occur, generally invisible to us and, so, generally below the level of consciousness. In an effort to make the invisible visible, media ecologists have identified a set of principles, a system of structural

229

analysis, to help us to step out of the picture of which we are a part and see it more objectively. These principles detail characteristics of all media and allow us to see how and why one medium affects us differently than another. And this is, of course, the underlying (and usually unspoken) rationale for the study of communication generally and mass communication specifically: all media are not alike. It is not necessary to make a qualitative judgment (to say, for example, "books are better than television"), although it certainly doesn't impede one's freedom to do so if he or she wishes. The point is, simply, that different media treat information (and us) differently.

Let us then take a look at some of the characteristics of media by which we can judge these differences.

First, media differ in their form. Form can be divided into two areas of investigation: symbolic form and physical form. Symbolic form refers to the characteristics of the code in which a medium conveys information (symbols, signs, gestures, icons, and so on) and the structures in which the information is conveyed (propositional or presentational). Physical form refers to the characteristics of the technology that conveys the code, and the physical requirements for encoding, transmitting, storing, retrieving, and decoding information.

The symbolic form of the book is very different from the symbolic form of, say, television (I do not mean to "pick on" television, but rather to contrast two media which structure information in radically different ways with radically different results). The symbolic form of the book is the written word, and more specifically the alphabetically written word. The symbolic form of television is somewhat more complex: it consists of spoken words, of course, on an aural channel, and sometimes visually we see written words. But by and large the word is overpowered by other channels of information conveyed through the television medium. We have visual images, colors, and movement on the level of visual information, and sound effects, music, and noises on the aural level. Visually, too, we see not only things and people, but things and people in relationship. We see people in interaction with one another and with the world around them. We can see their posture, read their kinesthetic cues (gesturing while performing, or remaining more or less emotionless), proxemic cues (people in situations of intimate contact with their world and the people in it, or maintaining physical and emotional distance), and pick up other paralinguistic cues (such as facial expression, tone of voice, loudness or softness of voice, and speed of speech). In short, the act of television viewing is a multisensory experience which mimics the experience of real life.

The book (and any product of literate culture) structures information propositionally. That is to say that the coin of common currency of the book is spoken language. Book information is subject to the same structure, rules, and logic of grammar, syntax, etc., as spoken language. This structure is linear and sequential, one idea following, and dependent upon, another. Syntactically, book information is organized into recognizable patterns which are easily interpretable and understandable (to those who have been trained in such structures), the most simple of which, subject/predicate/object, can yield patterns far more complex—to deal with ideas far more complicated.

Furthermore, spoken language consists of spoken words. Words are abstract symbols, sounds to which humans have arbitrarily assigned meaning. Written words share this characteristic with spoken words, but added to this is the fact that these abstract aural symbols are themselves mediated into abstract visual symbols. The complexity of this situation suggests that it will take years and years of training, practice, and study to assimilate such a system of communication.

The recent investigations into cognitive processes made possible by fMRI technologies described elsewhere in this book (see, for example, Chapter Two and Chapter Five) give powerful evidence that this situation is not merely a behavioral one demanding cognitive training, but a neurological one upon which an individual's lifelong relationship with propositionally structured information will be based.

Propositionally structured information is relatively clear and unambiguous. This is not to say that it cannot be misused, either deliberately or accidentally. But the statement, "the monkey is hanging from the tree" is clearer and less ambiguous than the illustration at right. That picture might, in fact, mean to some that "the monkey is hanging from the tree," or it might mean "the monkey is hanging from the branch." Indeed, seeing the look on the monkey's face, it would not be indefensible to suggest that to some observers the picture means "the monkey is lonely" or "the monkey is lost," or maybe he's hungry, or his arm is getting sore. There's just no way to be certain on the basis

of this picture. But the propositional statement "the monkey is hanging from the tree" probably means just that. While it would not be impossible to come up with alternate interpretations of a linguistic statement (for example, your friend's nickname is "the monkey," changing entirely the meaning of the sentence), the very nature of its structure raises the level of certainty one can have in interpreting it.

The very clarity and lack of ambiguity of propositionally structured information is, paradoxically, probably due to the abstract nature of linguistic symbols. Spoken words, as we've noted, are but abstract aural symbols. And written words are abstract aural symbols "encased" in abstract visual symbols. Because they bear no relationship, except an entirely arbitrary and consensual one, to reality (that is to say, we must all agree to a definition), word symbols are fairly clear and unambiguous.

By contrast, it should be clear now that television is a medium which structures information presentationally, since it so strongly avoids abstraction and instead presents an image to us very much like reality itself. And presentationally structured information, like life itself, is much more open to interpretation exactly because of the removal of abstraction.

Other differences between propositional and presentational structures in symbolic form include a high degree of linearity and sequence in the former and spontaneity, instantaneity, or simultaneity in the latter, dependence on intellect in the former as opposed to an appeal to emotions in the latter. And while propositionally structured information generally demands a high degree of training and education for the use and interpretation of symbols, presentationally structured information is generally universally available and understandable.

This brings us to the question of a medium's physical form. To state the case as briefly as possible, the question of physical form comes down to being a question of hardware. Some media have a simple physical form, and some are highly technologically complex. The significance of this apparently innocent difference will become apparent as we look to the next set of differences among media.

The second characteristic to investigate is that of a medium's conditions of attendance. Asking the following questions can identify these conditions: To whom does this medium make information available? Under what circumstances does one gain access to this information? What prerequisite skills or knowledge are necessary to make meaning of this information?

Let's begin with the first question: To whom does a medium make information available? This is a question, largely, of hardware. A medium can be small, simple, even invisible (for example, speech), and so, ultimately, inexpensive. Or a medium can be big, complex, and extremely expensive (there seems to be a direct relationship between technological complexity and expense). Obviously, the less complex and less expensive media are more universally available than the more complex and expensive ones.

But wait, you might say, what could be more universally available than television, and television is fairly complex and relatively expensive. True enough. But just because almost everyone has a television should not tempt us to make the mistake of thinking that this means everyone uses the television to communicate. If you and I want to communicate (in the truest sense of the word), we can meet in person and speak, write each other letters, call each other on the phone, even e-mail each other. All of these communication events are facilitated by media with relatively simple and inexpensive physical forms, thereby encouraging person-to-person and group communication. But when we turn on the television, we become receivers of mass messages, not really communicators.

The physical form of the television medium is so complex, there are so many pieces of technology involved—cameras, lights, microphones, video switchers, audio mixers, VCRs, editors, character generators, distribution amplifiers, broadcast transmitters (and this is all before it comes into our homes!)—that only the tremendously wealthy, and usually tremendously wealthy corporations, have control of the transmitting end of the communication process. The poor, the humble, the lowly (you and I) are destined to be only a small part of the receiving end. Even a person like myself, one who worked in the television industry for two decades, never had the opportunity to express my own views, my own opinions, my own experiences to a mass audience through the medium of which I was a very small part. I was a mere functionary in the transmission of someone else's message. On the other hand, it is no accident or coincidence, I think, that the television receiver itself is the least expensive single part of the medium's physical form. The mass audience is meant to be nothing more than a receiver of information.

So whether or not a person will have the means (usually economic) to use a particular medium, or will have free access to both the sending and receiving portions of the communication act, are functions of a medium's conditions of attendance dependent upon physical form, and say much about a medium's democratic qualities. (Who will be able to use it, and in what ways might we use it—to send information, or merely to receive it?)

On the level of symbolic form, now, we must again approach the first question. To whom does television make information available, and to whom does print make it available?

The powerfully presentational quality of visual images makes information available to almost anyone. We have mentioned elsewhere (see Chapter Seven) the proliferation of "screen media" (television, DVDs, videogames, the Internet, the I-Phone) among younger and younger children, as described by the Kaiser Family Foundation in its 2003 study, *Zero to Six: Electronic Media in the Lives of Infants, Toddlers, and PreSchoolers.* Parents are likely to use television as a "babysitter," simply because television is incredibly effective in that role.[2]

Television, as a profoundly presentational medium, is the quintessential non-limiting medium. Anyone can use it, for any purpose. We can, indeed, watch it for the express purpose of gaining information (a point I have tried to make throughout this book). But we don't have to. We can watch it to relax, to unwind, to fall asleep, as background noise, to relieve boredom, to fill the quiet voids of our lives.

The same cannot be said (certainly not in the same way) of print. The propositional structure of print creates a set of circumstances (which we describe below) which suggest that information will not be as universally available through a print medium as through a visual screen medium. A book will never be, for instance, a babysitter.

Consider the second question: Under what circumstances does one gain access to information in a given medium? Every medium comes with its own set of operating instructions, as it were, which more or less dictate when, where, and how we will use them. The book and television differ in a number of significant ways. The physical form of the book makes it usable just about anywhere, while that of the television limits our viewing to certain indoor venues (yes, I know this is changing).

The book can be taken on the train or in a car or bus; it can be read at an airport or at a sporting event. But many people don't like to read under those circumstances. These are not the best conditions for reading. For my part, I know that I like to read in a controlled environment, one that is cut off from distractions and noise. I like to sit comfortably in a quiet room, which is dark, except for the light that illuminates the page. Of course, I do read on the train or subway (I once had a friend who told me she liked to read while driving, but I don't recommend it), or in other environments unlike the one I prefer, but I find that the greater the level of distraction, the greater the likelihood that I will have to reread the page when I finish it and realize I don't know what I just read! Reading—and especially the activity of "deep reading" described by Sven Birkerts—takes concentration, time, and effort.

We do not have this problem, generally speaking, with television. Whereas the book is content-intensive, television is context-intensive. We don't generally watch television to learn something; we watch it to do something. (I'm aware of the paradox present in the minds of those of you who see television-watching as the antithesis of action.) We watch television to relax, to be lulled, to be entertained, to be amused, to be titillated, to be aroused,—in short to effect us on an emotional, rather than an intellectual, level. And if we should doze off in the middle of a comedy, or soap, or a mystery, and wake up at the ending, we don't ever really feel like we've missed anything. We simply do not have to attend to television the way we must attend to books.

This is not to say that television *cannot* be content-intensive, *cannot* teach us (the PBS Civil War documentary by Ken Burns was one of the best educational productions of any type on its subject), but that, most often, it does not choose to. This is a function of television's physical form. Such a technologically complex, labor-intensive medium naturally has to make money, and content-intensive programming has not historically been profitable.

Another difference concerning conditions of attendance relates to a fact we noted earlier: a two-year-old can and will watch television, but cannot and will not read a book. In fact, most ten-year-olds would watch television before they would read, for instance, the collected works of John Donne. Content, once again, and the desire to gain from specific content, is far more crucial to the book than to television. This fact is well known to anyone who has ever traveled to a country where English is not the native language. A decade ago I traveled to Poland for some friends' wedding and had the opportunity to watch a good deal of Polish television. I know some Polish, but am far from fluent. Yet I found I could watch a comedy, or drama, or soap opera, or even the news, and follow the story line, and understand what was happening, and interpret the actors' meanings, if not their words.

This point allows us to look at the third question: Does the recipient of the information have the prerequisite skills or knowledge to make use of the information? This question refers directly to symbolic form, for some media demand a certain level of skills and a certain amount of background or contextual information in order to successfully interpret, and find meaning in, symbols.

The book, as we've continually seen, is not an easy medium to use. In fact, it's downright difficult. Someone with no training and/or education in the rudiments of literacy will find it entirely indecipherable. And even then, when a young child learns how to read, and perhaps is even a fairly good reader for his or her age, we cannot expect that child to handle pieces of literature whose content is aimed at one with a far greater range and number of life experiences. A ten-year-old, no matter how good a reader she is, will probably not get much out of a text on, say, quantum physics. Nor is she likely to fully comprehend, let alone appreciate, a novel by Gore Vidal.

Television, however, is a powerfully presentationally structured medium that has few, if any, prerequisites. It is a curriculum unto itself. One does not have to learn how to watch television, any more than one has to learn how to watch the real world. This does not mean that there cannot be content on television that is beyond a very young child's comprehension (after all, there is content in life that is beyond a young child). It means simply that it doesn't matter as much with television if a person doesn't have all the prerequisite skills or knowledge to fully make use of the information contained in any given program. Being context- rather than content-intensive, the very act of watching television is nearly as important as any content that the television might present.

The third characteristic difference among media concerns the flow of information. Because of their differences in form, media differ in their speed of dissemination, quantity or volume of information disseminated, and direction of information flow.

Until very recently, information was physically connected to a medium. Writing is connected to the piece of paper that carries it, a voice is connected to a human body, and so on. Before electricity, information could move no faster than the medium that conveyed it. About a century and a half ago, however, Samuel Finley Breese Morse developed the telegraph and in the bargain accomplished something that continues to have profound consequences for the process of communication: the *disembodiment* of information. With the advent of electronic media, information is no longer embodied in some physical medium, but rather is modulated on some magnetic wave or translated into a digital code. The medium no longer moves; it moves the information, and does so at the speed of light (give or take a couple of miles per second). Even while we have electronic media that move information with unimaginable speed, we still have older media that move information rather slowly, and we need to investigate how these different types of media influence how we think about information differently.

Some media move a great deal of information. Others move relatively little information. Most people look at newspapers and say, "When I want a lot of information, a lot of background, a lot of detail, I read the newspaper." We believe that print gives us more information because the paper can give more space to an important story than television can give it time. And in fact, newspapers give us far more propositionally-structured textual information about any given story than television can afford to give us. The average front-page newspaper story (roughly 25 column inches) consists of anywhere from five hundred to one thousand words and takes several minutes to read. The average television story is roughly a minute long and consists of less than a hundred words.

Clearly, print gives us more information, right? This is not necessarily so. Print is a single-level, single-sensory medium, and all of the detail we are given comes from one linguistic channel. Television, on the other hand, is multi-level and multisensory, and while there may be fewer words used to tell a story or describe a scene, much of the story-telling in television derives from the images and sounds themselves. So, if we are viewing a report on a four-alarm fire, we can see the building itself, see the pandemonium, the look of fear on the faces of apartment dwellers, the sweat and soot on the faces of firemen. We also hear the sirens, the yelling of police, perhaps the terrified screams of tenants trapped on an upper floor. Which medium gives us more information? The answer is no longer clear. The point is that we must think hard about this question when comparing different media.

Information can flow in many different directions. It can flow in one direction, two directions, or in all directions simultaneously. Bi-directionality is easy to picture. Two people sitting together, chatting, engaged in conversation, sharing ideas. This is our most obvious and common example of bi-directional information flow. The telephone is also a medium that encourages the bi-directional flow of information. A classroom (my classroom, at least) is the ideal venue for a multidirectional flow of information—group discussion of topics, debates, bull sessions, etc. Anywhere groups of people share and discuss ideas you will find multidirectional information flow. The Internet is developing into a powerful new tool for the multidirectional flow of information. One of the defining characteristics of multidirectionality, however, is that there is no center; no authority. Without a strict protocol or set of guidelines for such a situation, chaos can reign, and communication will be impeded, rather than facilitated. At the same time, however, it is the very lack of a center that allows for the free, multidirectional flow of information.

I point these things out for a reason. Most people mistake the mass media for being multidirectional, when in fact they are the most strongly unidirectional of all. We see people all over the country, all over the world, watching the same programs and movies, listening to the same music, reading newspapers whose reports are supplied by the same news agencies, and it appears that we have a multi-directional flow of information. But shift your focus for a moment from the society of users (us) to the medium. Ask yourself how much information is being transmitted and, once received, how much is being returned? Mass media are strongly unidirectional, that direction being from some center, out (to the mass). Very little information returns to that center. As we noted earlier, we all watch television, but very few people get to make television (and the vast majority who make television are functionaries, as I was, not decision makers).

It is the centered-ness (if you will) and top-down authoritarianism of mass media, the ability to saturate a society with information emanating from one central authority, which allows for stability, but hampers the free, multidirectional flow of information. As Jacques Ellul points out in his seminal work, *Propaganda: The Formation of Men's Attitudes,* propaganda is impossible without the presence of some mass medium.[3]

The fourth characteristic we shall look at returns our attention to a medium's physical form. Because of differences in their physical form, different media have different temporal and spatial biases. This idea comes to us from the work of the Canadian economist and communication theorist, Harold Adams Innis. Innis states that media focus our attention, and bias our perceptions and thoughts in one of two ways: towards time or towards space. Time-biased media are those that more efficiently store information than transmit it. Space-biased media are those that more efficiently transmit information than store it.

Time-biased media, according to Innis, are heavy, durable, not prone to corruption or degradation by the elements, and not easily transportable. Space-biased media are light, easily transportable, prone to degradation and not very durable. He points out examples of each in history: the pyramids in ancient Egypt, monuments to the sacred life (and afterlife) of the Pharaoh, were meant to proclaim his greatness to posterity; the printing press, which took writing and mechanized it, transforming the book into the first mass medium and allowing for the mass distribution of information over vast areas.

What Innis mentions only in passing, and too few observers notice, is the profound influence a medium's bias has on a culture's epistemology. Space-biased and time-biased media tend to be most efficiently used with different categories of information. Time-biased cultures (that is, those cultures primarily dependent upon time-biased media) tend to put a great deal of emphasis on information that is eternal and unchanging. This is only natural because you would not dedicate to stone (for example) a piece of information that will be outdated and useless tomorrow. Space-biased cultures tend to focus attention on information that is more dynamic and changing. Such a culture has at its disposal a medium that allows them to administer large-scale organizations across wide areas. So space-biased cultures tend to be more dynamic and constantly changing than time-biased cultures. Time-biased cultures, by contrast, are more traditional and conservative.

Time-biased cultures put their stock in myth, tradition, and folklore; in concerns of religion or spirituality; in pursuits that touch upon the questions of time—not just human time, but eternal time, the afterlife. They are generally politically decentralized and unstable, but culturally quite cohesive. Such information/thought structures encourage a social structure wherein we will find among the strongest of the social institutions that of religion and/or some sort of priesthood, poetry and the bards/folklorists who keep traditions alive and spread them, historians, musicians, and artists.

Space-biased cultures emphasize, engender, support, and are dominated by organized institutions that build upon the utility of space-biased media: government, commerce, and the military—all institutions intimately concerned with space. These cultures are generally highly politically and economically centralized, though potentially culturally impoverished. Space-biased media give such cultures the impetus and wherewithal to create empire.

Because of their differences in symbolic form, different media have different sensory biases. Simply put, some media "train us" to perceive with our eyes or our ears, while some media are multisensory. Once again, it is not a matter of which isolation or combination of our senses is "better," but rather that we recognize that if we allow one sense or set of senses to predominate, we are in a different situation than if we function with a more or less balanced sensorium.

The meaning and significance of this particular principle is, I think, the focus of some controversy and, frankly, up for grabs. McLuhan and Ong, for instance, insist the changeover from a state of orality to one of literacy involves trading "an eye for an ear."[4] McLuhan says of printing:

> Psychically the printed book, an extension of the visual faculty, intensified perspective and the fixed point of view. Associated with the visual stress on point of view and the vanishing point that provides the illusion of perspective there comes another illusion that space is visual, uniform, and continuous. The linearity, precision, and uniformity of the arrangement of movable types are inseparable from these great cultural forms and innovations of Renaissance experience. The new intensity of visual stress and private point of view in the first century of printing were united to the means of self-expression made possible by the typographic extension of man.[5]

Ong makes a similar point:

> Hearing rather than sight had dominated the older noetic world in significant ways, even long after writing was deeply interiorized. Manuscript culture in the West remained always marginally oral. . . .Eventually, however, print replaced the lingering hearing-dominance in the world of thought and expression with the sight-dominance which had its beginning with writing but could not flourish with the support of writing alone.[6]

To be sure, the visual nature of print was a powerful medium through which to focus on the linearity and uniformity, as well as on the linguistic, grammatic, and syntactic structure of speech; these both created a context for the assimilation of the concept of standardization of the grapholect or written form of a language, as Eisenstein points out,[7] as well as the social standardization characterized by the behaviors "put on" or adopted by the "man of letters."[8]

Finally, because of both their physical and symbolic forms, different media exhibit different social, economic, and political biases. We have seen how both the physical and symbolic forms of different media create different conditions of attendance for their users. The symbolic form of television, being extremely nonlimiting in terms of its low threshold in both linguistic and intellectual demands, is accessible to nearly everyone in a society—young, old, rich, poor, male, female, different ethnic groups, and different linguistic traditions.

Print, on the other hand, presents us with a set of significant limitations: linguistic, neurological, sociological, economic, and many others. Young children untrained in the skills of literacy cannot read. Disadvantaged segments of society, with insufficient resources to have books on hand, with underfunded and overcrowded schools, and without the free time necessary to inculcate habits of deep reading, will not read—if they read at all—at the same level as children raised in a deeply literate environment (if there is such a thing left in our space-biased culture).

Yet the technologically complex and—ultimately—prohibitively expensive physical form of the television medium limits our participation in the act of communication to one of passive reception of information. Television's physical form supports a top-down, authoritarian structure of information dissemination which inhibits true sharing of information and has a normative influence on social attitudes, behaviors, and knowledge.

For this reason, many in the "progressive" movement today see a pronounced "corporate bias" in the industry that has grown around the television medium.[9]

Notes

Preface

1. McLuhan, *Forward Through the Rearview* Mirror, 66. I think, by the way, that McLuhan was being disingenuous in saying this. As someone who worked for more than two decades creating television and video programs, radio news broadcasts, recorded musical performances, films, and photographic slide/tape presentations, I must say with all objectivity and no false modesty that I'm pretty certain that I have more of an "understanding of technological matters" than the great prophet of the age of electonic information. But technological understanding is not the issue. It is not really what McLuhan was referring to, and I think he knew that. What we're really talking about when trying to understand the effects of media are not technological matters, but psychic and social matters, and to say that a moral point of view in such matters is irrelevant is, I think, grievously wrong. See Ellul, *The Technological Society,* for a full discussion of the tendency in mass society to put technological understanding before and above the moral point of view.

2. Postman, *Building a Bridge to the Eighteenth Century,* 7–20.

3. Ellul, *The Presence of the Kingdom,* 79–112.

4. I'm reminded of what is perhaps the first self-referential, postmodern television advertisement for a nonprescription over-the-counter medicine of some sort. Peter Bergman of the soap opera, *The Young and the Restless,* appears at fade-up, dressed in a white lab coat, a stethoscope hanging from his neck, and intones authoritatively, "I'm not a doctor, but I play one on TV."

5. Ellul, *The Humiliation of the Word,* 1.

6. "Immanent: remaining or operating within a domain of reality or realm of discourse; inherent; *specif:* having existence or effect only within the mind or consciousness. . . ." *Webster's Ninth Collegiate Dictionary* (Springfield, MA: Merriam-Webster, 1991).

7. "Transcendent: 1 a: exceeding usual limits; surpassing b: extending or lying beyond the limits of ordinary experience c; *Kantianism:* being beyond the limits of all possible experience and knowledge

2: being beyond comprehension 3: transcending the universe or material existence. . . ." Ibid.

8. Logan, "The Five Ages of Communication," 14–15. Logan sees a mimetic, pre-verbal era preceding the oral age, an interesting and certainly valid point, but rather unpromising for the purposes of this study.

Introduction:
Why a Metaphysics of Media? Why Should Anyone Care?

1. Strangely enough, I did remember two names that JFK kept referring to, names which meant absolutely nothing to me until I studied the period in an American History class many years later: Quimoy and Matsu. Those two names—names of islands held by nationalist Chinese against a communist bombardment—swirled in my head for years like music, a melody that had no inherent meaning other than its pure form.

2. Kraus (ed.), *The Great Debates.*

3. This makes the fact that in the intervening four decades there has arisen a rapidly growing movement denying this accomplishment—"The moon landing was a hoax!"—all the more ironic.

4. How early it is impossible for me to say right now, for these were ideas that had a long gestation. Indeed, it was not until college that I actually made a conscious decision to major in mass communication and media studies. But I also know that I felt a fascination with television, and particularly with television news, and I felt intuitively that we had on our hands a profoundly powerful agent of social change.

5. For a greater explanation and illustration of these ideas, see "Appendix: An Explanation of the Media Ecological Principles" at the end of this book.

6. Ong, *Interfaces of the Word*, 17.

7. Perez-Rivas, "Bush Vows to Rid the World of 'Evil-Doers.'"

8. Leakey and Lewin, *People of the Lake*, 189.

9. Ibid.

10. Gould, *The Mismeasure of Man.*

11. Herrnstein and Murray, *The Bell Curve.*

12. Aristotle, *Nicomachean Ethics*, Book 3, 52.

13. Ibid., 55.

14. Ibid., 55–56 and note. Ostwald explains that Aristotle's argument references a practical syllogism, which consists of a major premise and a minor premise. The major premise is always universal, that is to say it is based on some absolute value or truth—for exmple, "to take someone else's property without their knowledge and without just cause is stealing, which is always and everywhere wrong." The minor premise is usually a particular circumstance: "That 1964 Mustang convertible is someone else's property." The logical conclusion would be this: "To take that 1964 Mustang convertible, without just cause, is stealing." Ignorance of the universal premise, Aristotle is saying here, is immoral and can be met with nothing but reproach. Ignorance of the particular premise, on the other hand, results in an involuntary act which can only be pardoned or pitied.

15. The Catholic University of America, *The New Catholic Encyclopedia,* vol. 7, 314.

16. Ibid., 315.

17. Ibid.

18. Ibid.

Chapter One:
On the Utility of the Media Ecological Perspective as a Tool in the Study of the Metaphysics of a Culture

1. McLuhan, *Understanding Media,* 23.

2. Ibid.

3. Postman, *Teaching as a Conserving Activity,* 167.

4. Innis, *The Bias of Communication,* 29.

5. Ibid., 55.

6. Ibid.

7. McLuhan, *The Gutenberg Galaxy,* 236.

8. Ibid., 158.

9. McLuhan, *Forward Through the Rearview Mirror,* 46.

10. Ibid., 48.

11. Ong, *Orality and Literacy,* 80.

12. Ibid., 96.

13. Ibid., 105.

14. Ibid., 117.

15. Ong, *Interfaces of the Word,* 42.

16. Eisenstein, *The Printing Press as an Agent of Change*, 151.

17. Ibid., 419.

18. Ibid., 420.

19. Postman, *Amusing Ourselves to Death*, 51.

20. Perkinson, *Getting Better*, 9.

21. Ibid., 119.

22. For a greater explanation and illustration of these ideas, see "Appendix: An Explanation of the Media Ecological Principles" at the end of this book.

Chapter Two
The Contentious Nature of Objective Reality
and the Inarguable Value of Truth

1. E-mail message sent by the author to the Media Ecology Listserv: mea-bounces@lists.ibiblio.org, Thu 1/29/2004, 2:42 PM.

2. E-mail response sent by Kenneth Rufo to the Media Ecology Listserv: mea-bounces@lists.ibiblio.org, Thu 1/29/2004, 3:33 PM.

3. Ibid.

4. E-mail message sent by the author to the Media Ecology Listserv: mea-bounces@lists.ibiblio.org, Thu 1/29/2004, 5:30 PM.

5. Sapir, *Language, Culture, and Personality*, 75–93.

6. Whorf, *Language, Thought, and Reality*, x.

7. Nietzsche, *The Genealogy of Morals*, vol. 3, 119.

8. Dennett, "Postmodernism and Truth."

9. Ibid.

10. Deacon, *The Symbolic Species*, 31.

11. *Synapsids* are a class of animals from which mammals evolved. They are one of two groups of *amniotes*, animals whose gestation is characterized by embryonic development in a protective sac or placenta—either externally in an egg or internally in a uterus. The synapsid class includes mammals and mammal-like reptiles, and the sauropsid class includes reptiles, dinosaurs, and birds.

12. The notable exception being the onomatopoeia: the word that sounds like the sound it represents—*buzz, crash, ding-dong, quack*, etc.

13. This proposition does not, of course, reflect the fact that specific words—discrete bits of propositionally structured information—

might have some emotional content of their own, and indeed we ought to expect that there will be, from time to time, functional crossover into the right hemisphere after the words have been processed in the left hemisphere. The point is not to suggest an automatistic model of human thought, but to emphasize that, unlike most other functions controlled by the human brain, language production, processing, and comprehension are primarily left-brain functions.

14. MacLean, *The Triune Brain in Evolution,* 9.

15. Cytowic, *The Man Who Tasted Shapes,* 159.

16. Ibid., 159–60.

17. Wolf, *Proust and the Squid,* 145–55.

18. Anderson, et al., "Cortical Activation While Watching Video Montage: An fMRI Study."

19. Bavelier, et al., "Sentence Reading."

20. Linguists like George Yule differentiate between learning and acquisition. Language acquisition occurs more or less naturally beginning at a very young age if certain requirements are in place: full use of sensory-motor functions, a language environment within which the cultural transmission of a speech tradition can take place, and so on. *Learning* a specific speech system (that is, a language) is unnatural and takes several years for a child to reach a high level of proficiency.

21. McLuhan, *Forward Through the Rearview Mirror,* 170.

22. Lyotard, *The Postmodern Condition,* xxiii–xxiv.

23. Wittgenstein, *Tractatus Logico-Philosophicus,* 73–74.

24. Rorty and Engel, *What's the Use of Truth?,* 34.

25. Ibid., 37.

26. Ibid., 38.

27. Frankfurt, *On Bullshit.*

28. Ibid., 55–56.

29. Ibid., 61.

30. Suskind, "Faith, Certainty and the Presidency of George W. Bush."

31. Boswell, *The Life of Samuel Johnson, LL.D.,* 545.

32. Vardy and Wattie, "Shopping is Patriotic, Leaders Say."

33. Frankfurt, *On Truth,* 98–99.

34. Loving concern or charity.

35. Truth.

36. Nietzsche, "Beyond Good and Evil," in *The Basic Writings of Nietzsche*, 262.

37. For example, see Harvey B. Sarles, Barbara DeConcini, William Van Dusen Wishard, David Trend, Peter Lamborn Wilson, Genrich Krasko, and others.

38. Rorty, *Philosophy and the Mirror of Nature*, 377–78.

39. McLuhan, *Forward Through the Rearview Mirror*, 168.

40. Ellul, *The Presence of the Kingdom*, 96.

Chapter Three
Orality

1. Plato, *The Republic*, 384.

2. Havelock, *Preface to Plato*, 46.

3. Ong, *Orality and Literacy*, 67.

4. Havelock, *Preface to Plato*, 159.

5. Ibid., 198.

6. Or perhaps not so difficult to imagine, as I intend to show later.

7. Ong, *Orality and Literacy*, 33.

8. Malinowski, "The Problem of Meaning in Primitive Languages," 310.

9. Ibid.

10. Innis, *The Bias of Communication*, 10.

11. Fallon, *Printing, Literacy, and Education in Eighteenth-Century Ireland*, 29.

12. Ibid., 34.

13. Ong, *Orality and Literacy*, 45.

14. Ibid., 55.

15. Ibid., 5.

16. Caesar, *The Gallic War*, 339.

17. Fallon, *Printing, Literacy, and Education in Eighteenth-Century Ireland*, 36; see also Scherman, *The Flowering of Ireland*.

18. Havelock, *Preface to Plato*, 71-73.

19. Ibid., 87.

20. Ibid., 41.

21. Campbell with Moyers, *The Power of Myth*, 71.

22. Ong, *Orality and Literacy*, 74.

23. Innis, *The Bias of Communication*. This statement is only slightly problematic, and not in the slightest inaccurate. While never executing an anthropological study of any kind, Innis nevertheless catalogues the characteristics of time-biased and space-biased cultures, and the particular social institutions supported and sometimes exalted in each.

24. Lucien Levy-Bruhl, paraphrased in Malinowski, *Magic, Science, and Religion*, 8.

25. Jaynes, *The Origin of Consciousness in the Breakdown of the Bicameral Mind*, 73–74, describes the human person in the era before bicamerality as living an experience of deep familiarity, even intimacy, with "gods"—objective voices and visions perceived outside the self. "Who then were these gods that pushed men about like robots and sang epics through their lips? They were voices whose speech and directions could be as distinctly heard by the Iliadic heroes as voices are heard by certain epileptic and schizophrenic patients, or just as Joan of Arc heard her voices."

26. Jung, *Man and His Symbols*, 41-42.

27. Cassirer, *Philosophy of Symbolic Forms*, 1-16.

28. Campbell, *Myths to Live By*.

29. Malinowski, *Magic, Science, and Religion*, 9.

30. Ibid., 48.

Chapter Four
The Metaphysics of Orality

1. Geertz, *The Interpretation of Culture*, 142–46.

2. Havelock, *Preface to Plato*, 61–86.

3. Goody, *The Interface between the Written and the Oral*, 157.

4. Rahner, in Kelly (ed.), *Karl Rahner: Theologian of the Graced Search for Meaning*, 110.

5. See, for instance, Schmidt, *Melancholy and the Care of the Soul;* Berrios, *The History of Mental Symptoms;* Linn and Schwarz, *Psychiatry and Religious Experience*.

6. Campbell, *Myths to Live By*, 79–80.

7. Cassirer, *Language and Myth*, 44–45.

8. Ogden and Richards, *The Meaning of Meaning*, 24.

9. Heidegger, *On the Way to Language*, 141.

10. Genesis 1:6–7.

11. John 1:1–3.

12. Qur'an 36:81–83.

13. Armstrong, *A History of God*, 149–50.

14. Kaplan and Bernays, *The Language of Names*, 16.

15. Cassirer, *Language and Myth*, 53.

16. Dieterich, Eine Mithrasliturgie, 111, 114, quoted in Cassirer, *Language and Myth*, 54.

17. Genesis 2:19–20.

18. Crawley, *Studies of Savages and Sex*.

19. Kratz, "Genres of Power: A Comparative Analysis of Okiek Blessings, Curses and Oaths," 639.

20. Squire, *The Mythology of the British Islands*, 82–83. See also Fallon, *Printing, Literacy, and Education in Eighteenth-Century Ireland*, 34.

21. Ibid.

22. Ong, *The Presence of the Word*, 309.

23. Ong, *Orality and Literacy*, 33.

24. Ibid., 32.

25. Ibid., 67–70.

26. Malinowski, *Magic, Science, and Religion*, 56–57.

27. Cassirer, *Language and Myth* points out that primitive tool-users embraced both pre-scientism and magic: "As soon as man employs a tool, he views it not as a mere artifact of which he is the recognized maker, but as a Being in its own right, endowed with powers of its own. Instead of being governed by his will, it becomes a god or daemon on whose will he depends—to which he feels himself subjected, and which he adores with the rites of a religious cult (p. 59)."

28. Malinowski, *Magic, Science, and Religion*, 11–14.

29. Frazer, *The Golden Bough*, 16–17.

30. Ibid., 61–62.

31. Ibid., 62.

32. Malinowski, *Magic, Science, and Religion*, 68.

Chapter Five
Literacy

1. On the surface, two thousand five hundred years might seem like a vast period of time, and the fact that the systematic development of writing forms took place in this space of time can appear little more than a coincidence. But when you consider that humans have walked the earth for roughly a million (or more) years, and that cave paintings all across Europe and Asia are dated from about 60,000 to about 15,000 B.C., it seems less coincidental and more systematic and evolutionary—at least in the cultural sense.

2. Gelb, *A Study of Writing*, 29.

3. The earliest human civilizations are dated from 10,000 B.C. Settled towns arose when humans assimilated the knowledge of animal domestication. An early agricultural revolution occurred which was facilitated by the discovery of the process of fermentation as a means of preserving grains. The first "economies of surplus" spurred trade and barter of crops and goods. Arbitrary markings that associated goods with their owner have come to be known by communication scholars as identifying/mnemonic devices, a precursor of writing.

4. Gelb, *A Study of Writing*, 36.

5. Of course, wholly pictographic systems, like Chinese script, have survived and flourished for thousands of years doing just that. It is not my point in this brief examination of the evolutionary development of writing systems to claim one form better than another. That would be a wholly subjective judgment and an exercise in futility. It will suffice for my purposes if the reader will recognize the significant differences in the forms and try to imagine the advantages and disadvantages of each one for the organization, storage, recall, manipulation, and use of information.

6. "The great Chinese dictionary of K'ang Hsi (Kangxi—1662-1722) contains nearly 50,000 characters, but most of these are archaic or highly specialized. In the modern language, basic literacy requires knowledge of some 2,000 characters. Similarly, in Japanese, 1,850 characters are prescribed by the Japanese Ministry of Education and adopted by law as those most essential for everyday use. Of these, 881 are taught during the six years of elementary school." Source: Chinese Cultural Studies: Chinese Logographic Writing, Brooklyn College History Department, http://acc6.its.brooklyn.cuny.edu/~phalsall/texts/chinlng4.html

7. McLuhan and Logan, "Alphabet: Mother of Invention" questions this proposition implicitly in looking at why the alphabet was developed in the West and not the East: "To understand why the alphabet developed in the West and not in the East, we need only consider the nature of the spoken Chinese language. All Chinese words are monosyllabic. As a consequence of the limited number of sounds possible for a word, there is an enormous amount of redundancy in the sounds of Chinese words. There are 239 words, for instance, with all the same sound, *shih.* There is little incentive for the development of an alphabet under these conditions. Western tongues, on the other hand, lend themselves to alphabetic transcription because they are more fractured (p. 374)." See also Gelb, *A Study of Writing,* 183–89.

8. Ong, *Orality and Literacy,* 92.

9. McLuhan, *The Essential McLuhan,* 284.

10. Ong, Orality and Literacy, 105.

11. Derrick de Kerckhove, "A Theory of Greek Tragedy," cited in Ong, *Orality and Literacy,* 91.

12. Ong, *Orality and Literacy,* 24.

13. Goody, *The Interface between the Written and the Oral,* 256.

14. Ibid., 69.

15. Muller, *The Uses of the Past,* 238–39.

16. Eisenstein, *The Printing Press as an Agent of Change.*

17. Carothers, "Culture, Psychiatry and the Written Word," cited in McLuhan, *The Gutenberg Galaxy, 19;* also in Ong, *Orality and Literacy,* 50.

18. Carothers, "Culture, Psychiatry and the Written Word," in *Psychiatry,* November 1959, Volume 22, 307–20.

19. McLuhan, *Understanding Media,* 86.

20. See "Appendix: An Explanation of the Media Ecological Principles" at the end of this book.

21. McLuhan, "'The Logos Reaching across Barriers: Letters to Ong, Mole, Maritain, and Culkin," in McLuhan et al. (eds.), *The Medium and the Light,* 66–74.

22. Anonymous, "The Art of Printing," quoted in Ernest Reginald McClintock Dix, "An Early Eighteenth-Century Broadside on Printing," Royal Irish Academy Proceedings, C section, vol. 27 (1908–09), 401–03. See also Fallon, *Printing, Literacy, and Education in Eighteenth-Century Ireland,* 107–08.

Chapter Six
The Metaphysics of Literacy

1. Havelock, *Preface to Plato,* 45.

2. I say this despite the fact that, in "The Phaedrus," Plato has Socrates explaining that writing is an inferior art to rhetoric, one that would "create forgetfulness in the learners' souls, because they will not use their memories; they will trust to the external written characters and not remember of themselves. . . . Writing has one grave fault in common with painting; for the creations of the painter have the attitude of life, and yet if you ask them a question they preserve a solemn silence. And the same may be said of books. You would imagine that they had intelligence, but if you require any explanation of something that has been said, they preserve one unvaried meaning."

It is difficult to know the extent of Plato's conscious awareness of the epistemological effects of writing on Greek culture based on his recounting of the Socratic dialogues. This is certainly a different—and perhaps surprising—perspective than we might expect from someone who banished poetry based on a fairly acute awareness of some of the debilitating effects of orality, to say nothing of someone who was the author of countless books. Perhaps he was merely recounting as accurately as he could the essence of Socrates' thoughts and words; and perhaps he did not, as his pupil Aristotle did, fully appreciate the advantages of the literate mode of thought and propositional thinking.

See Plato, "The Phaedrus," sec. 275, in *The Dialogues of Plato,* 184–85.

3. Havelock, *Preface to Plato,* 3–49.

4. Plato, *The Republic,* 377–78.

5. It may be a pedantic point, but I see the process Jaynes is describing to us more as a unification than a breakdown. Only when the two hemispheres started working together rather than separately do we find the beginnings of consciousness as he defines it.

6. Jaynes, *The Origins of Consciousness in the Breakdown of the Bicameral Mind,* 130. In addressing the objections of linguists who believe that speech, a defining characteristic of the human being, was present at the first moment of our existence as a distinct species, Jaynes explains:

Sometimes the reaction to a denial that early man had speech is, how then did man function or communicate? The answer is very simple: just like all other primates, with an abundance of visual and vocal signals which were very far removed from the syntactical language we practice today. And when I even carry this speechlessness down through the Pleistocene Age, when man developed various kinds of primitive pebble choppers and hand axes, again my linguist friends lament my arrogant ignorance and swear oaths that in order to transmit even such rudimentary skills from one generation to another, there had to be language. But consider that it is almost impossible to describe chipping flints into choppers in language. This art was transmitted solely by imitation, exactly the same way in which chimpanzees transmit the trick of inserting straws into ant hills to get ants. It is the same problem as the transmission of bicycle riding; does language assist at all?"

7. Ibid., 85.

8. Ibid., 93.

9. Ibid., 93–94.

10. Goody, *The Domestication of the Savage Mind*, 51.

11. Deacon, *The Symbolic Species*, 321–22.

12. Wolf, *Proust and the Squid*, 216–17.

13. Ong, *Orality and Literacy*, 29

14. Armstrong, *A History of God*, 27.

15. Jaspers, *Way to Wisdom*, 99–100; cf. Mumford, *The Transformations of Man*, 57.

16. Mumford, *The Transformations of Man*, 60.

17. Ibid., 69.

18. Armstrong, *A History of God*, 27.

19. Mumford, *Transformations of Man*, 59.

20. Jaspers, *Way to Wisdom*, 100.

21. Ibid., 105–06.

22. Livingston, *An Anthropology of Reading*, 59–71.

23. Birkerts, *The Gutenberg Elegies*, 74.

24. Ibid., 75.

25. Ibid., 79–80.

26. Ibid., 91.

27. Ibid., 85.

28. Armstrong, *A History of God*, 49.

29. Goody, *The Logic of Writing and the Organization of Society*, 9–10.

30. Ibid., 5.

31. Mumford, *The Transformations of Man*, 63–64.

32. Ong, *Orality and Literacy*, 132.

33. Ibid.

34. Ó Fiaich, "The Beginnings of Christianity," 62.

35. Herm, *The Celts*, 261.

36. Caesar, *The Gallic War*, 339.

37. John 1:1.

38. Goody, *The Logic of Writing and the Organization of Society*, 17.

39. John 14:6.

40. Goody, *The Logic of Writing and the Organization of Society*, 20.

41. Ibid., 19.

42. Ibid.

43. Plato, *The Republic*, 349-408.

44. Tertullian, *The Prescription Against Heretics*, vii.

45. Ibid.

46. Rubinstein, *Aristotle's Children*, 28.

47. Plato, *The Republic*, 549.

48. Ibid., 29.

49. Ibid.

50. Aristotle, *Nicomachean Ethics*, 10.6, 1177a 12–18.

51. Aristotle, *Metaphysics*, 49–50.

52. Ibid., 330–31.

53. Aristotle, *De Anima*, 430a 20-26, 297–99.

54. Knox, "Books and Readers in the Greek World," 166.

55. Ibid.

56. Pieper, *Guide to Thomas Aquinas*, 153.

57. Armstrong, *A History of God*, 68.

58. Romans 1:16–23.

59. 1 Corinthians 1:19–25.

60. Erskine, "Culture and Power in Ptolemaic Egypt."

61 Man, *Alpha Beta*, 234–35.

62. Knox, "Books and Readers in the Greek World," 166.

63. Erskine, "Culture and Power in Ptolemaic Egypt," 39.

64. Perkinson, *Since Socrates,* 37.

65. Augustine, *The City of God,* vol. 1, book VIII, 10, p. 319.

66. 1 Corinthians 13.

67. Copleston, *A History of Philosophy,* vol. 2, 70.

68. Augustine, *Against the Academicians,* 63.

69. Fremantle, *The Age of Belief,* 26.

70. Augustine, *The City of God,* 55.

71. Ibid., 305.

72. Rubinstein, *Aristotle's Children,* 61–62.

73. Boethius, *The Consolation of Philosophy,* xi.

74. Pieper, *Guide to Thomas Aquinas,* 118.

75. Rubinstein, *Aristotle's Children,* 62.

76. Boethius, *The Consolation of Philosophy,* 7.

77. Rubinstein, *Aristotle's Children,* 59.

78. Copleston, *A History of Philosophy,* vol. 2, 134.

79. Ibid.

80. John Scotus Eriugena, *Patrilogia Latina,* CXXII, ed., Jacques-Paul Migne, trans. by George Bosworth Burch in *Early Medieval Philosophy* (New York: Columbia University Press, 1951), cited in Fremantle, *The Age of Belief,* 86–87.

81. Fremantle, *The Age of Belief,* 98.

82. Deane (trans.), *Works of St. Anselm,* 6.

83. Anselm of Canterbury, "De Veritate," in Hoskins and Richardson (trans. and eds.), *Truth, Freedom, and Evil,* 106–07.

84. Copleston, *A History of Philosophy,* vol. 2, 213.

85. Fremantle, *The Age of Belief,* 112.

86. Watt, *Muhammed at Mecca,* 3.

87. Armstrong, *A History of God,* 132.

88. Ibid., 133.

89. Sale (trans.), *The Koran,* 96:1 (p. 494).

90. Armstrong, *A History of God,* 143.

91. Copleston, *A History of Philosophy,* vol. 2, 217–18.

92. Rubinstein, *Aristotle's Children,* 183.

93. Copleston, *A History of Philosophy,* vol. 2, 224.

94. Herbermann et al. (eds.), *The Catholic Encyclopedia,* 151.

95. Qur'an 3:6.

96. Kraemer, "Maimonides' Use of (Aristotelian) Dialectic," in Cohen and Levine (eds.), *Maimonides and the Sciences,* 113.

97. Gilson, *Reason and Revelation in the Middle Ages,* 50–51.

98. Ibid.

99. Maimonides, *The Guide of the Perplexed,* 79–80, 288.

100. Copleston, *A History of Philosophy,* vol. 2, 230.

101. Armstrong, *A History of God,* 195–96.

102. Fremantle, *The Age of Belief,* 99.

103. Aquinas, *Summa Theologica,* I, q.84, a.5, p. 628.

104. Aristotle, quoted in Freemantle, *The Age of Belief,* 149.

105. Hebrews 1:3.

106. Aquinas, *Summa Theologica,* qq.[2]-26, pp. 16-17.

107. Muller, *The Uses of the Past,* 254.

108. Rubinstein, *Aristotle's Children,* 250.

109. Grant, *The Foundations of Modern Science in the Middle Ages,* 71–72.

110. Gilson, *Reason and Revelation in the Middle Ages,* 64.

111. John of Jaudun, quoted ibid., 62.

112. Ibid., 63.

113. Ibid., 87.

114. Frost, *Basic Teachings of the Great Philosophers,* 26, 90.

115. Thomas à Kempis, *The Imitation of Christ,* 29–30.

116. High, *Language, Persons, and Belief,* 9.

117. Dickens, *Reformation and Society in Sixteenth-Century Europe,* 51. See also Eisenstein, *The Printing Press as an Agent of Change,* 303.

118. Eisenstein, *The Printing Press as an Agent of Change,* 367–68.

119. Ong, *Ramus, Method, and the Decay of Dialogue,* 37–39.

120. Bacon, *The Advancement of Learning,* 87.

121. Davies, *The Mind of God,* 20.

122. Eisenstein, *The Printing Press as an Agent of Change,* 652.

123. Armstrong, *A History of God,* 289.

124. Hampshire, *The Age of Reason,* 36.

125. Hobbes, *Leviathan,* 1.

126. Ibid., 2.

127. Ibid., 14–15.

128. Frost, *Basic Teachings of the Great Philosophers*, 32.

129. Copleston, *A History of Philosophy*, vol. 4, 47–48.

130. Frost, *Basic Teachings of the Great Philosophers*, 36–37.

131. Ibid., 66.

132. Kant, *Critique of Pure Reason*, 38.

133. Ibid., 42.

134. Ibid., 54–55.

135. Copleston, *A History of Philosophy*, vol. 7, 202.

136. Ibid., 207.

137. Ibid., 208.

138. Bury, *The Idea of Progress*, 345–46.

139. Ong, *Interfaces of the Word*, 17.

Chapter Seven
Electric Culture

1. Postman, *Amusing Ourselves to Death*, 28.

2. See the explanation of presentationally structured and propositionally structured codes in "Appendix: An Explanation of the Media Ecological Principles" at the end of this book.

3. Postman, *Amusing Ourselves to Death*, 27.

4. Meyerowitz, *No Sense of Place*, 181.

5. Ibid., 160.

6. Ibid., 246.

7. Ibid., 247.

8. Postman, *The Disappearance of Childhood*, 85.

9. Birkerts, *The Gutenberg Elegies*, 119.

10. McLuhan, *The Medium and the Light*, 34.

11. Meyerowitz, *No Sense of Place*, 166.

12. Ong, *Orality and Literacy*, 160.

13. Ibid., 136.

14. Ibid., 8–9.

15. National Endowment for the Arts, "Reading at Risk," xii.

16. Rideout et al., *Zero to Six*, 4.

17. Ibid., 7.

18. Ibid., 10.

19. Sowell, *Inside American Education*, 3.

20. Ibid., 9.

21. Office of Educational Research and Improvement, "Scholastic Assessment Test Score Averages," 153.

22. Lasch, *The Culture of Narcissism*, 227.

23. National Endowment for the Arts, "Reading at Risk," ix.

24. Ibid., xii.

25. "Future of the First Amendment" website, Department of Journalism, Ball State University, Muncie, IN, and the John S. and James L. Knight Foundation, 2007, accessed February 8, 2008, http://firstamendment.jideas.org/findings/findings.php

26. *USA Today* online, March 1, 2006, "Study: More know 'The Simpsons' than First Amendment rights," accessed February 8, 2008, http://www.usatoday.com/news/nation/2006-03-01-freedom-poll_x.htm

27. Postman, *The Disappearance of Childhood*, 85.

28. "Advertising Agencies," *Encyclopedia Americana* (New York: Encyclopedia Americana, 1918), 169.

29. O'Brien, *The Story of the Sun*, 167.

30. Trotter, *Life of the Marquis of Dalhousie*, 99.

31. Plum, *The Military Telegraph During the Civil War*, 293.

32. Beauchamp, *A History of Telegraphy*, 86.

33. Fang, *A History of Mass Communication*, 259.

34. Petersen, *The Telecommunications Illustrated Dictionary*, 442.

35. Ketupa.net media timeline: 1861-1900, http://www.ketupa.net/timeline2.htm

36. Kingsbury, *The Telephone and Telephone Exchanges*, 430.

37. Meza, *Coming Attractions?*, 29.

38. Towers, *Masters of Space*, 208.

39. Nunes and Johnson, *Mass Affluence*, 213.

40. Veblen, *The Theory of the Leisure Class*, 68–100.

41. Estabrooks, *Electronic Technology, Corporate Strategy, and World Transformation*, 23.

42. Gillham and MacLean, *The Limitless City*, 31.

43. Kurzweil, *The Age of Spiritual Machines*, 266.

44. University of Minnesota, "Media History Project," 1900–1909, http://www.mediahistory.umn.edu/timeline/1900-1909.html

45. Hughes et al. (eds.), *Music Lover's Encyclopedia*, 803.

46. Bognar, *International Dictionary of Broadcasting and Film*, 269.

47. Axelrod and Phillips, *What Every American Should Know about American History*, 206.

48. Folkerts and Lacy, *The Media in Your Life*, 184.

49. Hogan, *Selling 'em by the Sack*, 6.

50. Gorman and McLean, *Media and Society in the Twentieth Century*, 50.

51. Honomichl, *Marketing/Research People*, 103.

52. Betts, *A History of Popular Culture*, 18.

53. Mogel, *Creating Your Career in Communications and Entertainment*, 140.

54. Kamarck and Nye, *Governance.com*, 83.

55. Sterling and Kittross, *Stay Tuned*, 118.

56. Fang, *A History of Mass Communication*, 155.

57. Curcio, *Chrysler*, 466.

58. Hegeman, *Patterns for America*, 23.

59. Roche, *Mega-Events and Modernity*, 162.

60. Butsch, *The Making of American Audiences*, 206.

61. Chandler et al., *Inventing the Electronic Century*, 29.

62. Sterling and Kittross, *Stay Tuned*, 315.

63. Ketupa.net media timeline: 1926-1950, http://www.ketupa.net/timeline4.htm

64. Gorman and McLean, *Media and Society in the Twentieth Century*, 128.

65. Straubhaar and Larose, *Media Now*, 217.

66. Jezer, *The Dark Ages*, 126.

67. Mithaug, *Self-Determined Kids*, 16.

68. Ibid.

69. *World Book Encyclopedia* (Chicago: World Book, 2000), 119.

70. Fang, *A History of Mass Communication*, 264.

71. Ewen, *Captains of Consciousness*, 53.

72. Lasch, *The Culture of Narcissism*, 136–37.

73. Ibid., 136.

74. Ellul, *The Technological Bluff*, 55.

Chapter Eight
The Metaphysics of Electric Culture

1. McLuhan, *The Gutenberg Galaxy*, 26.

2. McLuhan and Logan, "Alphabet, Mother of Invention."

3. Ong, *Orality and Literacy*, 136.

4. McLuhan, *Understanding Media*, 149.

5. Nietzsche, *Der Froelische Wissenschaft*, quoted in Morrison, "God is Dead: What is Next? A Buddhist Response to Nietzsche" in *Western Buddhist Review*, vol. 1, http://www.westernbuddhistreview. com/vol1/god_is_dead.html

6. Nietzche, *The Gay Science*, 125.

7. Hitschmann, *Freud's Theories of the Neuroses*, 148.

8. Freud, *The Future of an Illusion*, 32.

9. Kung, *Freud and the Problem of God*, 140.

10. The Harris Poll #11, February 26, 2003: *The Religious and Other Beliefs of Americans 2003,* http://www.harrisinteractive.com/ harris_poll/index.asp?PID=359

11. The Harris Poll #59, October 15, 2003: While Most Americans Believe in God, Only 36% Attend a Religious Service Once a Month or More Often, http://www.harrisinteractive.com/harris_poll/index. asp?PID=408

12. National Science Foundation survey, reported in *Science & Engineering Indicators 2008,* Chapter 7, "Science and Technology: Public Attitudes and Understanding," http://www.nsf.gov/statistics/seind08/ c7/c7s2.htm

13. *Parascope: On-line Journal of the Paranormal,* http://www. parascope.com/articles/0597/gallup.htm

14. CNN.com, June 15, 1997, Poll: "U.S. Hiding Knowledge of Aliens," http://www.cnn.com/US/9706/15/ufo.poll/index.html?iref=newssearch

15. Nielsen Media Research, 2003, cited at: Media Information Center, http://www.mediainfocenter.org/compare/penetration/

16. Nielsen Media Research, "Average U.S. Home Now Receives a Record 118.6 TV Channels," June 6, 2008, http://www.nielsenmedia. com/nc/portal/site/Public/menuitem.55dc65b4a7d5adff3f65936147a06 2a0/vgnextoid=fa7e220af4e5a110VgnVCM100000ac0a260aRCRD

17. Ibid.

18. Nielsen Media Research, "Led by Teen Girls, Americans Con-

tinue to Watch TV at Record Levels," September 21, 2006, http://www.
nielsenmedia.com/nc/portal/site/Public/menuitem.55dc65b4a7d5adff3
f65936147a062a0/vgnextoid=4156527aacccd010VgnVCM100000ac0a2
60aRCRD

19. Ibid.

20. Media Use Statistics Resources on media habits of children,
youth and adults, "2007 Media Habit Prediction," http://www.frankw-
baker.com/mediause.htm

21. Norman Herr, Ph.D., "Television and Health," in *The Source-
book for Teaching Science*, California State University, Northridge,
http://www.csun.edu/science/health/docs/tv&health.html

22. Postman, *Amusing Ourselves to Death*, 119.

23. Bell, Ritual: *Perspectives and Dimensions*, 243.

24. Ibid., 245.

25. Ellul, *The Technological Bluff*, 346.

26. Ibid., (footnote).

27. Tillich, "Our Ultimate Concern," in *The Essential Tillich*, 32–
38.

28. Postman, *Amusing Ourselves to Death*, 117.

29. Reiter, "Juicy Bits," *Salon.com* (on-line magazine) people
column, http://www.salon.com/people/col/reit/1999/09/03/reitfri/print.
html

*Note: the program in question was actually titled "The Miracle
Maker."*

30. Kung, *Freud and the Problem of God*, 143–44.

Chapter Nine
In the Dark:
The Survival of Ignorance in an Age of Information

1. Postman, "The Humanism of Media Ecology," 11, http://www.
media-ecology.org/publications/MEA_proceedings/v1/postman01.pdf

2. Ibid.

3. Ibid., 16.

4. Teilhard de Chardin, *The Future of Man*, 131–32.

5. 1 John 2:11, paraphrased.

6. A 1970s advertisement by New York Telephone and the
Midwestern US company Ameritech made this hyperbolic claim,

http://en.wikipedia.org/wiki/New_York_Telephone#Wholly_owned_
Subsidiary

7. Perkinson, *Getting Better.*

8. Maddox, "Ad Ratios and Budgets Grow" in *Advertising* (July 14, 2006), 12, http://www.btobonline.com/apps/pbcs.dll/article?AID=/20060710/FREE/607100724

9. Postman, *Amusing Ourselves to Death,* 106.

10. Ibid.

11. Ibid., 100.

12. Brainard, *Television: The Limits of Deregulation,* 61.

13. Ibid., 62.

14. By June 3, 2003, the Federal Communications Commission under the chairmanship of Michael Powell (son of former President George W. Bush's first Secretary of State, Colin Powell) had voted to further deregulate media ownership, opening the broadcasting industry to further corporate consolidation and monopolization. The vote allows corporations to own newspapers, radio stations, and multiple TV stations in the same city.

The FCC's latest deregulatory thrust allows individual corporations to own enough TV stations to reach 45 percent of U.S. households. Before this vote, they were limited to 35 percent.

Critics argue that, among other things, the public will end up with fewer independent sources of information as a result of the rule changes, and there will be more and more important world news stories ignored.

15. Postman, *Amusing Ourselves to Death,* 156.

16. Ellul, *The Presence of the Kingdom,* 81–82.

17. For a more thorough explanation and illustration of these ideas, see "Appendix: An Explanation of the Media Ecological Principles" at the end of this book.

18. Harris Poll (2003, #11), http://www.harrisinteractive.com/harris_poll/index.asp?PID=359

19. Harris Poll (2003, #59), http://www.harrisinteractive.com/harris_poll/index.asp?PID=408

20. Harris Poll (2003, #11), http://www.harrisinteractive.com/harris_poll/index.asp?PID=359

21. Roper Poll, "UFOs & Extraterrestrial Life: Americans' Beliefs

and Personal Experiences," prepared for the SCI FI Channel, September 2002 (Roper Number: C205-008232), http://scifipedia.scifi.com/index. php/Roper_Poll_on_UFOs_and_Extraterrestrial_Life

22. Alberta UFO Study Group, "Summaries of Some Recent Opinion Polls on UFOs," http://www.ufoevidence.org/documents/doc999. htm

23. It is important to note that in ancient Greek, the word *psyche* represented not only the mind or the intellect, but also the soul, the essence, and the animating spirit.

24. Postman, *Amusing Ourselves to Death*, 27.

25. John 1:5.

26. John Sheehan, Press Release from the Center for Media and Public Affairs, March 4, 1994, cited in *Media Monitor* (Washington: The Center for Media and Public Affairs, 1994), 6.

27. The Center for Media and Public Affairs, "The Media at the Millennium: The Network's Top Topics, Trends, and Joke Targets of the 1990s," in *Media Monitor* (Washington, DC: The Center for Media and Public Affairs, 2000), 1–2.

28. Ibid.

29. Klite et al., "Pavlov's TV Dog."

30. Gleditsch et al., "Armed Conflict 1946-2001."

31. The World Health Organization, *The World Health Report 2001*, 148–49. While no Americans were killed in active warfare in 2000, we should not necessarily assume that we were at peace. In the year 2000, 66,000 Americans took their own lives.

32. *SIPRI, SIPRI Yearbook 2008*, "Appendix 6A," http://www.sipri. org/contents/milap/milex/aprod/top100/SIPRI_TOP100.pdf

33. "Annex Table 1: Basic Indicators for All WHO Member States," in The World Health Organization, *The World Health Report 2004*, 112–18.

34. "Comparative International Statistics," in Statistical Abstract of the United States, 826.

35. "Violations of the ILO (International Labor Organization) conventions," http://www.transnationale.org/anglais/transnationale/tiersmonde/bit.htm

36. Campbell, *Myths to Live By*, 19–42.

37. O'Connor, *A Terrible Beauty is Born,* 86.

38. Allt and Alspach (eds.), *The Variorum Edition of the Poems of William Butler Yeats,* 391–92.

39. Ibid., 289.

40. "Address of John Paul II to the Plenary Assembly of the Pontifical Council for Culture," Saturday, 16 March 2002, http://www.vatican.va/holy_father/john_paul_ii/speeches/2002/march/documents/hf_jp-ii_spe_20020316_pc-culture_en.html

41. Havel, "The Need for Transcendence in the Postmodern World." See also *The Journal for Quality and Participation,* September 1995.

42. Kaplan, "Hellwig: Education Should be 'For Practice,'" The Observer On-Line, February 15, 2000, http://www.nd.edu/~observer/02152000/News/7.html

43. John 3:16.

44. King, "Remaining Awake through a Great Revolution."

APPENDIX:
An Explanation of the Media Ecological Principles

1. This explanation is mine and mine alone, and to the extent that there are omissions, inaccuracies, or other faults to be found in the interpretation of the six principles, I take full responsibility. The principles themselves come from my coursework in the Doctoral Program in Media Ecology at New York University in the 1980s. To my knowledge, they were never published, and their authorship remains a matter of speculation. They are a distillation of the work of many researchers whose findings make up the canon of media ecology. For instance, the fourth principle, having to do with time and space biases, flows directly from the work of Harold Innis, specifically *Empire and Communication,* and *The Bias of Communication.* The first principle's focus on symbolic form comes from the work of both Suzanne Langer (*Philosophy in a New Key*) and Ernst Cassirer (*Philosophy of Symbolic Forms*).

Some versions of the principles include more than six. One which I received a few years ago (from Janet Sternberg in response to a query I posed on the media ecology Listserv, August 1, 2007) includes the following principle: "Because of the ways in which they organize time and space, different media have different metaphysical biases." For some reason, that one was missing at the time I entered the program.

Most graduates of NYU's Media Ecology program credit Dr. Christine Nystrom with this amazingly useful—yet up until now, unpublished—act of synthesis. Having worked under Dr. Nystrom, having read her work, and having heard her on numerous occasions synthesize diverse, complex ideas and speak about them clearly and understandably, I am inclined to agree. If they and I are wrong in this assumption, I will humbly and enthusiastically give credit to the appropriate party.

2. Kornblum, "Study: More Parents Use TV as an Electronic Babysitter," *USA Today* (online), May 24, 2006, http://www.usatoday.com/tech/news/2006-05-24-kids-media_x.htm

3. Ellul, *Propaganda: The Formation of Men's Attitudes*.

4. McLuhan, *Understanding Media*, 84.

5. Ibid., 157.

6. Ong, *Orality and Literacy*, 121.

7. Eisenstein, *The Printing Press as an Agent of Change*, 80–88.

8. McLuhan, *Understanding Media*, 162.

9. See, for instance, the Media Channel's "Who Owns the Media?" chart, http://www.media-ecology.org/publications/MEA_proceedings/v1/humanism_of_media_ecology.html; the Media Reform Information Center's "Links and Resources on Media Reform," http://www.corporations.org/media/; and the National Organization for Women's Digital TV Project website, "Who Controls the Media?" http://www.nowfoundation.org/issues/communications/tv/mediacontrol.html

Bibliography

Allt, Peter, and Russell K. Alspach (eds.), *The Variorum Edition of the Poems of William Butler Yeats* (New York: MacMillan, 1977).

Anderson, Daniel R., et al., "Cortical Activation While Watching Video Montage: An fMRI Study," in *Media Psychology* 8:1 (2006), 7–24.

Anselm of Canterbury, "De Veritate," in Hoskins, Jasper, and Herbert Richardson (trans. and eds.), *Truth, Freedom, and Evil: Three Philosophical Dialogues* (New York: Harper Torchbooks, 1967).

Aristotle, *De Anima,* ed. by Sir David Ross (Oxford: Clarendon, 1961).

———, *Metaphysics,* trans. by Rev. John H. M'Mahon (London: George Bell and Son, 1896).

———, *Nicomachean Ethics,* Book III, ch. 1, translated with an introduction and notes by Martin Ostwald (Upper Saddle River, NJ: Prentice Hall, 1999).

Armstrong, Karen, *A History of God* (New York: Ballantine, 1993).

Augustine, *Against the Academicians,* trans. by Sister Mary Patricia Garvey, R.S.M. (Milwaukee, WI: Marquette University Press, 1942).

———, *The City of God,* vol. 1, trans. by Marcus Dods (New York: Hafner, 1948).

Axelrod, Alan, and Charles Phillips, *What Every American Should Know about American History: 200 Events That Shaped the Nation* (Avon, MA: Adams Media, 2004).

Bacon, Francis, *The Advancement of Learning* (London: Parker, Son, and Bourne, 1858).

Bavelier, D., et al., "Sentence Reading: A Functional MRI Study at 4 Tesla" in *The Journal of Cognitive Neuroscience* 9, 664–86.

Beauchamp, K. G., *A History of Telegraphy* (London: The Institution of Electrical Engineers, 2001).

Bell, Catherine, *Ritual: Perspectives and Dimensions* (Oxford: Oxford University Press, 1997).

Berrios, G. E., *The History of Mental Symptoms: Descriptive Psychopathology since the Nineteenth Century* (Cambridge: Cambridge University Press, 1996).

Betts, Raymond F., *A History of Popular Culture: More of Everything, Faster, and Brighter* (New York: Routledge, 2004).

Birkerts, Sven, *The Gutenberg Elegies* (New York: Fawcett Columbine, 1994).

Boethius, Marcus Anicius Severinus, *The Consolation of Philosophy*, trans. by Richard Green (Indianapolis, IN: Bobbs-Merrill, 1962).

Bognar, Desi K., *International Dictionary of Broadcasting and Film* (Burlington, MA: Focal, 2000).

Boswell, James, *The Life of Samuel Johnson*, LL.D., vol. 1, ed. by George Birbeck Hill (New York: Harper & Brothers, 1891).

Brainard, Lori, *Television: The Limits of Deregulation* (Boulder, CO: Lynne Rienner, 2004).

Bury, J. B., *The Idea of Progress: An Inquiry into Its Origin and Growth* (London: MacMillan, 1920).

Butsch, Richard, *The Making of American Audiences: From Stage to Television, 1750-1990* (Cambridge: Cambridge University Press, 2000).

Caesar, *The Gallic War*, trans. by H. J. Edwards (Cambridge, MA: Harvard University Press, 1917).

Campbell, Joseph, *Myths to Live By* (New York: Viking, 1972).

———, with Bill Moyers; *The Power of Myth*, ed. by Betty Sue Flowers (New York: Doubleday, 1988).

Carothers, J. C., "Culture, Psychiatry and the Written Word," *Psychiatry* (Nov. 1959), 307–20.

Cassirer, Ernst, *Language and Myth* (New York: Dover, 1953).

———, *Philosophy of Symbolic Forms* (New Haven, CT: Yale University Press, 1955).

The Catholic University of America, *The New Catholic Encyclopedia*, second edition, vol. 7 (Washington, DC: The Catholic University of America and Thomson/Gale, 2003).

The Center for Media and Public Affairs, "The Media at the Millennium: The Network's Top Topics, Trends, and Joke Targets of the 1990s," in *Media Monitor* (Washington, DC: The Center for Media and Public Affairs, 2000).

Chandler, Alfred D., Jr., Takashi Hikino, and Andrew Von Nordenflycht, *Inventing the Electronic Century: The Epic Story of the Consumer Electronics and Computer Industries* (Cambridge, MA: Harvard University Press, 2005).

Cohen, Robert S., and Hillel Levine (eds.), *Maimonides and the Sciences* (Boston: Kluwer Academic, 2000).

Copleston, Frederick, S.J., *A History of Philosophy*, vol. 2, "Medieval Philosophy," Part 1, "Augustine to Bonaventure" (Garden City, NY: Image, 1962).

———, *A History of Philosophy*, vol. 4, "Modern Philosophy: Descartes to Leibniz" (Garden City, NY: Image, 1963).

———, *A History of Philosophy*, vol. 7, "Modern Philosophy," Part 1, "Fichte to Hegel" (Garden City, NY: Image, 1963).

Craig, Edward (ed.), *Routledge Encyclopedia of Philosophy*, vol. 6 (London: Routledge, 1998).

Crawley, A. E., *Studies of Savages and Sex* (Manchester, NH: Ayer, 1969).

Curcio, Vincent, *Chrysler: The Life and Times of an Automotive Genius* (Oxford: Oxford University Press, 2000).

Cytowic, Richard E., *The Man Who Tasted Shapes: A Bizarre Medical Mystery Offers Revolutionary Insights into Emotions, Reasoning, and Consciousness* (New York: G. P. Putnam's Sons, 1993).

Davies, Paul, *The Mind of God* (New York: Touchstone, 1992).

Deacon, Terence, *The Symbolic Species: The Co-Evolution of Language and the Brain* (New York: Norton, 1997).

Deane, Sidney Norton (trans. 1903), *Works of St. Anselm,* (Peru, IL: Open Court, 1962), at sacred-texts.com, http://www.sacred-texts. com/chr/ans/ans006.htm

de Kerckhove, Derrick, "A Theory of Greek Tragedy," in *SubStance* (Madison: University of Wisconsin Press, 1981).

Dennett, Daniel C., "Postmodernism and Truth," paper presented to the World Congress of Philosophy, August 13, 1998, http://ase. tufts.edu/cogstud/papers/postmod.tru.htm

Dickens, Arthur Geoffrey, *Reformation and Society in Sixteenth-Century Europe* (New York: Harcourt, Brace & World, 1968).

DeConcini, Barbara, "The Crisis of Meaning in Religion and Art," in *The Christian Century* (March 20–27, 1991), 223–326.

Dieterich, Albrecht, *Eine Mithrasliturgie* (Leipzig, Germany: B. G. Teubner, 1903).

Eisenstein, Elizabeth, *The Printing Press as an Agent of Change* (Cambridge: The Cambridge University Press, 1979).

Ellul, Jacques, *The Humiliation of the Word* (Grand Rapids, MI: William B. Eerdmans, 1985).

———, *The Presence of the Kingdom,* second edition (Colorado Springs, CO: Helmers and Howard, 1989).

———, *Propaganda: The Formation of Men's Attitudes* (New York: Alfred A. Knopf, 1965).

———, *The Technological Bluff,* trans. by Geoffrey Bromiley (Grand Rapids, MI: William B. Eerdmans, 1990).

———, *The Technological Society* (New York: Alfred A. Knopf, 1967).

Erskine, Andrew, "Culture and Power in Ptolemaic Egypt: The Museum and Library of Alexandria," in *Greece & Rome,* 2nd ser., 42:1 (1995), 38–48.

Estabrooks, Maurice, *Electronic Technology, Corporate Strategy, and World Transformation* (Westport, CT: Greenwood, 1995).

Ewen, Stewart, *Captains of Consciousness: Advertising and the Roots of the Consumer Culture* (New York: McGraw-Hill, 1976).

Fallon, Peter K., *Printing, Literacy, and Education in Eighteenth-Century Ireland: Why the Irish Speak English* (Lewiston, NY: Edwin Mellen, 2005).

Fang, Irving E., *A History of Mass Communication: Six Information Revolutions* (Burlington, MA: Focal, 1997).

Folkerts, Jean, and Stephen Lacy, *The Media in Your Life: An Introduction to Mass Communication* (Needham Heights, MA: Allyn and Bacon, 2000).

Frankfurt, Harry G., *On Bullshit* (Princeton, NJ: Princeton University Press, 2005).

———, *On Truth* (New York: Alfred A. Knopf, 2006).

Frazer, J. G., *The Golden Bough: A Study in Magic and Religion* (London: MacMillan, 1900).

Fremantle, Anne, *The Age of Belief* (New York: George Braziller, 1958).

Freud, Sigmund, *The Future of an Illusion* (New York: W. W. Norton, 1961).

Frost, S. E., Jr., *Basic Teachings of the Great Philosophers* (New York: Doubleday, 1962).

Geertz, Clifford, *The Interpretation of Culture* (New York: Basic Books, 1973).

Gelb, I. J., *A Study of Writing* (Chicago: The University of Chicago Press, 1963).

Gillham, Oliver, and Alex S. MacLean, *The Limitless City: A Primer on the Urban Sprawl Debate* (Washington, DC: Island, 2002).

Gilson, Etienne, *Reason and Revelation in the Middle Ages* (New York: Charles Scribner's Sons, 1938).

Gleditsch, Nils Petter, et al., "Armed Conflict 1946–2001: A New Dataset," in *Journal of Peace Research* 39:5 (Sept. 2002), 615–37.

Goody, Jack, *The Domestication of the Savage Mind* (Cambridge: Cambridge University Press, 1977).

———, *The Interface between the Written and the Oral* (Cambridge: Cambridge University Press, 1987).

———, *The Logic of Writing and the Organization of Society* (Cambridge: Cambridge University Press, 1986).

Gorman, Lyn, and David McLean, *Media and Society in the Twentieth Century: A Historical Introduction* (Malden, MA: Blackwell, 2003).

Gould, Steven Jay, *The Mismeasure of Man* (New York: W. W. Norton, 1981).

Grant, Edward, *The Foundations of Modern Science in the Middle Ages: Their Religious, Institutional, and Intellectual Contexts* (Cambridge: Cambridge University Press, 1996).

Hall, Edwin T., *The Silent Language* (New York: Doubleday, 1959).

Hampshire, Stuart, *The Age of Reason* (New York: George Braziller, 1958).

Havel, Vaclav, "The Need for Transcendence in the Postmodern World" (text of a speech delivered at Independence Hall, Philadelphia, Pennsylvania, July 4, 1994), http://www.worldtrans.org/whole/havelspeech.html

Havelock, Eric A., *Preface to Plato* (Cambridge, MA: The Belknap Press of the Harvard University Press, 1963).

Hegeman, Susan, *Patterns for America: Modernism and the Concept of Culture* (Princeton, NJ: Princeton University Press, 1999).

Heidegger, Martin, *On the Way to Language* (New York: Harper and Row, 1971).

Herbermann, Charles G., et al. (eds.), *The Catholic Encyclopedia: An*

International Work of Reference on the Constitution, Doctrine, Discipline, and History of the Catholic Church (New York: The Encyclopedia Press, 1913).

Herm, Gerhard, *The Celts: The People Who Came Out of the Darkness* (New York: St. Martin's, 1975).

Herrnstein, Richard, and Charles Murray, *The Bell Curve* (New York: The Free Press, 1994).

High, Dallas M., *Language, Persons, and Belief* (New York: Oxford University Press, 1967).

Hitschmann, Eduard, *Freud's Theories of the Neuroses,* trans. by C. R. Payne (New York: Journal of Nervous and Mental Disease, 1913).

Hobbes, Thomas, *Leviathan* (Cambridge: The University Press, 1904).

Hoskins, Jasper, and Herbert Richardson (trans. and eds.), *Truth, Freedom, and Evil: Three Philosophical Dialogues* (New York: Harper Torchbooks, 1967).

Hughes, Rupert, Deems Taylor, and Russell Kerr (eds.), *Music Lover's Encyclopedia* (Garden City, NY: Doubleday, 1939).

Hogan, David Gerard, *Selling 'em by the Sack: White Castle and the Creation of American Food* (New York: New York University Press, 1997).

Honomichl, Jack J., *Marketing/Research People: Their Behind-the-Scenes Stories* (Chicago: Crain, 1984).

Innis, Harold A., *The Bias of Communication* (Toronto: The University of Toronto Press, 1952).

————, *Empire and Communication* (Toronto: The University of Toronto Press, 1950).

Jaspers, Karl, *Way to Wisdom: An Introduction to Philosophy* (New Haven, CT: Yale University Press, 1951).

Jaynes, Julian, *The Origin of Consciousness in the Breakdown of the Bicameral Mind* (New York: Houghton Mifflin, 1976).

Jezer, Marty, *The Dark Ages: Life in the United States 1945-1960* (Cambridge, MA: South End, 1982).

Wendell Johnson, *People in Quandaries: The Semantics of Personal Adjustment* (New York: Harper & Brothers, 1946).

Jung, Carl G., *Man and His Symbols* (London: Aldus, 1964).

Kamarck, Elaine Ciulla, and Joseph S. Nye, *Governance.com: Democracy in the Information Age* (Washington, DC: Brookings Institution, 2002).

Kant, Immanuel, *Critique of Pure Reason,* ed. by Norman Kemp Smith (New York: Random House, 1958).

Kaplan, Justin, and Ann Bernays, *The Language of Names* (New York: Simon & Schuster, 1997).

Kaplan, Stacey, "Hellwig: Education Should Be 'For Practice,'" in *The Observer* On-Line, February 15, 2000, http://www.nd.edu/~observer/02152000/News/7.html

Kelly, Geffrey B. (ed.), Karl Rahner: *Theologian of the Graced Search for Meaning* (Minneapolis, MN: Fortress, 1993).

King, Martin Luther, Jr., "Remaining Awake through a Great Revolution," sermon delivered at the National Cathedral, Washington, DC, 31 March 1968 (in *Congressional Record,* 9 April 1968).

Kingsbury, John E., *The Telephone and Telephone Exchanges: Their Invention and Development* (London: Longmans, Green, 1915).

Klite, Paul, et al., "Pavlov's TV Dog: A Snapshot of Local TV News in America Taken on September 20, 1995," *Rocky Mountain Media Watch Content Analysis #7* (Denver, CO: Rocky Mountain Media Watch, 1995).

Knox, B. M. W., "Books and Readers in the Greek World: From the Beginnings to Alexandria," in *The Cambridge History of Classical Literature,* vol. 1, part 4 (Cambridge: The Cambridge University Press, 1989).

Kraemer, Joel L., "Maimonides' Use of (Aristotelian) Dialectic," in Cohen and Levine (eds.), *Maimonides and the Sciences,* 111–30.

Krasko, Genrich, *This Unbearable Boredom of Being: A Crisis of Meaning in America* (New York: iUniverse, 2004).

Kratz, Corinne A., "Genres of Power: A Comparative Analysis of Okiek Blessings, Curses and Oaths," *Man* 24:4 (series 2, December 1989), 299-317.

Kraus, Sidney (ed.), *The Great Debates* (Bloomington: Indiana University Press, 1962).

Kung, Hans, *Freud and the Problem of God* (New Haven, CT: Yale University Press, 1979).

Kurzweil, Ray, *The Age of Spiritual Machines: When Computers Exceed Human Intelligence* (New York: Penguin, 2000).

Langer, Suzanne, *Philosophy in a New Key* (Cambridge, MA: Harvard University Press, 1957).

Lasch, Christopher, *The Culture of Narcissism* (New York: Warner, 1979).

Leakey, Richard E., and Roger Lewin, *People of the Lake* (New York: Avon, 1978).

Linn, Louis, and Leo Walder Schwarz, *Psychiatry and Religious Experience* (New York: Random House, 1958).

Livingston, Eric, *An Anthropology of Reading,* (Bloomington: Indiana University Press, 1995).

Logan, Robert K., "The Five Ages of Communication" in *EME—Explorations in Media Ecology: The Journal of the Media Ecology Association* 1:1, 14–15.

Lyotard, Jean-François, *The Postmodern Condition: A Report on Knowledge,* trans. by Geoff Bennington and Brian Massumi (Minneapolis: University of Minnesota Press, 1979).

MacLean, Paul, *The Triune Brain in Evolution* (New York: Springer, 1990).

Maimonides, Moses, *The Guide of the Perplexed,* trans. by M. Friedländer (London: Trübner, 1885).

Malinowski, Bronislaw, *Magic, Science, and Religion* (Glencoe, IL: The Free Press, 1948).

———, "The Problem of Meaning in Primitive Languages," in Ogden, C. K., and I. A. Richards, *The Meaning of Meaning.*

Man, John, *Alpha Beta: How 26 Letters Shaped the Western World* (New York: John Wiley & Sons, 2000).

McLuhan, Marshall, *The Essential McLuhan, ed. by Eric McLuhan and Frank Zingrone* (New York: Basic Books, 1996).

———, *The Gutenberg Galaxy* (Toronto: The University of Toronto Press, 1962).

———, et al. (eds.), *The Medium and the Light: Reflections of Religion* (Toronto: Stoddart, 1999).

———, *Understanding Media* (New York: New American Library, 1964).

———, *Forward Through the Rearview Mirror: Reflections on and by Marshall McLuhan,* (Cambridge, MA: The MIT Press, 1997).

———, and R. K. Logan, "Alphabet, Mother of Invention" in *Et Cetera,* December 1977, 373–83.

Meyerowitz, Joshua, *No Sense of Place: The Impact of Electronic Media on Social Behavior* (New York: Oxford University Press, 1985).

Meza, Philip E., *Coming Attractions?: Hollywood, High Tech, and the Future of Entertainment* (Palo Alto, CA: Stanford University Press, 2007).

Mithaug, Dennis E., *Self-Determined Kids: Raising Satisfied and Successful Children* (Lanham, MD: Lexington, 1991).

Mogel, Leonard, *Creating Your Career in Communications and Entertainment* (Mahwah, NJ: Lawrence Erlbaum, 1998).

Moody, T. W., and F. X. Martin (eds.), *The Course of Irish History* (Cork, Ireland: Mercier, 1967).

Muller, Herbert J., *The Uses of the Past: Profiles of Former Societies* (New York: Oxford University Press, 1957).

Mumford, Lewis, *The Transformations of Man* (Gloucester, MA: Peter Smith, 1978).

National Endowment for the Arts, "Reading at Risk: A Survey of Literary Reading in America," Research Division Report #46 (Washington, DC: National Endowment for the Arts, 2004).

Nietzsche, Friedrich Wilhelm, "Beyond Good and Evil," part 3, section 60, in Walter Kaufman (trans.), *The Basic Writings of Nietzsche* (New York: The Modern Library, 1968).

———, *Der Froelische Wissenschaft,* quoted in Morrison, Robert, "God is Dead: What is Next? A Buddhist Response to Nietzsche" in *Western Buddhist Review* 1, http://www.westernbuddhistreview.com/vol1/god_is_dead.html

———, The Gay Science (Der Froelische Wissenschaft), trans. by Walter Kaufmann (New York: Random House, 1974).

———, *The Genealogy of Morals*, vol. 3, sec. 12, trans. by Walter Kaufmann and R. J. Hollingdale (New York: Random House, 1967).

Nunes, Paul, and Brian Johnson, *Mass Affluence: Seven New Rules of Marketing to Today's Consumer* (Cambridge, MA: Harvard Business School Press, 2004).

O'Brien, Frank Michael, *The Story of the Sun: New York, 1833-1918* (New York: George H. Doran, 1918).

O'Connor, Ulick, *A Terrible Beauty is Born: The Irish Troubles, 1912-1922* (Bedford, VA: Hamilton, 1975).

Ó Fiaich, An t-Athair Tomas, "The Beginnings of Christianity," in Moody and Martin (eds.), *The Course of Irish History,* 61-75.

Office of Educational Research and Improvement, "Scholastic Assessment Test Score Averages For College-Bound High School Seniors, By Sex: 1966–67 To 2000–01," in *Digest of Education Statistics, 2001* (Washington, DC: Office of Educational Research and Improvement, February, 2002).

Ogden, C. K., and I. A. Richards, *The Meaning of Meaning: A Study of the Influence of Language upon Thought and of the Science of Symbolism, Second Edition* (New York: Harcourt Brace, 1927).

Ong, Walter J., S.J., *Interfaces of the Word: Studies in the Evolution of Consciousness and Culture* (Ithaca, NY: Cornell University Press, 1977).

———, *Orality and Literacy: The Technologizing of the Word* (London: Methuen, 1982).

———, *The Presence of the Word: Some Prolegomena for Cultural and Religious History* (New Haven, CT: Yale University Press, 1967).

———, *Ramus, Method, and the Decay of Dialogue: From the Art of Discourse to the Art of Reason* (Cambridge, MA: Harvard University Press, 1958).

Perez-Rivas, "Bush Vows to Rid the World of 'Evil-Doers.'" CNN.com, http://archives.cnn.com/2001/US/09/16/gen.bush.terrorism/

Perkinson, Henry J., *Getting Better: Television and Moral Progress* (New Brunswick, NJ: Transaction, 1991).

———, *Since Socrates: Studies in the History of Western Educational Thought* (New York: Longman, 1980).

Petersen, Julie K., *The Telecommunications Illustrated Dictionary* (Boca Raton, FL: CRC, 2002).

Pieper, Josef, *Guide to Thomas Aquinas* (San Francisco: Ignatius, 1991).

Plato, "The Phaedrus," sec. 275, in *The Dialogues of Plato,* trans. by Benjamin Jowett (Oxford: Clarendon, 1953).

———, *The Republic,* the complete and unabridged translation by Benjamin Jowett (New York: Vintage Classics, 1991).

Plum, William Rattle, *The Military Telegraph during the Civil War in the United States: With an Exposition of Ancient and Modern Means of Communication, and of the Federal and Confederate Cipher Systems* (Chicago: Jansen, McClurg, 1882).

Pope John Paul II, "Address of John Paul II to the Plenary Assembly of the Pontifical Council for Culture," Saturday, 16 March 2002, http://www.vatican.va/holy_father/john_paul_ii/speeches/2002/march/documents/hf_jp-ii_spe_20020316_pc-culture_en.html

Postman, Neil, *Amusing Ourselves to Death: Public Discourse in the Age of Show Business* (New York: Penguin, 1986).

———, *Building a Bridge to the Eighteenth Century: How the Past Can Improve Our Future* (New York: Vintage, 1999).

———, *The Disappearance of Childhood* (New York: Vintage, 1994).

———, "The Humanism of Media Ecology" in Proceedings of the Media Ecology Association 1 (2000), 11, http://www.media-ecology.org/publications/MEA_proceedings/v1/humanism_of_media_ecology.html

———, *Teaching as a Conserving Activity* (New York: Dell, 1979).

Rideout, Victoria J., et al., *Zero to Six: Electronic Media in the Lives of Infants, Toddlers, and Pre-Schoolers* (Henry J. Kaizer Family Foundation, 2003).

Roche, Maurice, *Mega-Events and Modernity: Olympics and Expos in the Growth of Global Culture* (New York: Routledge, 2000).

Rorty, Richard, *Philosophy and the Mirror of Nature* (Princeton, NJ: Princeton University Press 1979).

———, and Pascal Engel, *What's the Use of Truth?* (New York: Columbia University Press, 2005).

Rubinstein, Richard, *Aristotle's Children: How Christians, Muslims, and Jews Rediscovered Ancient Wisdom and Illuminated the Middle Ages* (Orlando, FL: Harcourt, 2003).

Sale, George (trans.), *The Koran* (Philadelphia: J. W. Moore, 1856).

Sapir, Edward, *Language, Culture, and Personality, Essays in Memory of Edward Sapir*, ed. by Leslie Spier (Menasha, WI: Sapir Memorial Publication Fund, 1941).

Sarles, Harvey B., *Nietzsche's Prophecy: The Crisis in Meaning* (Amherst, NY: Humanity Books, 2001).

Scherman, Katherine, *The Flowering of Ireland: Saints, Scholars, and Kings* (Boston: Little, Brown, 1981).

Schmidt, Jeremy, *Melancholy and the Care of the Soul: Religion, Moral Philosophy and Madness* (London: Ashgate, 2007).

SIPRI (Stockholm International Peace Research Institute), *SIPRI Yearbook 2008: Armaments, Disarmament and International Secu-*

rity, "Appendix 6A. The 100 largest arms-producing companies, 2006," (Oxford: Oxford University Press, 2008), 281–85.

Sowell, Thomas, *Inside American Education* (New York: Simon and Schuster, 1992).

Squire, Charles, *The Mythology of the British Islands* (London: Gresham, 1905).

Statistical Abstract of the United States, (Washington, DC: United States Census Bureau, 2000).

Sterling, Christopher H., and John M. Kittross, *Stay Tuned: A History of American Broadcasting* (Mahwah, NJ: Lawrence Erlbaum, 2002).

Straubhaar, Joseph, and Robert Larose, *Media Now: Understanding Media, Culture, and Technology* (Belmont, CA: Thomson/Wadsworth, 2006).

Suskind, Ron, "Faith, Certainty and the Presidency of George W. Bush," The New York Times Magazine, October 17, 2004, http://www.nytimes.com/2004/10/17/magazine/17BUSH.html

Teilhard de Chardin, Pierre, *The Future of Man,* trans. by Norman Denny (New York: Harper and Row, 1964).

Tertullian, The Prescription Against Heretics, vii, Rev. Peter Holmes, D.D., found on the website of The Tertullian Project, http://www.tertullian.org/anf/anf03/anf03-24.htm#P3208_1148660 accessed January 15, 2008.

Thomas à Kempis, *The Imitation of Christ,* trans. by W. Benham (Leipzig, Germany: Bernhard Tauchnitz, 1877).

Tillich, Paul, "Our Ultimate Concern," in Church, F. Forrester (ed.), *The Essential Tillich: An Anthology of the Writings of Paul Tillich* (Chicago: University of Chicago Press, 1987).

Towers, Walter Kellogg, *Masters of Space: Morse and the Telegraph, Thompson and the Cable, Bell and the Telephone, Marconi and the Wireless Telegraph, Carty and the Wireless Telephone* (New York: Harper and Brothers, 1917).

Trend, David, *The Crisis of Meaning in Culture and Education* (Minneapolis: The University of Minnesota Press, 1995).

Trotter, L. I., *Life of the Marquis of Dalhousie* (London: W. H. Allen, 1889).

United States Census Bureau, "Comparative International Statistics," *Statistical Abstract of the United States,* (Washington, DC: United States Census Bureau, 2000).

Vardy, Jill, and Chris Wattie, "Shopping is Patriotic, Leaders Say," National Post (Canada), September 28, 2001, http://www.commondreams.org/headlines01/0929-04.htm

Veblen, Thorstein, *The Theory of the Leisure Class* (London: MacMillan, 1912).

Watt, W. Montgomery, *Muhammed at Mecca,* third edition (Oxford: Oxford University Press, 2000).

Watzlavick, Paul, Janet Beavin-Bavelas, and Don D. Jackson, *The Pragmatics of Human Communication: A Study of Interactional Patterns, Pathologies, and Paradoxes* (New York: W. W. Norton, 1967).

Whorf, Benjamin Lee, *Language, Thought, and Reality* (Cambridge, MA: The M.I.T. Press, 1956).

Wilson, Peter Lamborn, "The Crisis of Meaning," http://www.hermetic.com/bey/crisis-meaning.html, retrieved June 6, 2008.

Wishard, William Van Dusen, *Between Two Ages: The 21st Century and the Crisis Of Meaning* (Bloomington, IN: Xlibris, 2000)

Wittgenstein, Ludwig, *Tractatus Logico-Philosophicus,* trans. by D. F. Pears and B. F. McGuinness (Atlantic Highlands, NJ: Humanities Press International, 1974).

Wolf, Maryanne, *Proust and the Squid: The Story and Science of the Reading Brain* (New York: HarperCollins, 2007).

The World Health Organization, *The World Health Report 2001* (Geneva: The World Health Organization, 2001).

———, *The World Health Report 2004* (Geneva: World Health Organization, 2004).

Index